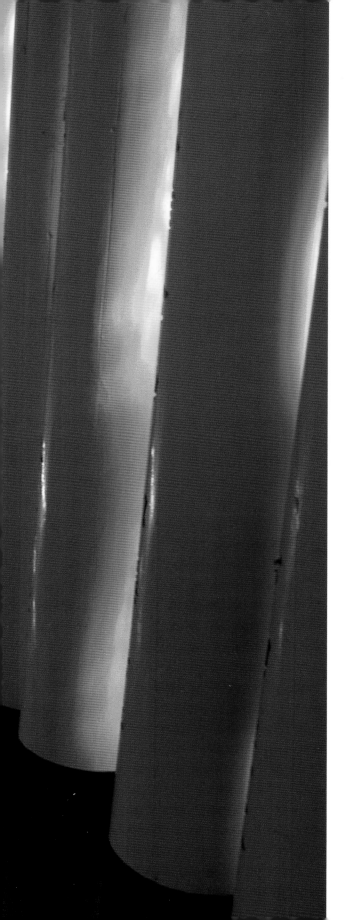

JAPANESE ARCHITECTURE

AN EXPLORATION OF ELEMENTS & FORMS

MIRA LOCHER
FOREWORD BY KENGO KUMA
PHOTOGRAPHY BY BEN SIMMONS

TUTTLE Publishing

Tokyo | Rutland, Vermont | Singapore

Published by Tuttle Publishing, an imprint of
Periplus Editions (HK) Ltd.

www.tuttlepublishing.com

Text copyright © 2010 Mira Locher
Photographs © Ben Simmons and Periplus
Editions (HK) Ltd

ISBN 978-4-8053-1328-2 Pb
ISBN 978-4-8053-0980-3 Hc

Distributed by

North America, Latin America & Europe
Tuttle Publishing
364 Innovation Drive
North Clarendon, VT 05759-9436 U.S.A.
Tel: 1 (802) 773-8930
Fax: 1 (802) 773-6993
info@tuttlepublishing.com
www.tuttlepublishing.com

Japan
Tuttle Publishing
Yaekari Building, 3rd Floor
5-4-12 Osaki, Shinagawa-ku, Tokyo 141 0032
Tel: (81) 3 5437-0171
Fax: (81) 3 5437-0755
sales@tuttle.co.jp
www.tuttle.co.jp

Asia Pacific
Berkeley Books Pte. Ltd.
61 Tai Seng Avenue, #02-12, Singapore 534167
Tel: (65) 6280-1330
Fax: (65) 6280-6290
inquiries@periplus.com.sg
www.periplus.com

Pb   16 15 14   10 9 8 7 6 5 4 3 2 1
Hc   14 13 12 11 10   10 9 8 7 6 5 4 3 2 1
Printed in Malaysia   1406TW

TUTTLE PUBLISHING® is a registered
trademark of Tuttle Publishing, a division of
Periplus Editions (HK) Ltd.

A Note on Language

Japanese names in the text are written to follow the
typical Japanese order of family name followed by
given name (the opposite of English). An exception
is Kengo Kuma's name, which is in reverse order on
the cover and introductory pages.

The Japanese words used in the text are written in
roman script (*romaji*), based on phonetic pronuncia-
tion using a modified Hepburn system. Consonants
are pronounced similarly to English, with *g* always
hard. A macron is used to denote a long vowel
sound, except for words such as Tokyo and Kyoto
which have become common in English. Vowels are
pronounced as follows:

a is ǎ as in father (ā denotes a lengthened sound, also
sometimes written as *aa*)
i is ē as in greet (ī denotes a lengthened sound, also
sometimes written as *ii*)
u is ū as in boot
e is ě as in pet (also sometimes written as *é*)
o is ō as in mow (ō denotes a lengthened sound, also
sometimes written as *oo* or *ou*)

The Glossary includes Japanese characters for each
word—*kanji* ideographs originally from China
and the two *kana* syllabaries based on phonetics,
hiragana (now used for Japanese words or parts of
words for which there is no *kanji*) and *katakana*
(now used primarily for foreign words).

Japanese nouns can be either plural or singular.

Inside front cover Kiyomizu Temple, Kyoto.
Inside back cover Jōmyōji Temple, Kamakura.
Page 1 Ryorijaya Uoshiro Restaurant, Mikuni, Fukui Prefecture.
Pages 2–3 Fushimi Inari Shrine, Kyoto.
Pages 4–5 Raikyūji Temple, Takahashi, Okayama Prefecture.
Pages 6–7 Ryōanji Temple, Kyoto.
Page 9 Kitano Tenmangu Shrine, Kyoto.
Pages 10–11 Ginkakuji Temple, Kyoto.
Pages 12–13 Yasaka Pagoda, Higashiyama, Kyoto.

Contents

ARCHITECTURAL TRUTH

Traditional Japanese architectural design, in terms of its building structure, is based on an important element that is not found in most other countries. This is the presence of an abundance of strong, beautiful timber. In Japan, there are many volcanoes, and the ash emitted from these creates rich soil. In addition, Japan's wet climate sustains beautiful forests, which provide a continuous supply of timber.

How to use that timber so that it is capable of achieving strength as well as beauty is something the Japanese people have considered and worked on repeatedly for many thousands of years. If the same issue is contemplated over a long period of time, it is natural that the details become refined as a matter of course. In order to enhance those fundamental and simple structural systems that support buildings, rigorous study has been carried out of the dimensions as well as the corresponding details of other structural elements, for example, the tiles mounted on roofs, the type of fitting affixed with *washi* paper called *shōji*, and the flooring material known as *tatami* that is spread out in the space between the columns. It is clear that a system in which the structure came first and everything else depended on it was generated and fostered because of the strong and beautiful trees that grew so abundantly in the country.

Furthermore, with this wood structural system there was no need to do anything with it, such as covering it with other construction materials or thickly coating it with paint. This is because the grain of the wood was sufficiently beautiful in itself. Since the structural materials were unadorned, and the other elements of the building also were unadorned, importance became attached to their natural quality.

It is unfortunate that a culture of ornamentation dominates the present-day world. Wood, for example, is used merely as one kind of ornamental material, such as fastening thin wood sheets over structures made of concrete and steel. To show "nature" as a symbol, this skin can be chosen. When showing authority and wealth, thin stone can be attached. When showing the existence of the very latest techniques, aluminum and glass can be affixed. The structure itself is completely ignored. It has become an era in which people compete for how highly priced buildings can be sold based on the manipulation of the skin. Global capitalism has fostered this "era of skin."

Now that the era of capitalism is reaching a major turning point, the time has come to search once more for the essence behind the skin, the truth the materials themselves must be hiding. When observed from this new viewpoint, it is quite likely that Japan's building tradition will be "rediscovered" as something very new. A great deal of knowledge to save the earth's environment also is hidden within this tradition. I believe that the power to solve the earth's environmental problems and the power to rescue the spirit of the people of this earth from the confusion of today is possessed within this tradition.

Kengo Kuma

隈 研吾

Through the lattice

時鳥
顔の出されぬ
格子かな

志太　野坡

Japanese cuckoo—
can't get my head
through the lattice.[1]

SHIDA YABA (1663–1740)

For an outsider, Japan can be like the Japanese cuckoo bird or
hototogisu—audible because of its melancholy song announcing the
arrival of summer, but visible only through fleeting glimpses of its
long spotted tail or curved bill. For many who have studied Japan, the
first glimpses of the country are very much like the changing of the
seasons—new and refreshing, suggestive of something more to come.
But the sense of the lattice is always present, stopping you just short
of understanding the whole—or seeing the *hototogisu*. Its mysterious
song draws you into the forest, but the bird rarely reveals itself. Yet,
the further into the woods you venture, the more the cuckoo discloses
aspects of the forest that are new to you.

Imagine the wonder of the foreign visitors to Japan who arrived
shortly after the ports were reopened in the latter half of the nineteenth
century, after the country had mostly isolated itself for more than 200
years. Japan was not yet industrialized—and not completely sure it
was ready to embark on the big changes its government was starting to
embrace. It was a country with dense cities of wood and plaster houses,
timber farmhouses with soaring thatched roofs, enormous temples
sheltering gigantic bronze statues, quiet shrines amid thick forests of
cryptomeria, angry volcanoes, peaceful rice paddies, and water lapping
at the coastline. Much of this is still there, and nearly 150 years later
many visitors feel that same sense of wonder when experiencing Japan.

Today, however, the visitor's first experience with the *hototogisu*
might be an electronic version of its song, piped into a subway station
or used as a "safe-to-cross" chirp at busy intersections. Yet, even in the
city, if you look beyond the throngs of people, the crowded concrete
buildings, and the barrage of information—giant screens streaming
dance videos, flashing neon signs one atop the other six or eight stories
above the street, cute animated characters bouncing along every store-
front, and electronic cuckoos—"traditional" Japan is still there. Hidden
like the *hototogisu*, it sings out to you when you listen for it.

Traditional wisdom and customs continue to play an important role
in contemporary life in Japan, and historic buildings, some hundreds of
years old, exist in most towns and cities. Traditional architectural forms
and construction methods still are in use for particular building types.
Yet, what we today understand as "traditional" was understood as such
only from the time the country reopened its doors to the outside world.

It was first the eyes of outsiders and then the eyes of Japanese trained in the ways of the West, which led to the understanding of the present concept of "tradition."

In the same way, what we now think of as "traditional Japanese" was not always purely Japanese, as the Japanese culture we know today has been informed and transformed over centuries of contact with China and other countries. What some Japanese elusively have defined as "Japanese taste" is built on a foundation of Chinese culture infused with ancient sensibilities stemming from the Japanese way of living with nature. Everything traditional goes back to nature and the ways of life that developed in concert with the seasonal climate and mountainous landscape. Any study of the architecture of Japan must start there, yet the definition of "Japanese taste" or "Japan-ness" remains as elusive as the *hototogisu*.

This sensibility, which imbues everything that we now call "traditional Japanese," has drawn many an observer into the forest that is Japan. The arts, architecture, and landscapes of traditional Japan intrigue and influence not only contemporary designers in Japan but all over the world. There is much we can learn, starting with the connection to the natural and cultural environments and how those relationships have transformed over time.

There is a history of identifying traditional Japanese architecture by classifying specific elements within historic buildings. This book builds on that history and the teachings and research of many who have followed the *hototogisu* before me. It is not meant to be an exhaustive compilation, and there are, no doubt, many details neglected. Rather, this book deals primarily with the common representative built elements found in the architecture and landscapes of traditional Japan and attempts to explore their connections to Japanese culture through the ways they are made and used. It is my hope that it may entice others to look beyond the lattice and wander into the forest drawn by the cuckoo's song.

Historic Periods in Japan

Ancient	縄文	Jōmon	c. 10000–c. 300 BCE
	弥生	Yayoi	c. 300 BCE–300 CE
	古墳	Kofun	300–c. 552
	飛鳥	Asuka	c. 552–710
Classical Japan	奈良	Nara	710–794
	平安	Heian	794–1185
Middle Ages	鎌倉	Kamakura	1185–1333
	室町	Muromachi	1334–1573
Pre-modern Japan	桃山	Momoyama	1573–1615
	江戸	Edo	1615–1868
Modern Japan	明治	Meiji	1868–1912
	大正	Taisho	1912–1926
	昭和	Shōwa	1926–1988
	平成	Heisei	1989–present

PART 1

Context

あさがほに
我は食くふ
おとこ哉

松尾　芭蕉

A man who eats his meal amidst
morning glories—that's what I am.

MATSUO BASHŌ (1644–94)

Chapter 1
Environment and culture

Above, figure 1 Matsushima.
Opposite The weathered wood structure of the Sanzenin Temple in Ōhara blends in with the natural surroundings.
Pages 14–15 The Nandaimon Great South Gate at Tōdaiji Temple, ensconced among trees at Nara Park, Nara.

Beginning his day by relishing the brief blossoming of a seasonal flower while enjoying a meal—that is how *haiku* poet Bashō described himself in the mid-seventeenth century. Bashō's words give form to an important idea in traditional Japanese culture: that humankind is inseparable from nature and its fleeting moments of beauty and inevitable decay. The theme of Bashō's poem resonates with the "strong 'native' Japanese belief that the only way to live in this world is to subject oneself to its natural immutable laws,"[1] along with the teachings of Buddhism as they were disseminated in Japan in the sixth century.

Japanese culture developed in concert with nature and as a result of a long stream of outside influences tempered by a constantly developing sense of aesthetics. Just as Bashō and his followers developed *haiku* into a high art in the seventeenth century, other Japanese arts and architecture were reaching their peak at the same time. After centuries of evolution, the arts and architecture of Japan—those which we now consider to be "traditional Japanese"—matured during the peaceful but politically and socially strict years of the Edo period (1603–1868).

The natural environment and the cultural context are so fully integrated in traditional Japanese architectural forms, materials, and construction that it is impossible to separate them. Nature was the source for traditional architecture—the construction materials were found locally, and the buildings were designed to fit into and work with the natural environment. The cultural context shaped the buildings through a strong respect for nature, combined with the influence of foreign forms and methods of construction, as they were brought into Japan and transformed over time

to suit both the Japanese landscape and Japanese aesthetic sensibilities.

The natural landscape of Japan is the foundation for any discussion of the traditional architecture, as the Japanese culture developed from the land and continues to be strongly connected to nature. The country of Japan is an archipelago made up of more than 3,000 islands (many which are uninhabited) stretching almost 4,000 kilometers (2,500 miles) along a roughly northeast to southwest diagonal line, with the Pacific Ocean on the east and the Sea of Japan on the west, separating Japan from the Korean Peninsula. The four main islands (from north to south: Hokkaido, Honshū, Shikoku, and Kyūshū) are home to the majority of the country's population,[2] with the main island of Honshū having the largest land area and population and featuring a temperate climate with four distinct seasons. The northern island of Hokkaido is cool temperate, with heavy snows in winter. The smaller island of Shikoku has a similar climate to that of the western part of Honshū, while the southern island of Kyūshū has a subtropical climate. The tropical Ryūkyū Islands, which include the island of Okinawa, are strung along a curve southwest of Kyūshū to a length of almost 1,000 kilometers (625 miles).

Like the climate, the landscape varies from island to island. In general, the central areas of the islands are mountainous, dotted with active volcanoes, and the coastline is rugged, often with little flat land between the mountains and the sea. Almost three-quarters of the land in Japan is mountainous, with the great majority of it too steep for agriculture or for buildings.[3] The cities and villages, as well as the majority of the agricultural fields, are built on the plains and other relatively flat areas, taking up only

about one-quarter of the total land area. Therefore, because of the rugged terrain, populated areas developed in a condensed fashion with a very economical use of land. In rural areas, multiple generations of a family typically shared a house (which might also have included spaces for domesticated animals), and the agricultural fields often extended right up to the edge of the house. In urban areas, the privileged class had large estates with multiple buildings set within gardens, but commoners lived in cramped quarters with shared walls and communal wells and sanitation—again, carefully planned to make the most of the little space available.

The rugged quality of the natural environment in Japan inspired awe and respect, and certain natural features became important aesthetic and spiritual landmarks. The venerable Mount Fuji, Japan's highest mountain,[4] is a prominent landmark on the island of Honshū, often featured in works of poetry and art, such as the artist Hokusai's famous early nineteenth-century series of *ukiyo-e* (woodblock prints), *36 Views of Mount Fuji*. Osore-zan (literally "dread mountain"), a sacred mountain in the far northern part of Honshū is considered to be the gateway to hell and a place where *itako* mediums can communicate with the spirit of the dead. The rugged volcanic terrain, sulfur haze, and plantless landscape is eerily beautiful—and the complete opposite of the more than 250 rock- and pine-covered islands of Matsushima, which are considered historically to be one of the three most famous scenic spots in Japan (*nihon sankei*).[5] Scenes of Matsushima (figure 1) have been featured in poems and paintings for hundreds of years—even inspiring a seventeenth-century poetry competition.[6]

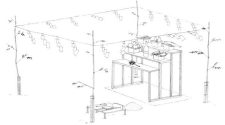

In addition to the awe-inspiring natural environment, Japanese culture developed with the constant threat of destructive natural forces—earthquakes, *tsunami* (tidal waves), typhoons, and active volcanoes. This very harsh natural environment did not result in a culture of fear and constant battle against nature, however, but rather a culture of respect for nature with an understanding and appreciation for the ephemeral quality of all life. This long-established cultural respect for nature is demonstrated by the daily rituals and seasonal festivals based in the indigenous Japanese religion, *shintō* ("the way of the gods").

Shintō deities, known as *kami*, are believed to reside in natural features like rocks, mountains, and trees, and daily, seasonal, and special offerings are made to show respect for local deities. Traditionally, houses have at least one *kamidana* ("deity shelf," figure 32) upon which the first bowl of rice and cup of tea are placed as daily offerings to the local deity. *Shintō* ceremonies are held seasonally to celebrate the preparations for planting in the spring as well as the bounty of the fall harvest. When starting construction of a new building, the traditional groundbreaking ceremony (*jichinsai*) is a *shintō* ritual. Offerings of nature's riches (fish, seaweed, fruit, vegetables, rice, salt, *sake*, and the like) are placed on a temporary altar

constructed of wood (figure 2). The altar is set up in the middle of a square oriented to the four cardinal directions and demarcated by four bamboo poles connected with a twisted rope made of rice straw, a *shimenawa*. The *shimenawa* is used to designate a sacred *shintō* place by separating the space of the everyday or profane world from that of the sacred world. The respect for the bounty of nature is obvious in the use of natural materials imbued with *shintō* reverence and symbolism.

This nature-based veneration in *shintō* is integrated into many aspects of Japanese life, from the annual New Year's trip to the local shrine to the blessing by a *shintō* priest at a wedding ceremony. Although *shintō* predates Buddhism in Japan, when Buddhist thought was introduced in the sixth century, it did not replace *shintō* ideas or rituals but rather was introduced in a way that allowed the two to coexist. That peaceful coexistence is obvious in the *shintō* shrines that are part of Buddhist temple complexes, such as the Asakusa Shrine within the Sensōji Temple precinct in Tokyo, and in the mingling of *shintō* and Buddhist rituals throughout a Japanese person's life—weddings are traditionally *shintō*, while funerals are Buddhist. This coexistence of *shintō* and Buddhism is clear in a traditional household, where the family maintains both the *shintō* deity shelf and a Buddhist family altar.

Buddhism, too, incorporates a strong respect for nature. Influenced by Buddhist thought, the transitory nature of life as it relates to Japanese aesthetic ideas is clear in the often used terms *aware* ("the aspects of nature (or life, or art) that move a susceptible individual to an awareness of the ephemeral beauty of a world

in which change is the only constant")[7] and *mujō* ("a Buddhist concept suggesting impermanence").[8] These terms have long been and continue to be utilized by writers, artists, and architects to express the awareness and acceptance of the transitory nature of all things. Falling cherry blossoms, the waning moon, one's own aging—these are popular themes incorporating the idea of ephemerality.

The transitory quality of nature is also apparent in traditional thought about the preservation of buildings, which were constructed using natural materials such as wood, paper, and bark—materials which disintegrate over time and must be maintained, repaired, or replaced. The idea of preservation was not one in which buildings must be kept intact, with elements replaced only when they outlived their useful life. Rather, buildings could constantly change, with pieces removed or added as needed for daily life or as required for maintenance. Buildings were understood as part of the changing environment rather than as permanent fixtures. Architect Kurokawa Kisho explains, "It is an ancient Japanese belief that a house is only a temporary abode. If it burns down it can be easily rebuilt."[9]

Nature that provides the canvas for architecture may at times be harsh, but it also provides an abundant supply of stone, wood and other plant materials, and mud—the primary construction materials for traditional Japanese buildings. The islands of Japan are thickly forested in many areas, and those forests provide various kinds of wood that can be used in construction. Japanese cypress (*hinoki*) is used most typically for the structure of buildings. Cedar (*sugi*), cherry (*sakura*), red and black pine

(*akamatsu* and *kuromatsu*), and zelkova (*keyaki*), as well as bamboo (*take*) and other grasses, among others, commonly are used as secondary structure or for ornamental uses. Japan is well known for the woodworking techniques and high level of skill developed by carpenters whose knowledge and training allowed them to take advantage of the stresses occurring naturally in trees to develop ingenious earthquake-resistant joints and structures that show off the natural beauty of the wood elements.

Like wood, mud too was the basis for a highly skilled craft, as solid walls are made from mud plaster (*tsuchikabe*) flecked with bits of straw and sand. These walls resplendently show the color of the earth, or sometimes are coated with a thin layer of bright white lime plaster (*shikkui*), troweled to a perfectly flat smooth finish. Like carpenters, master plaster craftsmen perfected their techniques over years of training and developed their craft to express the beauty of the natural quality of the earthen material.

Wood and mud provide the basic enclosure for traditional Japanese buildings, but other natural materials are used in combination with them to create spaces. Roofs are frequently made of a thick thatch of rice straw (*wara*), a highly useful by-product of rice-based

agriculture. Floors are made of tamped earth (*tataki*) to create a hard flat indoor–outdoor floor at ground level, or they are made of lengths of bamboo or wood planks or woven rush-covered *tatami* mats set above the ground on a wood substructure. *Washi*, paper made by hand from the inner bark of the mulberry tree, is attached to sliding wood lattice *shōji* screens to filter the light. *Washi* also is applied on two sides of sliding wood frames to create opaque sliding partitions (*fusuma*, figure 27).

The surface of the *fusuma*, as well as wood panels on walls and openings, became the canvas for paintings of natural scenery or famous faraway places. Ornament enhances the architecture and supports its connection to nature. Mother-of-pearl, gold and silver leaf, ink, paint, pigments like iron oxide (*bengara*), and handmade *washi* paper are applied to the architectural elements in aristocratic residences and important temple and shrine buildings in patterns and scenes that relate to nature but also are utilized to show wealth and power.

Buildings not only incorporate many different natural materials in their construction, but the forms of the buildings, especially the *minka* (literally "people's house"), are directly related to the climate and environment of the place where they are built (figure 10). *Minka* in cold mountainous areas with heavy snowfall typically have steep, thickly thatched roofs to avoid the build-up of snow on the roof, and wood exterior siding because of the prevalent availability of nearby trees. *Minka* in hot climates feature removable exterior wall partitions to allow breezes to pass through the house and overhanging roof eaves to shade the interior spaces.

Buddhist temples, as well as some *shintō* shrines and aristocratic residences, have substantial ceramic tile roofs with extended eaves. Heavy timber framing holds up the roof and gives a sense of strength and permanence. The weight of the tiles makes roofs resistant to strong winds, and the long eaves provide shade from the summer sun. The winter sun, lower in the sky than the summer sun, often reflects off an adjacent pond or gravel forecourt into the interior. The relative darkness of the interior of a traditional building came to suit the Japanese taste, and other arts developed within this context of shadows. Gold and silver leaf, smoothly finished lacquerware, and mother-of-pearl inlay are used to reflect small amounts of light and bring moments of brightness into the shadows. Novelist Tanizaki Jun'ichirō remarked, "Darkness is an indispensable element of the beauty of lacquerware."[10] He continued, "The quality that we call beauty, however, must always grow from the realities of life, and our ancestors, forced to live in dark rooms, presently came to discover beauty in shadows, ultimately to guide shadows towards beauty's end."[11]

This awareness of the qualities of space, along with the high caliber of craft in construction and the attention to detail that are hallmarks of traditional Japanese architecture, are apparent as the architecture reached its final phase in the Edo period. However, the beginnings of Japanese architecture were much more humble. As buildings developed in harmony with the natural surroundings and the seasonal and daily changes in nature, as well as influences from abroad, the forms that we now recognize as embodying a Japanese sense of beauty slowly emerged.

Chapter 2

The evolution of Japanese architecture

Before the ancient Japanese began to settle and construct dwellings they were nomadic, moving with the seasons, changes in climate and available food sources, and sustained by hunting, fishing, and gathering. With the advent of systematic agriculture, especially wet rice farming from about 500 BCE,[12] communities formed to work the fields, and permanent dwellings were constructed. These early eras, known as the Jōmon period (c. 10000–c. 300 BCE), are characterized by ceramic pots, many adorned with rope patterns from which the era gets its name (Jōmon means "rope mark"), and the energetic design of *haniwa* ceramic funerary images that remain from that era, and the Yayoi period (c. 300 BCE–300 CE), distinguished by its more sedate, smoothly finished pottery and bronze mirrors, bells, and tools. The contrast of the rough, creative energy of the Jōmon people and the relatively more refined lifestyle of the Yayoi has been used by a number of Japanese architects and historians to explain the two-sided character of the Japanese people, as well as to categorize certain buildings.[13]

Ancient Buildings

The earliest buildings in Japan can be considered to have been of three distinct types: earthen-floored flat-land dwellings (*heichi jūkyo*), pit dwellings (*tateana jūkyo*, "vertical hole dwelling," figure 3), and wooden-floored buildings either with the floor built directly on the ground (*hiraya tatemono*, "one-story building") or constructed above the ground (*takayuka*, "high floor"), as found in the raised-floor storehouse (*takakura*, "high storehouse," figure 4). Because these early structures were made entirely of wood and

thatch, the buildings themselves naturally no longer exist. However, many dwelling sites have been located, and the pits and postholes excavated. The building forms have been deduced using the excavations, as well as images of buildings found on ancient bronze mirrors and in the forms of some *haniwa*.

All three types of building were constructed using wooden posts and thatched roofs, with the posts resting on top of or set directly into the ground. Since many daily activities took place outside, the buildings were small and enclosed a single space. In the case of the pit dwellings, the typical construction consisted of an excavated pit with four posts set into the

Opposite The expanse of gravel adjacent to the Kazenomiya auxiliary sanctuary awaits the ritual twenty-year rebuilding at the Geku Outer Shrine of the Ise Shrine. Only the sacred central column, submerged in the ground and hidden from view by a small structure in the middle of the gravel expanse, remains permanent.

Above left Nestled into a hillside, the mausoleum of Gosamatu Seishun, the Lord of Nakagusuku, Okinawa Island, who ordered the construction of Nakagusuku Castle, displays the stone front wall and gently curved roof typical of a fifteenth-century turtleback-style tomb.

Above right Light filters between the large stone blocks into the interior space of the seventh-century Ishibutai Tumulus burial chamber in Asuka.

Top Displaying the appropriate permanence and power, huge boulders create the stage-like roof of the Ishibutai Tumulus burial chamber.

ground and beams connecting the posts at the top. The floor was earthen, tamped to create a hard surface, with a fire pit placed within the small space. Timber rafters rested on the ground, leaning against the beams to meet at a central ridge, and were covered with a thick layer of thatch. The flat-land dwellings were constructed in a similar manner but without the sunken floor—the floor was at ground level and the roof rested directly on the ground, serving as both roof and wall. The *hiraya tatemono* improved upon this by lifting the roof above the ground on posts and enclosing the interior space with wood plank walls and a wood floor built directly on the ground.

The *takakura* storehouses, which primarily were used to hold grain, also were based on a four-post configuration, but the floor was raised about two meters above the ground to keep out moisture and rodents. The storage space was accessed by a stair carved out of a log, with a flat board at the top that created a barrier for rodents (*nezumi-gaeshi*, "rat turn-around"). The structure of the four vertical walls and the roof was made of timber. The roof was covered with thatch, and the walls enclosed with wood planks, perhaps with overlapping corner joints. The corner joints and mortise-and-tenon joints believed to be used elsewhere in the structure suggest a relatively advanced knowledge of carpentry techniques and tools.[14] It is thought that the form of the raised-floor storehouses may have been influenced by buildings from elsewhere in Asia, in particular granaries from Southeast Asia or the Pacific Islands,[15] and may have influenced early *shintō* shrine architecture.

Minka

The building type that eventually developed from the ancient dwellings is the *minka* or "people's house" (often translated as "folk house"). Since *minka* were constructed using natural materials, primarily wood, mud, and thatch, few examples exist that are more than 200–300 years old. Although the number of *minka* in use decreases every year, many fine examples can still be seen in Japan. The existing *minka* represent the final stage of the development of the common dwelling from

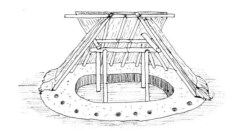

Top, figure 3 *Tateana jūkyo* pit dwelling.
Above, figure 4 *Takakura* raised storehouse.

the pithouse and flat-land dwelling, one in which political stability and relative prosperity led to an increase in communication within the country and a diminishing of many regional variations.[16]

The typical *minka* features an earthen floored space or *doma*, but unlike in pit dwellings the tamped earth floor is at ground level rather than sunken below. The *doma* is often large and is the location of the kitchen and where many of the household tasks are completed. Some *doma* are spacious enough to include storage areas and even stables for domesticated animals.

The structure of the *minka* is heavy timber, with columns placed on stone foundations rather than set into the ground as in the ancient dwellings. Beams connect the tops of the columns and sometimes also join the columns at intermediate heights. The beams support a truss system which, in turn, supports the roof. The roof of the *minka* is the most prominent architectural feature—and therefore is most important in terms of social status. It is also the strongest regional expression of the

dwelling. Diverse styles of roofs developed in different areas (figure 10), and historically the size and form of the roof was evidence of a family's social standing in the community. The typical *minka* roof is large and thickly thatched with rice straw, but some roofs are covered with wood planks held in place with wood battens and heavy stones. Others feature ridges covered with rows of ceramic tiles or perhaps planted with flowers.

The large roofs of the *minka* enclose grand spaces, sometimes incorporating multiple levels of floors and other times remaining open to the soaring roof. Originally, the interior space of the *minka* was one large room with a tamped earth floor. This developed into one room with a separation of the floor plane—half of the space had an earthen floor and half had a floor raised above the ground and covered with wood planks or bamboo poles. Eventually, the floor plan became more complex, with the raised floor area growing larger than the earthen floor and being divided into several spaces separated by sliding partitions (figure 28).

The focus of the interior space is the hearth, in which a fire is always kept burning. The smoke and carbon from the fire keep insects out of the thatched roof and help to preserve the exposed wood structure. Typically, the hearth is set within the semi-public space of the *minka*, on a wood plank floor raised above the ground level, adjacent and open to the *doma*. Private rooms are located to one side of the hearth space, while the earthen floored *doma* entrance and working area is on the other side. The form of the *minka* allows for multiple activities to take place within the house, as there is space for cooking and working in the *doma*, private rooms for living and sleeping, and sometimes even space in the uppermost level of the house for silkworms to be grown in the winter.

The exterior walls of *minka* typically are covered in rough mud plaster, although some are faced with wood planks, depending on the local availability of the materials. The interior surfaces of these walls are finished in the same fashion as the exterior, with a textured plaster of mud, straw, and sand. Interior walls, when permanent, also are covered with mud plaster

Above A *jizaikagi* adjustable kettle hanger with a simple carved wood fish and a *kamado* cook stove covered with a mud plaster are typical elements of a *minka* kitchen.

Right Characteristic of a single-story *minka*, the overhanging eave is supported by a straightforward structure of wood columns on base stones and protects the raised floor of the house.
Below The thick thatch and steep roof of this three-story *gasshō-zukuri minka* protect the farmhouse from the winter weather.

or paneled with wood. Movable interior partitions, used to separate living spaces, started out as simple wood panels but later developed into wood lattices covered with handmade paper, influenced by upper-class residential architecture.

Shinto Shrines

"Shrines are a spontaneous manifestation of the people's faith in *kami* [deities],"[17] and the early *shintō* shrines were simple structures sited in nature to create places where people could leave offerings and pay their respects to the local deities. Often erected temporarily, these small local shrines consisted of four poles of bamboo or *sakaki* (a Japanese ever-green tree, *Cleyera japonica*) connected with a *shimenawa* (twisted rice straw rope) and decorated with strips of folded paper (*shide*) and lengths of tree bark fiber (*yū*). This type of shrine either was built around the object of veneration or was erected near it and had a small wooden altar in the center.[18] The first shrine buildings were constructed of wood and were based on the form of the raised-floor

storehouses, because that was the form of non-residential architectural which was most common at the time. The entrances to the sacred precincts were marked by simple post-and-beam gates, called *torii*, which are still in use today.

As *shintō* became more systematized, large-scale shrines were built to show respect to important deities and to reinforce the tradi-tional connection of the imperial family to the *shintō* gods. This imperial tie to *shintō* dates back to the myth of the creation of Japan, as documented in the *Kojiki* ("Records of Ancient Matters"), recorded in 712 CE. The story relates that Izanami-no-mikoto and Izanagi-no-mikoto, a female and a male *kami*, created the Japanese archipelago by dipping a spear into the ocean floor and dripping the mud to form an island. They then descended from the heavens and planted a stick vertically in the ground—the first column in Japan—danced around it, and mated. Their offspring include the eight main islands of Japan and many deities, including the goddess of the sun, Amaterasu-omikami ("heaven-illuminating

deity"), whose divine descendants are the legendary ancestors of the imperial family.

Because of this strong connection between *shintō* and the imperial family, important shrines were built on a large scale with the finest materials and craftsmanship. The most venerated *shintō* shrine in Japan, built in the ancient forests of Ise, is separated into two distinct precincts, an inner and an outer shrine, with both precincts comprised of buildings based on the *takakura* raised-floor storehouse form that was prevalent in ancient Japan. The Naiku Inner Shrine at Ise, which venerates the goddess of the sun, generally is thought to have been founded in the late third century and the Geku Outer Shrine, built for the goddess of agriculture, in the late fifth century. The build-ings are constructed almost completely from *hinoki* (Japanese cypress) grown in sacred forests and have thatched roofs with ridges distinctively reinforced with wood billets and finials, wood plank walls, and floors raised more than two meters above the ground. The shrines stand in a courtyard of white gravel, surrounded by four layers of fences.

Opposite A grand wood *torii* gate, on axis with the primary entrance gate and main hall, marks the entrance to the Meiji Shrine in Tokyo.
Top right The ornamented roofs of the Izumo Shrine reflect both the grandeur associated with an important *shintō* shrine and remnants of earlier methods of construction.
Center right Four bamboo posts supporting a *shimenawa* delineate the sacred space of two conical sand mounds in front of the Ujigami Shrine.
Below right An enormous *shimenawa* marks the entrance to the Izumo Shrine. Visitors throw coins, attempting to lodge them in the oversized tassels.
Below Stately stone stairs lead through a majestic *torii* gate to the second gate, where wind lifts the *noren* curtain, giving a view to the third of the four gates at the Kōtaijingu Shōgu Main Sanctuary of the Naiku Inner Shrine at the Ise Shrine.

Because ritual purification is an important element in *shintō* beliefs, both the inner and outer Ise Shrines are completely rebuilt on adjacent sites every twenty years—a process which continues today. This act of renewal assures that the secret methods used in the buildings' construction are passed down from generation to generation, but it does not guarantee that the forms of the buildings may not have been altered slightly over the centuries, especially as Buddhism was introduced to Japan and became powerful.

Shintō shrines throughout Japan take a variety of forms. Some show the direct influence of Ise and the *takakura* raised-floor storehouse, while others expressly follow the forms of Buddhist temples—only recognizable as *shintō* because of the *torii* gate marking the entrance to the shrine precinct. Most shrines reflect the style of architecture that was popular at the time the shrine was built. This sharp variation in the forms of *shintō* shrines demonstrates—with the exception of a few examples such as the Ise Shrine—a lack of specific religious significance in the architectural form, as the buildings were considered sacred because of their function to "provide a dwelling place for one or more *kami* and a place where the *kami* can be served,"[19] not because of their particular form.

Buddhist Temples

Buddhism was introduced to Japan in the mid-sixth century, and by the end of the century was accepted by the Japanese rulers for its structure and practice of scholarly teaching and learning. This included a system of writing—which did not exist in Japan at that time—as well as a religious philosophy that seemed compatible with the Japanese people's way of life. The Buddhism that was brought to Japan had developed in China based on Mahayana Buddhism from India, was tempered with Chinese Confucian and Taoist ideas, and had spread to the Korean Peninsula. Together with the teachings of Buddhism, the Japanese imported the forms of the Chinese Buddhist temples. The Chinese temples initially were derived from Indian temple forms (this is most obvious in the

transformation of the Indian stupa into the Chinese pagoda) and later were altered based on the forms and planning of Chinese imperial architecture. These early temple complexes feature a series of gated courtyards entered from the south, with buildings placed along a north–south axis. The complexes are laid out according to principles of Chinese geomancy (*feng shui*), specifically with the buildings oriented toward the sun or toward a particular view, and are designed "to harmonize with the cosmic forces of the environment."[20]

The temple buildings are grand constructions of heavy timber, featuring large roofs covered with ceramic tiles and walls surfaced with white lime plaster between the exposed columns and beams. Layers of decorative ceramic tiles line the ridges of the roofs, and tiers of carved wood brackets extend from the upper part of the thick round columns to support the deep eaves of the roof. The most splendid buildings, like the *kondō* or golden hall at the seventh-century Yakushiji Temple in Nara, may be several stories in height and have multiple layers of roofs. Originally, the exposed wood of the structure, paneled doors, and balustrades was painted in vivid hues of red, green, and yellow (as in the *kondō* at Yakushiji, rebuilt in 1976). The juxtaposition of the bright white plaster and the lively polychromatic wood structure and ornamentation is quite eye-catching and adds to the grandeur of the buildings.

Set several steps above the ground on stone plinths, the buildings are imposing and monumental. They well served the purpose of showing the strength of Buddhism and the power permitted the religion by the Japanese government. Although Buddhism was introduced into Japan in a way that allowed it to coexist with *shintō*, it is easy to imagine that over time the powerful Buddhist forms effected changes in the forms of *shintō* shrines, including even the most important and oldest shrine buildings, such as those at Ise.[21]

The early temple buildings in Japan are constructed exactly like the Chinese Buddhist temples of the time, and Chinese and Korean

Top Incense is prepared in a metal cauldron in front of the stone-surfaced forecourt of Tōdaiji Temple in Nara. Originally built in the eighth century CE to be the headquarters of Buddhist teaching in Japan, the temple suffered damage from multiple fires and earthquakes. The present building dates from the early nineteenth century, and although just two-thirds of the original size unmistakably expresses the monumentality and formalism of a grand Buddhist temple.

Center The Jikidō Hall of the Tōji Temple shows the typical architectural features of a Buddhist temple with a symmetrical and formal composition of elements, including a stone plinth foundation, an articulated structure of heavy timber columns and beams, and a curved ceramic tile roof.

Left Multiple levels and layers of space merge and open unto another, yet maintain the spatial hierarchy vital to the functions of a Buddhist temple.

craftsmen were brought to Japan for the specific purpose of building temples. However, over the centuries, as Buddhist ideals changed, the strong symmetry and monumentality of the architectural forms began to break down. As the forms of the temples changed, the transformations were reflected and developed in the architecture used for aristocratic residential compounds, especially those of the Heian period (794–1185 CE), known as *shinden*.

Shinden Complexes

Shinden-style architecture derives its name from the *shinden* or central hall of aristocratic residential complexes, which reached their full development in the Heian period. The architecture of the *shinden* style reflects the school of Buddhist thought that was prevalent at the time, Pure Land Buddhism (*jōdoshū*). In Pure Land Buddhism, "a rich spirituality is cultivated, endowing a person with endless energy and boundless vitality.... It challenges people to discover the ultimate meaning of life in the abyss of the darkness of ignorance."[22] It

emphasizes "the here and now cherished as a gift of life itself to be lived creatively and gratefully."[23] The architecture and landscapes of the *shinden* style reflect that energy, vitality, and creativity with forms that appear to be lighter and more open than previous Buddhist buildings and which have a strong connection to a designed landscape.

The buildings are still grand and impressive, but they are less imposing than the earlier Chinese-style Buddhist architecture. *Shinden*-style architecture is built on a slightly smaller scale, with lighter timber framing and greater curvature to the roofs, which imparts an impression of weightlessness. The main hall is in the center of the complex, maintaining the symmetry of the earlier architecture, and is constructed atop a stone podium, giving a sense of grandeur to the central entrance. The main hall, or *shinden*, typically is flanked by L- or I-shaped corridors ending in pavilions within the space of the garden. The corridors and pavilions often were built without walls, adding to the sense of lightness. The *shinden*

Above Intricate wood bracketing and carved balustrades are both ornamental and functional elements of a *shinden*-style building.
Left The reflection of the curving roofs in the pond enhances the sense of lightness of the mid-eleventh century *shinden* Phoenix Hall of the Byōdōin Temple.

building itself served as a reception and living space for the master of the house. In some cases, such as at Byōdōin in Uji, the *shinden* later was converted into a Buddha hall, with an image of the Amidha Buddha in the center of the hall looking out to the garden (figure 29). Other residential buildings were reached by covered corridors connected to the *shinden* and generally maintained the overall symmetry of the complex.

Not only are the buildings less imposing than the earlier architecture, but the landscape is used in a less formal and more playful manner and has a strong connection to the architecture. The side pavilions of the *shinden* reach out to the main garden, located in the front part of the complex. The garden, used for both ceremonial and leisure activities, typically is designed with a large pond, which reflects the image of the *shinden*, and has a central island connected by bridges to the land. The first view of visitors to the complex was from the main gate, still usually located on the south, and they moved through or around the garden to reach the entrance to the main hall. This movement through the garden became an important part of the building–garden relationship in later architectural styles.

Life at the time of the Heian period was generally peaceful, and signs of privilege and prosperity were obvious in the architecture and landscapes of the *shinden* complexes. The daily life of the aristocratic class was fastidiously chronicled in the *Genji monogatari* ("The Tale of Genji"), written by Murasaki Shikibu in the early eleventh century. Murasaki wrote in detail of the activities within a *shinden* mansion, describing the intrigue and splendor of court life, scenes such as "morning when mist lay heavy over the garden," the maid "lifted part of the folding-shutter, seemingly to invite her mistress to watch the Prince's [her lover, Genji's] departure."[24]

Shoin Complexes

Over time, Japan's sociopolitical situation transformed from one in which the governmental structure was highly informed by Chinese customs and ideas,[25] which led to relative peace and prosperity during the Heian period, to a feudal system with a strong sense of militarism in the late twelfth century. Naturally, the lifestyles of Japanese aristocrats and the forms of their residences and places of worship reflected the changing circumstances. Simplicity and restraint became important

aesthetic concepts, as did the significant role of nature in architecture, especially with the emergence of Zen Buddhism. The *shinden* style of building had begun to move away from the symmetry and strict formality of the earlier Chinese-style Buddhist forms, and this development continued as the earlier architecture transformed into the *shoin* style.

Like the *shinden* style, the *shoin* style is named after the most important space in a residential complex. The *shoin* is a study room with a writing desk called a *tsukeshoin* (from which the room also gets its name). The low desk, often projecting out onto a veranda, faces the garden and is used while seated on the floor, as is typical in traditional Japanese buildings. In addition to the writing desk, the *shoin* room has several important distinguishing features, which developed throughout the thirteenth and fourteenth centuries and attained their final forms in the fifteenth century[26] (figure 30). These features include a decorative alcove (*tokonoma*), staggered shelves (*chigaidana*), and an ornamental doorway (*chōdaigamae*). Other features typical of the *shoin* style are a coffered coved ceiling, square posts, a *tatami* mat floor, and sliding panels of *shōji* (wood lattice screens covered

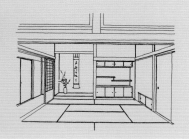

with translucent paper), *fusuma* (wood lattice screens covered with opaque paper), and *amado* (wood shutters used to protect openings in exterior walls).

A *shoin*-style complex includes elements from the earlier Chinese-style Buddhist architecture, such as the main gate on the south leading to a walled-in gravel courtyard on the south side of the formal reception hall. Whereas in the *shinden* complexes the gravel court was replaced with a garden, the *shoin* compounds brought back the formal entry court and moved the garden to the more private spaces toward the sides and rear of the complexes. The formality of the public front of the *shoin* complex is reinforced by the stately forms and elaborate ornamentation of the buildings. Yet, the elaboration and formality of the *shoin* buildings is very different from that of the early Buddhist temples. The curving ceramic tile roofs supported by layers of wood brackets that are so typical of the earlier style are transformed into straight or gently curving roofs covered with wood shingles or bark and supported with minimal bracketing. Rather than being positioned atop stone podia, many *shoin*-style buildings are supported by wood columns on stone bases.

Another important change from the earlier styles is the transformation of the symmetrical arrangement of buildings. The *shoin*-style buildings are no longer situated on a strict north–south axis, nor are they connected only by covered corridors. Instead, some buildings are connected to one another by smaller buildings attached at their corners, creating a zigzag movement in plan. This continues in the private spaces of the complex, where the formality of the public buildings diminishes. The private quarters, though still constructed on a grand scale, are less ornate and are designed with a strong relationship to the landscape. These buildings typically look out onto a garden with paths for strolling, pavilions for resting, and ponds for boating. The zigzag connection of buildings and the relationship of the buildings to the garden are two important elements that matured in the next phase of architectural development, the *sukiya* style.

Sukiya Complexes

Sukiya-style buildings are often considered to be the epitome of traditional Japanese architecture, the most complete form of its development which best reflects the Japanese culture, environment, and taste. The reason for

this is twofold. First, while the *sukiya* style is part of the continuous development of Japanese architecture that began after Chinese-style architecture was introduced in the sixth century and continued through the *shinden* and *shoin* styles, it is the final historical style that emerged before Japan began to industrialize in the late nineteenth century. Before that time, in the Edo period, the Japanese government had closed the country to outside influences for more than 200 years. This period of isolation, known as *sakoku* or "closed country," was also a time of strict government rule which produced relative peace and prosperity. Within that sociopolitical context, architecture and the other arts of Japan flourished. After the Edo period, Japan saw an abrupt change in its politics and a rapid move toward industrialization and emulation of the West, putting a sudden halt to the development of traditional arts and architecture.

The second reason is that twentieth- and twenty-first century architects in Japan and abroad have found inspiration in the *sukiya* style and have made connections to contemporary architectural styles and ideas of their day. This influence is especially evident in the regularity of the structural grid, the expressive use of materials, the informal aesthetic (compared to the *shoin* style), and the strong connection between inside and outside. The *sukiya* style continues to thrive, whether used in its most traditional form for a new teahouse or restaurant or adapted to contemporary taste and lifestyle in a residence or inn.

The style of *sukiya*, which often is translated as "abode of empty" or "abode of refinement," moves away from the symmetry and formality of earlier styles and builds on the zigzag layout first implied by the *shoin*-style architecture and the strong relationship to the landscape started with the *shinden* architecture and reinforced in the *shoin* style. Although the *shoin* style continued to be used for formal buildings in the Edo period, the less formal *sukiya* style was favored for residential architecture among the aristocratic class. *Sukiya*-style residential compounds are grand complexes of buildings set within elaborate gardens, not unlike the Buddhist temples of the time. However, while many temples were built with the main halls facing walled-in gardens, aristocratic residences tended to have expansive gardens. In both cases, the relationship between the buildings and gardens was very important, with rooms opening up to the gardens or framed views of the gardens designed as part of the important spaces of the buildings.

As with previous styles, the architecture features timber construction, but the framing is lighter, and the materials are used in ways that best show off their natural characteristics. Roofs are covered with wood shakes or shingles or thick layers of cedar bark, giving a quality of softness. Permanent walls are plastered with clean white lime plaster or roughly textured mud plaster. Other walls are made from movable partitions, sliding opaque paper-covered panels called *fusuma* or translucent paper-covered lattice screens known as *shōji*, which are used to filter light coming in from outside. Floors are covered with *tatami* mats or wood planks and are separated by sliding *shōji* screens from the *engawa*, an indoor–outdoor veranda-like extension of the floor plane that reaches out toward the garden and is shielded by the overhanging eaves.

The interiors of *sukiya*-style buildings also reflect the change toward expressing the beauty inherent in the natural construction materials. The *sukiya*-style *shoin* room (known as the *sukiya-shoin*, figure 5) still contains the *tsukeshoin* desk, the *chigaidana* staggered shelves, and the *tokonoma* alcove, but these features are constructed with less formality and greater creative freedom than in the *shoin* style (figure 30). This creative freedom is best represented in the *tokobashira*, the column that separates the *tokonoma* alcove from the alcove containing the staggered shelves. A fine *tokobashira* might be a cherry wood column with the beautifully figured bark left intact or perhaps a wonderfully gnarled length of pine, used in a way that expresses the time-worn character of the wood. This creative use of materials and the expression of their natural qualities are two unique and essential features of *sukiya* buildings.

Teahouses

The most evocative examples of *sukiya*-style buildings are teahouses, designed to reflect the aesthetic ideals of the era in small contained spaces complemented by accompanying gardens. Most teahouses are separate buildings set in gardens constructed specifically for the purpose of the tea ceremony, although some are rooms with independent entries within larger buildings. The aesthetic of the teahouse developed to reinforce the ideals of the ritual of tea, as they developed from the first tea gatherings in China until the high point in the development of tea culture in Japan under tea master Sen no Rikyū in the sixteenth century.

The tea plant may have been brought to China from India with Buddhism, or it may have grown naturally,[27] but its first use in China was medicinal. With the publication of tea connoisseur Lu Yu's three-volume *Chajing* ("The Classic of Tea") in the mid-eighth century, tea gained popularity with the elite classes, who began to serve it at social functions. It was this custom of drinking tea socially that first entered Japan through Korea in the Asuka period (c. 552–710 CE), but its popularity was brief. Tea reemerged in the twelfth century, when it was used by monks

Above Typical architectural elements found in teahouses include the low *nijiri-guchi* entrance, an expressed wood structure with mud plaster infill walls (the lower part of the wall is covered with *washi* paper to protect the surface), *shōji* screens to block the view and filter sunlight, and floors covered with *tatami* mats with an inset *ro* (hearth) for heating water.
Near right Adjacent to the *tokonoma* decorative alcove displaying a scroll and flower arrangement, a *fusuma* partition slides open to reveal the host's preparation space.
Far right, figure 6 An *okoshi-ezu* folding drawing used by master carpenters to study spaces and proportions when designing teahouses.

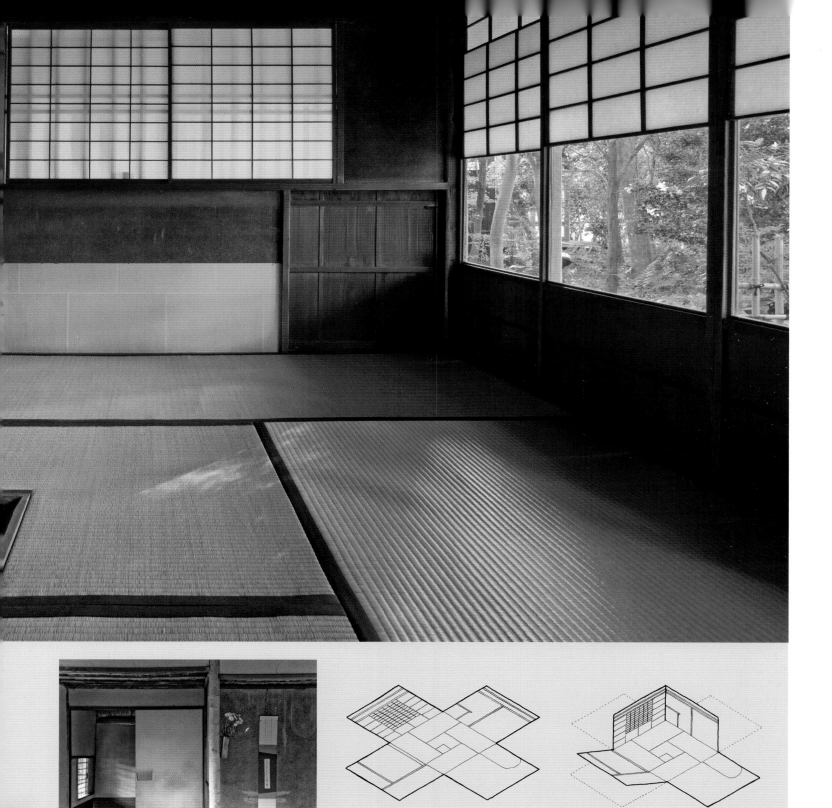

Top A shaggy thatched roof partially conceals an overscaled circular window, reflecting the playful character often found in *sukiya*-style teahouse architecture.
Center Traditional teahouses are designed to express the intrinsic qualities of the natural materials used in their construction. Tree trunks set on uneven stone bases serve as columns, and walls are covered with roughly textured plasters.
Above Water sprinkled on the path leading to a teahouse indicates to the guests that the tea ceremony and its accordant spaces have been carefully prepared in honor of their visit.

as a medicinal drink and stimulant before it became popular as a social drink for the elite classes. From the fourteenth century, aristocrats held gatherings specifically for the drinking of tea that were grand affairs with dozens of people. These parties developed into tasting contests, where guests tried to determine the geographic origin of the tea. As the popularity of tasting contests waned, the drinking of tea was transformed into the ritualistic tea ceremony promulgated by fourteenth to sixteenth-century influential tea masters such as Murata Jukō, Takeno Jōō, and Sen no Rikyū. Along with developing and perfecting the art of *wabicha*, the style of tea that informs most contemporary tea ceremonies, Jōō, Rikyū, and others designed landscapes and buildings used for the tea ceremony.

These tea masters cultivated informality and asymmetry, which became hallmarks of the *sukiya* style, and were inspired by the beauty of the roughly textured architecture of the vernacular *minka* and the idea of isolation in a hermit's primitive hut in the woods. Developing a refined version of the *minka* and primitive hut, the tea masters sought to create small buildings in gardens that represent the entire cosmos in a contained space, "a corner however humble, where a man can rise above the limits of relativity and have even a glimpse of eternity."[28] Although the inspiration for these buildings and landscapes came from rough, sometimes primitive forms, the teahouses are sophisticated and highly refined, and the gardens are carefully manipulated and maintained to emulate nature and enhance the architecture.

Teahouses typically are constructed with an exposed timber frame with walls coated with textured mud plaster and roofs covered with thatch or wood shakes. The wood and other construction materials are utilized in ways that show off their natural qualities as much as possible. For example, structural columns may have only the bark removed to expose the silky uneven surface of the wood underneath. The columns may sit on rough foundation stones, with the base of the column carved to fit perfectly to the shape of the stone. In this way, all materials utilized in the construction of the

teahouse are chosen for their natural beauty and used in ways that emphasize that beauty. The materials accentuate the interior spaces, which are designed with a specific proportional system used to determine the dimensions of every element. Designers often used a specialized type of drawing called an *okoshi-ezu*, with the elevations of the four walls drawn adjacent to the floor plan, which could be cut out and folded to verify the space of the tea house in three dimensions (figure 6).

Machiya Merchant Houses

In addition to the aristocratic residential compounds found in the cities, another urban residential building type—a form of urban *minka*—developed. Called a *machiya*, literally a "townhouse," the typical merchant's house in a town or city usually included a small shop connected to a residence. Although it is difficult to determine just when this housing style developed, single-story *machiya* are depicted in twelfth-century scroll paintings and two-story *machiya* appeared by the end of the Heian period but were not common until the Muromachi period (1334–1573 CE).[29] In Kyoto and some other cities, land was divided into long narrow lots with the short end facing the street, and the *machiya* typically developed side by side, with shared wells and sanitary spaces in a communal backyard area. Although some fine examples of *machiya* still exist, especially in preserved historic areas of cities such as Kyoto, the *machiya,* like the *minka*, is an endangered species.

The *machiya* fill the space of the lots, with the front of the building taken up by the shop, which is directly connected to the residential spaces behind. Early *machiya* were quite small and primitively constructed, but as the merchant class grew wealthier in the Edo period, their *machiya* developed to incorporate multiple rooms, including baths and toilets and one or more *kura* storehouses, which are separated from the living quarters by a back garden or open space used for shop-related work and often contain the family's well. A long earthen-floored corridor connects the front of the house to the open area in back and encompasses the kitchen, bath, and toilet spaces.

Left The street façade of the Yoshijima house in Takayama features fine latticework, exemplifying the skilled carpentry for which the region is famous.
Below The entrance to this *sake* brewery in Hida Furukawa leads into an earthen-floored (*doma*) space where *sake* is sold, which has views into the less public spaces beyond.

Bottom The layers of space from the interior to the exterior are demarcated by sliding *shōji* screens, which open to give views to the courtyard garden.
Above A courtyard garden brings light and air into the surrounding rooms, each of which has a different view of the natural beauty of the garden.

Above A gently rounded mound of closely clipped azalea bushes is juxtaposed with the flat white surfaces of the gravel bed and garden walls. Beyond the wall, the distant Mount Hiei is brought into the garden as borrowed scenery (*shakkei*).
Right The expansive view and contrast of the raked gravel and the naturalistic plantings can be viewed from the long compressed space of the covered veranda-like *engawa*.
Far right A composition of raked gravel, stone groupings, clipped bushes, and carefully trained trees creates the image of islands and an ocean shoreline in the garden at the Mimurodōji Temple in Uji.

Machiya merchant houses utilize the forms and materials found in higher class residences, including timber structures, mud and lime plaster walls, ceramic tile roofs, and *tatami* mat floors, but the forms are adapted to the size and shape of the urban site. Because the lots are narrow and the houses are built right next to one another, the house and shop could not be built as separate buildings within a larger garden. Instead, small courtyard gardens or *tsuboniwa* (literally "*tsubo* garden"—a *tsubo* is a unit of measure equal to two *tatami* mats, about 3.24 square meters or 36 square feet), are designed into the buildings to bring in light and air and create a tie to nature. The inclusion of the *tsuboniwa* in the *machiya* transposed the well-developed paradigm of the house in the garden to a new type: the garden in the house.

Landscapes and Gardens

Traditional Japanese architecture, especially the *sukiya* style, said by some to be the high point of palace architecture in Japan, is well known to have a strong connection to the adjoining landscape. The extended roof eaves and verandas of the buildings seem to reach out to the surroundings and, together with the exposed structural columns and beams, frame views of the landscape that combine aesthetic pleasures with a feeling of religious profundity. More than vistas of far-off nature in its pristine state, the prized views feature carefully designed landscapes, finely crafted to create an idealized version of nature. Even in the *machiya*, which were built on constricted lots with little open space, diminutive gardens were designed within the buildings to allow

Above A white lime plaster wall with a ceramic tile roof is the backdrop for a composition of clipped bushes, colorful trees, and huge rocks.

for the flow of air and light and to maintain that important connection to nature. These tiny gardens were hardly examples of nature in its pure state but rather were refined representations of the natural environment.

The shaping of the land in Japan began with agriculture, especially the terracing of the land for wet rice farming, and the marking of the land for religious purposes, as in the demarcation of a sacred *shintō* place. The obvious reverence for nature and care used when altering natural landscapes in ancient times developed over centuries into the art of the Japanese garden. Like the architecture, the designs of Japanese gardens initially evidence significant influence from China, especially from the relationship of the building to the land in Chinese-style imperial residences and

Buddhist temple complexes. These landscapes are marked by formality and symmetry, with a succession of white gravel-covered courtyards, perhaps planted with a minimal number of symbolic trees, surrounded by buildings. In contrast, the early Chinese-style gardens that entered Japan through Korea by the seventh century are expansive *sansui* ("mountain–water") landscapes, which featured meandering streams, ponds with islands, and expressive outcroppings of rough rock. Many of these features remained as the Japanese gardens developed, but they were transformed over time to comprise subtle but meticulously controlled—and sometimes very small and carefully contained—compositions of water, plants, and rocks. Some of the best known Japanese gardens are in the *karesansui* ("dry

mountain–water") style, where both water and mountain are represented using rock, and few if any plantings are incorporated into the design.

By the end of the Edo period, two dominant garden styles had developed—expansive gardens with paths and pavilions (also known as "stroll gardens") and contained gardens for seated viewing and meditation (sometimes called "scroll gardens" as they are viewed from a fixed position like a scroll painting). In both types, the architecture played an important—though different—role in the viewing and appreciation of the garden. By the end of the lengthy development of the designs of landscapes and architecture, the relationship between garden and building became so intrinsic that they could no longer be understood or experienced separately.

Chapter 3
The role of tradition

Many different aspects of Japanese architecture reflect tradition—architectural forms can be "traditional," as can the conception of space, the construction materials, and the methods of construction. In Japan, the materials, construction methods, spaces, and forms that we now identify as "traditional" were not labeled as such by the Japanese themselves until the Meiji period (1868–1912), when Japan opened its ports to trade with the outside world after more than two centuries of self-imposed isolation during the Edo period. Historians have noted that the sudden changes of the Meiji era required the Japanese to look at themselves with the eyes of "the other" and to give names to concepts that previously may have been understood inherently but had gone unidentified. "Tradition" may well have been one of those unnamed concepts.[30]

The English word "tradition" derived, in the fourteenth century, from the Latin *traditio*. The generally accepted meaning is "the handing down of information, beliefs, and customs by word of mouth or by example from one generation to another without written instruction."[31] In pre-modern Japan (before 1868), although there may not have been a word for it, this same concept of handing down information orally was prevalent and has been recorded in detail in relation to various aesthetic and technical pursuits, including the design and construction of buildings and gardens.

Top, figure 7 Kuma Kengo's design sketch for the Museum of Hiroshige Ando emphasizes the space captured between the floor and roof planes, learned from traditional buildings in Japan.
Above Sliding *shōji* screens separate the *tatami*-matted interior living spaces from the veranda-like *engawa* at the perimeter of a traditional Japanese house.

An important example of this type of communicating information is one way that apprentice carpenters learned their trade from the masters. Skills and information were taught verbally, often in combination with a demonstration by the master and long hours of practice by the apprentice. However, many skills were passed down through "stolen lessons" (*nusumi-geiko*), when the apprentice watched the master at work and picked up techniques to refine through his own practice.[32]

In pre-modern Japanese society, the general concept of "the handing down of information, beliefs, and customs" was well understood. However, it is unclear whether the Japanese had a specific word for the concept, or if they used different words, like "*nusumi-geiko*," for

particular situations. Scholars working in the modern period in Japan, including folklorist Yanagita Kunio, who published his influential book *Dentō ni tsuite* ("On Tradition") in 1937, believe that the combination of ideographs now used for *dentō* ("tradition," 伝統, literally "transmit control") were brought to Japan from China in *The Analects of Confucius*, as well as in calligraphy manuals, and had been developed in China by the early fourth century CE, perhaps 1,000 years earlier (approximately contemporaneous to the Latin *traditio*). Yanagita reasons that the word *dentō* came to be translated as "tradition" in the Meiji era following Japan's isolationist period, when many foreign words and concepts were introduced to Japan and translated into Japanese.[33]

Along with the need for new words brought about by the advent of foreigners and foreign things after the first Japanese port reopened in 1858, came the country's quest for rapid industrialization in order to catch up with its counterparts in the West. At the time, a Japanese citizen famously told a German physician, "We have no history. Our history begins today."[34] This idea of closing the door on a country's history (and with it, the traditions and customs) and starting fresh was especially clear in the building arts. Design and construction, which previously had been the domain of the carpenter, were separated (as in the West), with design and its related subjects taught as an academic discipline called "architecture," which was initially translated in the Meiji period as *zōkajutsu* ("building arts"), later as *zōkagaku* ("building studies"), and then finally as *kenchiku*[35] (which also means "building" or "construction"). Along with the new profession and academic discipline based directly on the Western paradigm came new architectural styles and construction methods and materials based on Western models. The Japanese government proclaimed Western-style architecture to be the proper architecture to express the newly industrializing Japan, and before long civic buildings in Japan's major cities appeared in authentic neo-classical style.[36]

Foreign experts were brought to Japan to assist in this sudden industrialization, including a young British architect, Josiah Conder, who arrived in 1877 as Japan's first professor of "architecture" for the newly formed university course in architecture at the Imperial College of Engineering (now the Tokyo University Faculty of Engineering). Along with his teaching duties, Conder practiced architecture, receiving commissions for a number of important public and residential buildings.

Change happened quickly in the public realm (though much more slowly in the private sphere), and building forms and materials embodied that change. The architecture that Conder taught and built, which was sanctioned by the Japanese government, was unlike anything that had previously been built in Japan. It furthered the government's industrialization agenda by mimicking the imposing neo-

Top With its steep stone foundation, white plaster walls, and layers of curved tile roofs, Himeji Castle is an exceptional example of Japan's brief but prolific period of castle building.
Above left Although completed in 1920, the Meiji Shrine in Tokyo is built in a centuries-old style that is common for *shintō* shrines.
Above right Sliding *shōji* paper and wood screens, floors covered with straw-filled *tatami* mats, roughly textured earthen plaster walls, and wood board-and-batten ceilings are typical of *sukiya*-style architecture.
Left A garden pavilion mixes modern forms and technology with traditional materials.

Top Buddhist temples maintain tradition through the continuity of the religious rituals, as well as the maintenance of the buildings and gardens.

Above Old and new are combined in the Hōnenin Temple in Kyoto. Traditional sliding *fusuma* panels are painted with a bold contemporary design.

Right An attendant at the Yasaka Shrine in Kyoto displays wooden plaques noting the names of recent donors.

classical architectural forms popular in Europe and the United States at that time, although Conder sometimes embellished them with exotic Asian-influenced motifs or combined them with elements derived from the French Second Empire or other styles. The heavy timber structures of the past gave way to grand masonry buildings with pilasters and rusticated bases in place of the wood columns and stone plinths.

One of the important public buildings Conder designed was the Rokumeikan ("Hall of the Baying Stag"), a grand "pleasure pavilion"[37] with an expansive lawn and small Japanese garden, where Japanese and foreigners could meet for social events. Completed in 1883, the building was indicative of the politics of the time—which have been referred to as "Rokumeikan politics," where foreigners were kept at a distance, living in separate neighborhoods and meeting and socializing with their Japanese counterparts in buildings erected specifically for those purposes.

It is interesting to note that, as is typical when the ideas that dominate a culture are suddenly shifted, an alternative to both the old and new paradigms developed. *Giyōfu* ("pseudo-Western style") architecture made its debut shortly after the reopening of the ports, led by the master carpenters who realized their roles as designers and builders would have to change. In an effort to keep up with the times, many carpenters began to design buildings by combining old and new forms, but they still constructed the buildings using their time-honored methods and materials. This new style of architecture, also sometimes called *kaikashiki* ("Restoration mode"),[38] is exemplified by buildings with eclectic combinations of Western and Japanese elements. They are mostly Western in scale and proportion but with details and ornamentation that often are very Japanese in style. The buildings are constructed with timber frames but are cleverly disguised to look like masonry buildings.

One of the finest examples of the *giyōfu* style is the Tsukiji Hotel built by master carpenter Shimizu Kisuke II in 1868. The hotel was designed to be used specifically by foreigners and featured a ceramic tile-covered roof with

an elaborate cupola topped with a weathervane. The heavy timber frame was completely covered on the exterior with a diagonal grid of plaster and tile in the *namako-kabe* style, punctuated by rows of shuttered windows.

It was during this time in Japanese architectural history, when building forms and construction methods were suddenly dramatically changing, that Western architects and historians—along with newly trained Japanese architects and historians—began to look at Japan's history from the outside, and the idea of tradition began to be defined. However, at that time the architecture curriculum of the Imperial College of Engineering focused on the new Western forms and construction methods and did not include any study of historic Japanese styles or ways of building.

It was not until a new style of architecture began to appear in the West—"modern" architecture that utilized industrial materials such as steel, concrete, and glass, and new construction techniques designed to take advantage of the qualities of those materials—that the young Japanese architects started questioning the appropriateness of neoclassical Western-style architecture in Japan. At the time, many young Japanese architects aspired to move beyond the Western-style architecture they were taught at university and instead work in the modern style. These architects were propelled by a group formed in 1920 calling themselves the *Bunriha Kenchikukai* (literally the "Secessionist Architects Group" but usually referred to as the Bunriha in English).

The Bunriha group "sought to break with the past as it had been constructed in recent architectural practice. At the same time, they proposed to replace this problematic 'past' with an architecture firmly situated in the present yet resonant with their own conception of a more vital and authentic 'tradition.'"[39] One of the leaders of the Bunriha group, Horiguchi Sutemi, declared that while it was impossible to break with one's tradition, which for him meant the architecture in Japan that predated the Meiji-era Western styles, it was necessary to push architecture forward based on newly available technology and ideas.[40]

While Horiguchi and the Bunriha were working toward a new style of architecture for twentieth-century Japan, an architecture rooted in tradition which would reflect the latest advances in architectural technology and style while not severing the connection to the architecture of the past, architect and historian Itō Chuta promoted working with the forms of Japan's historical architecture. Itō suggested that the historical styles could be combined with Western styles to produce an appropriate architecture for Japan. Itō's idea of suitable historical precedent for early twentieth century architecture in Japan included important Buddhist buildings and the *shintō* shrine at Ise. An article written by Itō for a daily newspaper in 1921 champions the simplicity of the Ise Shrine as an authentic Japanese quality.[41] These kinds of ideas regarding the role of tradition in architecture were central in a difficult debate among Japanese architects relating national identity and architectural form.

While the architects were deliberating the role of tradition, the Japanese government was promoting the idea of national identity and pushing for a partial return to historic styles as a way to ensure Japanese character in major buildings designed to represent the Japanese government at home and abroad. Japan began flexing its colonizing muscle in Asia in the 1920s and 1930s, and "as Japan encountered mounting hostility in the world, and as the sense of isolation grew, the government's appeals for patriotic sacrifice grew more insistent and more strident."[42] The Japanese government's desire for patriotism as it was manifest in architecture came to be known as the *teikan yōshiki* ("imperial crown") style because of the focus on a Japanese-style roof. The style is best represented by Watanabe Jin's 1931 competition-winning design for the Imperial Household Museum in Tokyo, a neo-classical building with pilasters and a porte cochere, topped with a Japanese-style roof with curved eaves covered with ceramic tiles.

As members of the first generation of Japanese architectural historians were completing their university studies, they were looking at Japan's historic architecture with fresh eyes—

eyes that had been trained in Western methodologies. Influenced by the ideas of tradition advanced by historian and ethnologist Yanagita Kunio in the 1930s,[43] they observed and researched what they understood to be traditional Japanese architecture. Architect and Tokyo Imperial University professor Kishida Hideto published a collection of modernist photographs of historic Japanese buildings, *Kako no kōsei* ("Composition of the Past"), in late 1929 and followed that in 1936 with an English-language pamphlet produced by the Japan Travel Bureau titled simply *Japanese Architecture*. In the first chapter, "Characteristics of Japanese Architecture," Kishida states that his goal is to explain the "distinct characteristics" of Japanese architecture so that readers will be able "to recognize the developments peculiar to Japanese architecture and to understand the necessity and rationality which lie behind these features."[44]

Kishida goes on to list seven features which he understands to be essentially Japanese: 1) construction based on the column, 2) materials featuring natural wood, 3) the function and expression of the roof, 4) prominently projecting eaves, 5) *masu-gumi* ("square framing") structural detail to support the eaves, 6) the natural color of building materials, and 7) an architectural feeling based on an admiration of the beauty in nature. He continues by stating that the Japanese people "are capable of a keen appreciation of refinement, elegance, simplicity, clearness, and frankness, which, I believe, are fully embodied in their architecture."[45] Like Itō Chuta and others before him, Kishida selected the *shintō* shrine at Ise as "the purest expression of original and genuine Japanese taste,"[46] and states, "None can reproduce its beauty in any picture, and to it ought all the world's architects make a pilgrimage, for this genuinely original expression of the Land of Nippon has become a work which belongs to the whole world."[47]

Many foreign architects of the time agreed with Kishida's assessment of the Ise Shrine, especially the German modernist architect Bruno Taut, who visited Ise on his 1933 trip to Japan. "The shrines at Ise are Japan's greatest and completely original creation in general

world architecture ... after the first visit to Ise one knows what Japan is."[48] Earlier architects who saw the Ise Shrine did not necessarily agree. Ralph Adams Cram visited Ise in 1898 and viewed it with the eyes of an architect trained in the classical tradition. The "rude contrivance of Ise," he wrote, is "ugly and barbarous."[49] But to the newly modernist Japanese architects and historians, Ise provided the important historical roots for an essentially Japanese modernism.

Bruno Taut was hosted in Japan by a group of young architects who were keen to promote modernism and were looking for a way to present modern architecture as part of the historical continuity of Japanese architecture. They took Taut to Ise as well as to the Katsura Imperial Villa, an example of the refined *sukiya* style. Acknowledgement of a connection between the Katsura villa and modernist ideas by a well-respected European architect would give credibility to their aspirations, and Taut obliged by "identifying Katsura as *the* masterpiece of functionalist architecture."[50]

As the nationalist and colonialist tendencies of the Japanese government increased in the late 1930s and early 1940s, construction materials went to military purposes, and opportunities for architects to design large projects decreased considerably. However, the state's nationalist pursuit of a characteristically Japanese architecture was demonstrated in the government sponsorship of design competitions for the Greater East Asian Memorial Hall in 1942 and the Japanese Cultural Center in Bangkok in 1943. Kishida Hideto served as a juror for both competitions, and in both cases the winning design was by Tange Kenzō.

Tange was a key player in the tradition–modernism debate and Kishida's former student at Tokyo Imperial University. For the Greater East Asian Memorial Hall, he based his design on the overall layout of the Ise Shrine, with a symmetrical arrangement of gable-roofed structures centered in enclosed courtyards. As inspiration for the Japanese Cultural Center, Tange looked to the *shoin-*style Kyoto Imperial Palace, designing a series of gabled-roofed buildings, with the floors raised above the ground, linked by enclosed

corridors. In *Japan-ness in Architecture*, architect Isozaki Arata discusses these competitions, as well as a third competition (post-World War II), also won by Tange, for the Memorial Peace Center in Hiroshima (for which Tange used the proportional system from the *sukiya-*style Katsura villa in addition to other historical elements). "All three projects were thought of as significant expressions of the Japanese nation-state, albeit reflecting various ideological phases of the war effort and its conclusion."[51]

After the war, Tange and others continued to consider the "problem of tradition" as the country and people of Japan struggled with sociopolitical reforms and the rebuilding of the nation. Again, the issue of finding and maintaining an authentic Japanese identity in the face of great change and modernization was a core issue for Japanese philosophers, writers, artists, and architects. Although some Japanese architects and historians include the great Chinese Buddhist-style temples and the later *shinden-*style buildings in their understanding of "Japanese taste," most primarily have looked

Left Long a symbol of the strength of the *shintō* religion, the Izumo Shrine stands proud with its great gently curving roof and perimeter veranda.
Below The moon-viewing deck of the Katsura Imperial Villa stretches out into the garden toward a pond where the reflection of the moon is visible on clear nights.
Right, figure 8 Early design sketches of the Jinchōkan Moriya Historical Museum by Fujimori Terunobu.

at buildings like the Ise Shrine and the Katsura Imperial Villa to determine what they believe to be essentially Japanese. In his 1960 book, *Katsura: Tradition and Creation in Japanese Architecture*, a collaboration with the German modernist architect Walter Gropius and the Japanese-American photographer Yasuhiro Ishimoto, Tange put his spin on Katsura by noting that its style is that which is "ordinarily described as 'Japanese,'"[52] and illustrating that quality with modernist photographs that emphasize the gridded façade compositions and flatten the sense of perspective.

Tange's *Katsura* and Kishida's earlier *Japanese Architecture* are two examples of scholarship on Japanese architecture published specifically for an English-language audience. From the time Japan ended its Edo-period isolation, Westerners had been interested in many aspects of Japanese culture, including architecture, and Japanese architects and historians published English language essays and books about Japanese architecture to satisfy this desire for knowledge. Of course, it also gave them the opportunity to promote their own ideas about

Japanese tradition and to take advantage of the international stage to give credence to their views, especially the idea of the architecture of buildings like Ise and Katsura being the roots of Japanese modernism.

In 1954, the Museum of Modern Art in New York corroborated the Japanese architects' idea that traditional Japanese architecture had a strong relationship to modern architecture by exhibiting a "traditional" Japanese house in the museum courtyard. In his 1955 book accompanying the exhibition of the Japanese house, *The Architecture of Japan*, curator Arthur Drexler identified the six elements he believed to be "of continuing relevance to our own [American] building activities."[53] They include 1) the post-and-beam skeleton construction system, 2) the expression of shelter through the large roof, 3) the decorative use of structural elements, 4) the preference for additive space, 5) the flexibility of plan, and 6) the close relationship of indoors and outdoors.[54]

This quest to define the essential Japanese elements in the historic architecture continued into the 1960s and beyond. In his essay in the

1965 book *Ise: Prototype of Japanese Architecture*, a collaboration between architect Tange Kenzō, architectural critic Kawazoe Noboru, and photographer Watanabe Yoshio, Kawazoe noted as being "Japanese" 1) the centrality of wood as a building material, 2) the preference for structures that relied on a grid of horizontal and vertical members and avoided diagonals and curved lines, 3) the tendency in Japanese building to perpetuate architectural form without undue concern for the preservation of the actual building itself, 4) an appreciation for the mutability of all things, and 5) the recognition that the practice of building should be attuned to natural processes.[55]

In the same book, Tange makes note that "the entire later course of Japanese architecture starts at Ise,"[56] based on 1) the use of natural materials in a natural way, 2) the sensitivity to structural proportion, and 3) the feeling for space arrangement, especially the tradition of harmony between architecture and nature.[57] Historian Jonathan Reynolds, writing about Tange's book, explains that Ise "resonates with cherished assumptions about Japanese culture.

Ise has come to serve as an exemplar of architecture devoid of unnecessary ornament; an architecture that reflects extraordinary sensitivity to building materials; an architecture that is integral with nature rather than being imposed on it."[58]

In another book from the mid-1960s that attempted to define traditional Japanese architecture, *The Roots of Japanese Architecture*, a collaboration between historian Itō Teiji, Japanese-American sculptor Isamu Noguchi, and photographer Futagawa Yukio, Itō lists ten elements of an "underlying system that gives [Japanese] architecture its validity:"[59] 1) the materials wood, stone, and earth, 2) setting limits to infinity, 3) dynamic space, 4) the garden as a miniature universe, 5) the linking of nature and architecture, 6) the pillar and the *tatami* mat, 7) teahouses, bamboo, and more pillars, 8) borrowing space; 9) the rhythms of the vertical plane, and 10) the roof as a symbol.

More recently, Nishi Kazuo and Hozumi Kazuo in their 1983 book, *What is Japanese Architecture?*, note a "core of shared traits that allows us to speak of 'Japanese architecture' in general, instead of isolated Japanese buildings."[60] They continue, "These fundamental consistencies are particularly remarkable considering the variety of climates that characterize the Japanese archipelago and the millennium and more that separates the earliest and latest examples of the nation's traditional architecture."[61] Nishi and Hozumi go on to list the following ten "traits:" 1) the choice of materials (wood, paper, straw, plaster and clay, tile; stone only for temple podia), 2) the post and lintel structural system, 3) the great roof (with extended eaves), 4) the interior core from which secondary spaces may radiate, 5) the preference for straight lines rather than curves, 6) the dim interiors due to the deep eaves, 7) the fluidity of interior partitions, 8) the inside–outside fluidity/integration of buildings and landscape, 9) the proportional system, and 10) decoration that embellishes rather than disguises basic construction.[62]

In his 1996 book, *Island Nation Aesthetic*, architect Isozaki Arata chooses not to follow the typical pattern of listing formal elements and instead looks toward composition and the perception of space as particular attributes of Japanese architecture. He emphasizes flatness, the Japanese way of sensing space, and the use of non-compositional non-hierarchical compositional principles.[63] Isozaki writes, "In Japan, traditional architecture had demonstrated virtually no concern with three-dimensional, solid spatial composition and had instead preferred to sever time into instances and space into floor areas, and to organise these fragments with intervals (*ma*) among them."[64]

Isozaki and other Japanese architects working in the late twentieth and early twenty-first centuries have dealt with the concept of tradition in many different ways. The space–time concept of *ma* is one aspect of tradition that Isozaki understands to be essentially Japanese and of continuing importance. "The concept of *ma*, or interval, for which we Japanese require no explanation, pervades our lives and our art in general, as well as our feelings, methods and artistic awareness."[65]

Right The building housing the Reihōden Museum nestles into the hillside and blends with its surroundings in the Kurumadera Temple complex in Kyoto.
Below With a contrasting but unified composition of raked gravel against carefully placed stones and plantings in the foreground, a wall-like hedge bounds the garden yet allows the borrowed scenery of Mount Hiei to be part of the garden view.

Like many Japanese architects, Isozaki also considers the teahouse or space for tea ceremony as essentially Japanese. In *The Contemporary Tea House: Japan's Top Architects Redefine a Tradition*, he writes, "The Japanese tearoom evolved into an architectural form found nowhere else."[66] The tea ceremony is one of the aesthetic traditions of Japan that has continued to the present day, and with it comes the need and desire to design appropriate spaces for tea. Considering a contemporary idiom for the building type that is the epitome of *sukiya*-style architecture is appealing to architects. Fujimori Terunobu unequivocally

states, "Asked to design a tearoom, no Japanese architect today would refuse the opportunity."[67] Current Japanese architects' designs and ideas for teahouses are good indicators of the many different ways in which tradition is embodied in contemporary architecture.

Teahouse design involves the challenge of creating, in Ando Tadao's words, "an infinitely expanding universe in an enclosed, very small space."[68] Within that context, Isozaki wishes "to explore to the utmost the boundaries of formalized tearoom architectural form of modern Japan,"[69] and his teahouses range from a "traditional" wood and mud plaster teahouse inserted into a contemporary building to a freestanding teahouse with rectangular walls of limestone set off by an undulating titanium wall. Ando's teahouses enclose "infinitely expanding" space not only with the fine concrete work for which he is famous but also with other materials, such as plywood, rattan, opaque glass, and *washi* paper.

The choice of building materials is fundamental to teahouse design, and Kuma Kengo

understands "the tearoom as a radical form of critique."[70] Kuma builds "tea rooms to critique the use of concrete as a building material.... [C]oncrete is by far the main reason for the terrible decline of Japan's traditional building culture."[71] As well as carefully considering materials, he also notes inspiration from historic examples, especially designs by Sen no Rikyū. Kuma's teahouses show great material breadth and ingenuity, from stone louvers and *tatami* in a converted stone warehouse to a portable *washi* paper tea space to an inflatable teahouse made from architectural fabric.

Fujimori Terunobu also uses materials in surprising ways, noting, "The most overt characteristic of my tearooms is the finish of the material."[72] His teahouses are highly textured compositions of plaster, bark, wood, metal, and glass. Fujimori declares, "I have not attempted to create the kind of traditional space used for tea ceremony with my designs."[73] Instead, he pushes design boundaries by planting teahouses on top of tree

trunks—as high as 6.5 meters (more than 21 feet) off the ground—and working with amateur artisans on their construction.

From the single example of the teahouse, it is clear that many Japanese architects today draw from tradition, incorporating and integrating traditional and contemporary forms, materials, and concepts into many different building types, while other architects consciously choose to break with tradition and search for new architectural expressions.

Over the decades, many architects have studied historic Japanese architecture and struggled to understand and define the potential roles of traditional elements and spatial concepts in their architectural designs, no matter the building type. The role of tradition in contemporary Japanese architecture is constantly changing as architects experiment with new forms, construction methods, and materials. It seems that in contemporary Japanese architecture, the role of tradition is no longer traditional.

PART 2
Forms and Materials

にほひくる
隣の風を身にしめて
ありし軒端の梅ぞこひしき

更級

From the neighboring garden comes a scented breeze.
Deeply I breathe it in, though longing all the while
For the plum tree by our ancient eaves.[1]

LADY SARASHINA (1008–AFT. 1064)

Chapter 4
Basic principles

Nature is at the heart of traditional life in Japan, just as it is the foundation for the architectural forms and construction materials of traditional Japanese buildings. Having developed within an environment that at times is very harsh yet provides an abundance of materials suitable for construction, the traditional architecture of Japan is an expression of the fundamental concepts of Japanese culture.

Traditional Japanese culture is built on a strong respect and reverence for nature. Despite the constant threat of natural perils, such as earthquakes, typhoons, and volcanic eruptions, Japanese culture did not develop a hostile stance toward nature. Instead, a fundamental reverence and awe for the power of nature underlies the relationship of humankind and nature in Japan. Rather than fighting nature, Japanese culture embraces it—the beauty and wonder of nature as well as its overwhelming power and severity. Humankind is understood as one of many species of living creatures in the natural world—part of nature, never separate from it.

This idea that humankind cannot be separated from nature lies at the very core of Japanese beliefs. Traditional life in Japan developed in concert with the seasons but also includes daily acknowledgment of the power and bounty of nature. In addition to the planting and harvesting of crops and the development of cultural festivals and rituals associated with those all-important activities, respect for nature in Japan is an essential part of everyday life, starting with simple morning offerings to the local *shintō* deities.

Two of the fundamental principles in *shintō* are the beliefs that deities have a strong

connection to nature—many, in fact, reside in nature, in trees, stones, mountains, and waterfalls—and that deities are local as well as communal. Therefore, a local god may reside in an unusual outcropping of rocks—and a road might be directed around the rocks to avoid disturbing its sacred nature. At the same time, communal deities, like those of the sun, wind, and agriculture, and deities that inhabit nationally revered places like Mount Fuji have equivalent importance in traditional life. The original belief that deities live among the people without barriers, and they are not to be feared but to be respected, reinforces the idea that humankind and nature are inseparable.

The respect for nature that is at the basis of the *shintō* religion fits well with the teachings of Buddhism. When Buddhist thought was brought to Japan in the sixth century, it was introduced in a way that would allow it to be compatible with the long-existing *shintō* beliefs. In Buddhism, like *shintō*, nature is

respected, and human life is understood to be part of the natural cycle of all living things. "Let us destroy all such artificial barriers we put up between Nature and ourselves, for it is only when they are removed that we see into the living heart of Nature and live with it—which is the real meaning of love."[2]

The respect for nature and the idea of human life as part of nature, as was supported by both *shintō* and Buddhist beliefs, is reflected in the ways traditional buildings were sited and constructed and in the understanding of the lifecycle of a building. Early builders responded to the need to keep out the cold winter wind and provide ventilation for the hot summer months and constructed buildings with those conditions in mind. The later Chinese-style architecture that accompanied the introduction of Buddhism in Japan incorporated principles of Chinese geomancy, a formalized—and somewhat mysticized—response to the same environmental issues.

Pages 44–5 Kumamoto Castle, Kumamoto, Kyūshū Island.
Opposite Carved wood in a floral motif over a wood lattice grid, ornamental bargeboard metalwork, and layers of ceramic tile come together in an ornate but unified combination on the roof gable of the Ninomaru Palace of the Nijō Castle in Kyoto.
Left A *shimenawa* ties together the sacred Meotoi-wa wedded rocks at Futami-gaura near the Ise Shrine.

Above left Village residents join together to replace the thatch on a *minka* farmhouse in Shirakawa-go. After the fall rice harvest, each family dries its rice straw to use for communal building maintenance.

Above center Wood shutters are propped open to limit the sunlight entering the Kyusuitei Pavilion at the Shūgakuin Imperial Villa in Kyoto, as well as to control the views out to the garden of the villa.

Above right In a multidimensional scene of white, the snow-covered landscape of the Sanzenin Temple expresses the movement-filled design of the garden.

Left, figure 9 A geomantic chart used with a floor plan drawing shows auspicious and inauspicious directions for different types of rooms and functions.

Geomancy is defined as "an aesthetic science dealing with the positive management of the landscape in accordance with the hidden forces within the earth."[3] Known as *feng shui* in Chinese and *fūsui* in Japanese, both literally meaning "wind water," geomancy gave a kind of mythical meaning to common responses to climate. The cardinal directions were represented by gods symbolized by a tortoise in the north, a dragon in the east, a phoenix in the south, and a tiger in the west. For certain uses or architectural elements, misfortune or sickness was associated with specific directions (such as from where the cold winter wind blew), and positive forces and good health were associated with others (the direction of the morning sun, for example).[4] Geomantic charts (figure 9) were developed to aid in the siting of buildings and the layouts of rooms in relation to one another and to the land. "The concern of geomancy for integrating structures of human origin with the great forces of nature made it the 'ecology' of its day."[5]

In addition to responding to the local climate and environment in their forms and siting, traditional Japanese buildings were

constructed using locally obtainable materials—and the variety of materials available entirely depended on the climate and environment. In much of Japan, the temperate climate and ample rainfall create excellent growing conditions for many different kinds of plants and trees. Much of the land is forested, so wood is an obvious choice for construction. Reeds and grasses, such as bamboo and miscanthus, are common and have many uses, including as versatile building materials.

Stone is prevalent in many regions and is an obvious choice for certain architectural elements, especially foundations and retaining walls. Because of frequent earthquakes, stone is not appropriate for structural walls, so most structural walls are built with timber framing. Soil is also abundant, and in many areas the soil contains sufficient clay so that it can be used as the base for mud plaster, which covers the walls between the timber framing. Soil also can be tamped to form a durable floor surface.

The earliest dwellings were simple constructions of commonly found materials—wood and thatch with earthen floors. These houses developed into the *minka* ("people's houses"), which incorporate stone, bamboo, mud plaster, and other local materials, in addition to wood, thatch, and earth. The methods for joining materials also developed based on the use of readily available materials. Rope, made from rice straw or vines, is used to bind; wood is cut into dowels or wedges; and bamboo is fashioned into nails. These straightforward solutions initially were used quite simply in the early *minka*, but they later developed into complex and elegantly sophisticated systems of joinery, especially in wood, for which traditional Japanese architecture has long been admired.

As the forms and construction of traditional Japanese buildings developed with the influence of spiritual ideas and geomantic principles, as well as the increased knowledge of and skill in working natural materials, the relationship of buildings to the land likewise progressed. This relationship changed from a simple response to the need for protection from the weather to a complex and intrinsic overlapping of interior and exterior space, as traditional Japanese buildings cannot be understood outside of the context of their relationship with the land.

The Development of Architectural Space

Early buildings in Japan were not understood in terms of the space they contained; rather, the focus was on the objects and activities that were contained within the space.[6] Prehistoric buildings, flat-land and pit dwellings in particular, were simple shelters to protect their inhabitants from the weather. Although a certain amount of space was necessary for people to eat and sleep, it is easy to imagine that the ancient dwelling was understood as a container for these activities and for the tools required to accomplish them. Life focused on survival, and there was little motive, need, or occasion for aesthetic pursuits.

Even as life for the early Japanese became easier, as is reflected in the advancement of architectural forms (religious buildings and houses for the upper class) from the early fourth century until the mid-sixth century CE, the focus still was on the objects contained within the space of a building, rather than on the space itself. These buildings, however, were more complex in construction and more comfortable than the earlier dwellings. Rather

than being sunken into the ground like the pit dwellings or built directly on the ground like the flat-land houses, some buildings had floors built above ground. However, each structure still contained only a single large space, and divisions of that space were made with movable partitions and platforms, which acted more like furniture than spatial dividers. These buildings, too, lacked a strong relationship to the land and to exterior space, thereby reinforcing the idea of the building as an object in space which contained objects within its interior space. This predilection for objects in space continued with the introduction of Chinese-style Buddhist architectural forms in the sixth century, as the great temple complexes were organized with the buildings as sculptural elements within the space of enclosed courtyards.[7]

It was not until the end of the Heian period in the late twelfth century that the Japanese conception of space began to change. With the development of the *shinden* style of architecture from that time, buildings started to reach out to the landscape, and rather than simply being surrounded by land, the buildings began to influence the intentional shaping of the landscape. This fundamental change from building as object within space to building as form that defines space was further developed in the *shoin* and *sukiya* architecture of the thirteenth through mid-nineteenth centuries.[8]

Above The silhouette of a *shintō* priest is veiled by a sheer *misu* blind in the Haidan Oracle Hall at the Izumo Shrine.
Below Each space in this residence is a tranquil composition of elements based on the proportions of the *tatami* mat.
Right A slightly crooked *tokobashira* column, a simple straight wood shelf, and a raised *tatami* platform demarcate the spaces of the *tokonoma* alcove.

The Japanese first distanced themselves from the damp ground by covering the tamped earth floors with "bran about two inches deep, with straw matting laid over it."[11] They later made raised floors surfaced with bamboo poles or wood planks, which eventually were replaced with thick straw-filled *tatami* mats. There was no need for specialized furniture such as beds and chairs, since sleeping, eating, and other activities could occur on the floor with the addition of a few easily moved and stored cushions. For the nobility, social hierarchy was expressed by placing raised platforms on the floor for the most esteemed, eliminating the demand for a special chair or throne.

As for the emulation of an advanced culture, the Japanese had no problem adopting the forms of Chinese Buddhist temples and over time adapting them to their own taste, but it was not the same with furniture. Perhaps chairs were playthings of the elite, "decorative items that never found their way into the daily life of the people."[12] Or perhaps "the coincidence of all the factors necessary to comfortable sitting is so unlikely, the probability of awkwardness and discomfort is so great, that it is not hard to imagine that [the Japanese, like] many cultures, having had a try at it, would abandon the effort and wisely resort to sitting on the ground."[13]

Since rooms contained little furniture that would dictate a specific use, such as a bedroom or dining room, they generally developed as flexible multipurpose spaces rather than for a single activity. The lack of large pieces of furniture reinforces the continued functional flexibility, which is a very important circumstance of traditional Japanese buildings, houses in particular. Not only are houses traditionally used for normal daily activities, they also are used for familial and neighborhood gatherings for special events like wedding parties and funerals. Removable partitions allow spaces to be opened up to accommodate large groups of people, and more people can share the space sitting on the floor than using tables and chairs.

Although many different activities take place in these flexible interior spaces, as the level of comfort and number of rooms increased, certain areas were designated for

While the spatial relationship of architecture and landscape developed, so did the Japanese conception of interior space. Starting from the initial understanding of objects within contained space, as the function of buildings developed from mere shelter to incorporate concerns for comfort and privacy, the space inside buildings became more complex. Changes in floor and ceiling levels and new and varied methods for dividing interior space and connecting interior and exterior space demonstrate a different understanding of interior space—one in which the interior space is contained within horizontal and vertical surfaces and is continuous with the space outside.

Life on the Floor

Despite the sophisticated development of the architectural forms and the relationship of interior and exterior space, it may seem surprising that the Japanese continued to live on the floor, rather than developing furniture that moved daily life activities to a slightly higher level. It is easy to understand how life began on the floor, as most primitive cultures use the ground for all daily activities, including eating, sleeping, preparing food, and playing, and the early Japanese were no different. It also is easy to understand that once the earthen floor was covered with another material, life might initially proceed on the ground as before. But it is perhaps more difficult to comprehend why the lifestyle did not change during the centuries of development of the architecture, especially with the strong influence of Chinese culture, in which high seating for the nobility began during the Han dynasty (206 BCE–220 CE) and was in common use by the T'ang dynasty (618–907 CE).[9]

Chairs were introduced into Japanese architectural spaces at various times, first from China as early as the end of the prehistoric period (c. 300–552 CE), again from China in the twelfth century, and later from Europe in the late sixteenth century. In each case, the chair enjoyed a brief period of popularity among the elite classes but never was accepted among commoners. In many cultures, the commencement of the use of chairs corresponded to at least one of three objectives: to be removed from the damp ground, to express social hierarchy, and to emulate a more advanced culture.[10]

Left The *tataki* tamped earth floor, a rough wood column and a beam structure resting on an uneven stone foundation and infilled with coarse mud plaster walls form texture and shadow.
Below Stepping stones lead from the raised wood *engawa* into the garden at the Shisendō Temple in Kyoto.
Bottom Two large granite blocks create a place of pause at the transition between the exterior and the interior.

specific purposes. This typically is reinforced through the types of floor materials used and the relative levels of the floors. For example, the area where much of the food preparation and cooking is done is the earthen-floored *doma*, which is at the same level as the ground outside the house. Work in the *doma* usually is accomplished standing up. Footwear is worn in the *doma* but removed when stepping up to the wood plank or *tatami* mat floors of the living spaces, where activities take place on the floor. Because of the separation of floor levels and the custom of removing shoes, the dirt brought in from the outside remains in the lower earthen-floored spaces, and the raised living spaces stay clean. In addition, the raised floor is often at a height that makes the eye level of a person sitting on the floor equal to that of someone standing in the *doma*, which allows for easy communication.

Within the living spaces, too, changes in floor materials and levels designate different uses. For example, the floor of the *tokonoma* decorative alcove, typically constructed from a single large wood plank, is raised slightly higher than the adjacent floor. This signals that the *tokonoma* floor is not for living purposes and not to be trod upon. This sort of signal from the materials and heights of certain architectural elements within traditional Japanese buildings is clearly understood, and often these same elements are imbued with strong symbolism.

Formal Symbolism

Symbolism is an important aspect of traditional architecture in all cultures. The symbolism inherent in certain architectural elements develops based on a combination of the forms and functions of the elements. Many symbolic elements initially have purely functional roles in buildings, and their symbolism grows out of the significance of their function. Others have spiritual or mythological symbolism associated with them from ancient times. Often a symbol "carries a greater wealth of associative meaning than its perceivable form indicates, representing concepts, ideas or beliefs that are sought or shared by a group or community. Some symbols may be graphic, while others may be ritualized, many may be ephemeral while others may persist over millennia. In certain cases they may be so ancient and so enduring as to be regarded by some as residing in the collective subconscious."[14]

The most obvious symbolic element in traditional Japanese architecture is the roof. The roof is the dominant feature of nearly all types of Japanese buildings, as it typically is built quite high and large with long overhanging eaves. The roof is a clear expression of shelter and of the containing of space for multiple activities. The greater the size of the roof, the more space it contains. Based on its size and form, the roof also expresses the wealth and social status of the inhabitants. This is further reinforced by the materials used to construct the roof and the amount of embellishment in the details. A ceramic tile roof is a sign of wealth and permanence, since tile is much more expensive than thatch and lasts longer. The ornamental end tiles at the edges of the roof, the pattern of the tiles used on the roof ridge, and the especially ornate *onigawara* demon tiles at the ends of the ridge are also expressions of wealth and power. Even a thatched roof may be embellished to show social class and wealth through the manner in which the ridge is constructed and finished and, in exceptional cases, with the carving of patterns and symbols into the thick thatch at the edge of the eave.

From outside a building—almost any type of building: house, temple, castle—the roof is the most prominently symbolic element. However, from the inside the most distinct feature is the exposed wood structure, especially the columns. Since the columns are the most obvious expression of the structure supporting the building, it is not surprising that they might take on symbolic roles. However, their symbolism also may stem from ancient *shintō* purification rites, in which sacred columns were erected in central locations in shrine compounds, "where they were placed as a means of approaching the gods.... The aura of strength given off by such pillars would have come to be perceived as

the divine authority that dwelled in them emanating into the surrounding space."[15] The column, after all, was the first architectural element constructed in Japan—by the *shintō* deities Izanami-no-mikoto and Izanagi-no-mikoto in the Japanese creation story. Two columns in particular, the *daikokubashira* and the *tokobashira*, both found primarily in residential architecture, acquired the strongest symbolism of all the columns.

The *daikokubashira* ("god of wealth column") is a central column that very often is exaggerated in size to express its strength and importance. Usually a different type of wood, often *keyaki* (zelkova), was used for the *daikokubashira* than for the other structural columns, and many times it was formed or finished differently than the others. Its position of centrality in the building developed gradually over time, and although its actual structural role is no different than that of other columns, the *daikokubashira* became a symbol of strength as well as status and was dedicated to the god of wealth, Daikoku.

The *tokobashira* ("alcove column") is the decorative column marking one side of the

tokonoma. The *tokobashira* typically is made from a different wood than other columns (cherry wood or bamboo, for example). The surface of the column reinforces its distinctive character, as the *tokobashira* may have its bark left intact, or the surface may be naturally shaped into an unusual finish. Though often smaller than the structural columns, the shape and finish of the *tokobashira* give it an air of importance and strengthen its role as a focal point in the space.

A third symbolic column, the *nakabashira* ("center column") is found only in tea ceremony rooms. It is an unusually shaped wood column near the *ro* (hearth) toward the center of the space that is attached to a thin partial wall (*sodekabe*) that limits the guests' view of the host's entrance. The *nakabashira* reinforces the dynamic spatial hierarchy of the small room, as well as serves as both a focal point and a decorative component. The form of the *nakabashira*, which may be a gnarled pillar of red pine or camellia wood, expresses the natural forces that formed it. The textured surface also reinforces this vital connection to nature.

Far left With motifs that strongly reference the natural world, the elaborate ornamentation of the Ninomaru Palace shows the power and prestige of the residents while maintaining a strong connection to nature.
Above left Bright white lime plaster walls contrast with the vermilion color of the painted structural members of the Jōmeimon Gate of the Kyoto Imperial Palace.
Left Complex combinations of structural columns and beams joined to layers of brackets supporting floors and roofs provide ornament through their intricacy and the refined skill evident in the joinery.

Chapter 5
Regional variations

The forms of the vernacular architecture of Japan, in particular the *minka* or "people's houses," vary greatly between different geographic regions. The root of these architectural variations is grounded in the specific regional environment and culture, and many cultural differences themselves stem from a region's distinct natural environment. The primary environmental factors affecting the forms of *minka* include the climate, topography, and available construction materials.

Since buildings are constructed first and foremost for shelter, the climate affects the amount of closed wall area of the building envelope, the required structural strength of the framing, and the selection of construction methods. Climate is an especially influential factor in Japan, as it varies greatly from the northern island of Hokkaido to the southern Ryūkyū Islands. *Minka* in the north are built to withstand the cold and heavy snows of the long winters and are designed to be tightly closed up in winter, with wood *amado* shutters that slide in front of the openings in the exterior walls. Many of these northern *minka* have larger openings on the upper stories than on the ground floor because of the significant annual accumulation of snow. Conversely, *minka* in tropical climates like the southern islands are constructed with low roofs and long eaves that shade the interior spaces and direct the breezes through the building. The exterior walls are constructed almost entirely of movable panels so that the buildings can be opened up and naturally ventilated.

Topography is a significant factor in the form of the *minka*, since building foundations are much simpler to construct on flat surfaces. Given that Japan is quite mountainous, and

Opposite In the forested mountains of the Hida region, bundles of rice straw dry in the sun in front of a tall *minka* farmhouse, which takes advantage of the locally available materials with its wood-paneled walls and roof covered with a thick thatch of rice straw.
Above A low eave shades the entrance to a traditional Okinawan house. Wood lattice doors open to allow breezes to enter the single-story space.

many villages are located in hilly areas, the local topography affects the size and construction of the vernacular houses, as well as the shaping of the land. For example, to build on a sloping site, typically the land first is leveled. The easiest way to level land is to dig into the slope, construct a retaining wall to hold back the high land, and use the soil that is removed to fill in the lower part of the site, which must also be held in place with a retaining wall. Since this process is very labor-intensive, land terraced in this way generally is limited to small plots, which naturally affects the size of the building that can fit on the flat area. To avoid having to terrace the land, in a few areas houses mimic the topography, stepping down the slope, with a single story on the uphill section of the building and two levels of floors on the downhill part. These houses often have two entrances—the main entrance on the level which faces the street and a secondary entrance on the other level.

The availability of natural materials that could be used in construction is another important determinant in the form of vernacular buildings in Japan. In the past, the country's mountainous topography made travel slow and arduous, so it was difficult to move construction materials over great distances. Needing to create shelter with as little extra effort as possible, people learned to make the most of the materials that were readily available in their locale.

Much of the Japanese countryside is forested, so lumber is often prevalent and typically is used for the building structure as well as the cladding for many surfaces (floors, walls, ceilings, even roofs). Bamboo and other grasses and reeds also grow well in most areas.

Left Interior and exterior spaces merge at the perimeter of the Sentō Imperial Palace. The *engawa* veranda is raised above the ground to the level of the interior floor and is covered by the roof, but at the same time remains open to the garden.
Above Coral sand is artfully swept around a single wood column. The column and the coral stone wall reflect the harsh climate of strong sun and winds on Taketomi Island in the far southwestern Ryūkyū Island chain.

Bamboo can be used for secondary structure and other applications, and grasses and reeds can be used for thatch or woven into blinds or coverings. Rice is a staple food, and rice stalks can be dried into straw that has many uses— it can be bundled for thatching roofs, twisted into rope, or added to plaster as a binder. Soil containing a high clay content is the main ingredient of mud plaster; and sea shells can be burned to produce lime for a bright white plaster. Stone typically is used for foundations, non-structural walls, and paths. Although these materials occur naturally and abundantly in many places, some areas, especially the small islands, have few forests or bamboo groves, so wood and bamboo are utilized only for the major structural elements, and other more prevalent materials, such as stone or mud plaster, are used extensively in construction.

Cultural Factors

In addition to the various natural factors that affect the form and construction of the *minka*, cultural influences also shape the *minka* differently from region to region. Because Japan is an archipelago consisting of more than 3,000 islands—some of which are quite small though still boast human populations (about 600 of the Japanese islands are inhabited)— it is natural to find differences in the local customs and lifestyles on the various islands.

Although many of the regional cultural variations architecturally are not so significant, the most obvious cultural differences can be found in the Ryūkyū Islands, which were heavily influenced through centuries of trade with China. Because of their proximity to Taiwan and China (and their distance from the Japanese mainland), these islands developed their own culture and language, and the architecture reflects the influence of Chinese forms and building materials. Two typical Okinawan practices not found on the Japanese mainland are the use of red roof tiles and rooftop guardian statues. The roofs of Okinawan *minka* are covered with red tiles set into light-colored mortar, a much more colorful roofing material than is found on mainland Japan, and *shīsā* lion-dog guardian sculptures on the roof and freestanding walls in front of entrances to the houses protect from evil spirits.

The far north also developed a separate culture, which is concentrated on the island of Hokkaido, as well as the northern part of Honshū, and the far north Sakhalin and Kurile Islands. The native people of this area, known as the Ainu, are considered to be the original inhabitants of Japan. Edward Morse, who recorded Japanese daily life in his 1886 book, *Japanese Homes and their Surroundings*, described the remaining houses of the Ainu as wood structures with roofs thatched in tiers, walls covered with mats of woven reeds, and low doorways that led into dark interiors.[16] Morse also noted that by the time he visited the Ainu territory of Yezo and recorded his observations, the Ainu had assimilated many aspects of the dominant Japanese culture, so it is difficult to know just how much of what Morse saw was original to Ainu houses prior to the nineteenth century. The living space of an Ainu house features a central hearth, where the fire goddess resides, and a small sacred window oriented toward the source of the local river, also the source of food. The sacred window allows for communication with the *kamuy* spirits in nature outside and faces a small exterior shrine. These two elements, the hearth and the window, are the most important spiritual and symbolic elements of the Ainu house. "Inside the house, allocation of space, such as areas for living and the placement of furniture, was made with reference to the location of the hearth and the sacred window."[17]

Specific building forms also developed to correspond to local lifestyles. An excellent example of this is the *minka* type that developed in the fishing village of Ine, on the Sea of Japan (described in detail below). The buildings in Ine are constructed out over the water, with the fishing boats pulled in under the shelter of the upper story. Not only does this configuration protect the boats during storms and provide covered spaces to maintain and repair the boats, it makes good use of the village's location along a thin strip of land between the mountains and the sea.

Vernacular Building Forms

"It is mainly to the roof that the Japanese house owes its picturesque appearance; it is the roof which gives to the houses that novelty and variety which is so noticeable among them in different parts of the country."[18] No matter whether the influences on vernacular architecture are natural or cultural, the most obvious result of those influences is the form of the roof, and there is great variation in the size and shape of *minka* roofs throughout Japan (figure 10). Because of the dominance of the roof as an architectural element, as well as the great differences in the style and construction of the roofs, *minka* typically are categorized based on their roof forms.

Some examples of *minka* that have names derived from their roof forms are *gasshō-zukuri* ("hand-clasp style"), *kabuto* ("helmet"), and *shihōbuta* ("covers on four sides").[19] Each of these distinct forms developed within the local environment and culture and is a clear expression of the relationship of the house to the local climate.

Gasshō-zukuri minka are prevalent in the Hida region of Japan, the mountains north of Nagoya in central Honshū. The huge roofs are distinguished by their steeply sloping sides, which resemble a pair of hands pressed together in prayer, or *gasshō*, giving the name *gasshō-zukuri*. These *minka* typically are quite large, with three or more stories accommodating multiple generations of a family, and often a population of silkworms in the upper spaces. Since the Hida area is resplendent with fine forests, the *minka* feature heavy structural

Above right The *hinpun* wall in front of this Okinawan *minka* blocks evil spirits from entering the house, while the heavy low tiled roof is sturdy against typhoon winds.

Center right The architecture of the *minka* farmhouse is multipurpose. Here, farmer's clothes and *daikon* radishes hang to dry in the sun on bamboo poles attached to the façade of the building.

Below right Like a white paper fringe growing on the tree, inauspicious fortunes are folded and tied so that bad luck will be left behind.

timbers and frequently are sided with wood panels. The steep roofs are thickly thatched with rice straw for insulation from the cold.

The helmet-style roof, or *kabuto-yane*, is a very unusual roof form that developed in the mountainous part of central Honshū, Japan's main island. The form of the roof, considered to resemble the shape of a traditional Japanese helmet, is a variation of a hipped roof, with four gently curving sloped sides, two of which are cut back to allow light and air into an upper loft space historically used for sericulture. For additional light and ventilation, some *kabuto* roofs have dormers cut into the long sides, while others feature variously shaped cut-backs of the curved gable ends. The complex and expressive shape of the roof suggests that the people in the village took pride in the unusual form and fine craft of their houses.

A *shihōbuta*-style *minka* has a thickly thatched hipped upper roof, with eaves below which skirt the perimeter of the roof. Since the roof is identified by having the same lower eaves on all four sides, it is named "covers on four sides." The lower eaves usually are covered with ceramic tiles, regardless of the family's social standing. However, the size of the roof corresponds to social status, with larger roofs expressing greater wealth and power, as is typical of many *minka*.[20]

Historically, *minka* were constructed by the villagers themselves in collaboration with traveling carpenters. The carpenters moved throughout a region and designed floor plans and built the main post-and-beam structures of the *minka*. The remainder of the construction was completed by the people in each village. "Men and women worked together in teams, performing the task of construction and periodic repair in the same spirit of community solidarity in which they planted and harvested rice."[21] The villagers built floors, roofs, and walls using the tools they had at hand—mostly farm implements—to work with wood, thatch, and mud plaster. The *minka* were adapted as lifestyles changed, forming "an interesting record of lives, times, tastes and skills in building,"[22] while remaining expressive of the local environment.

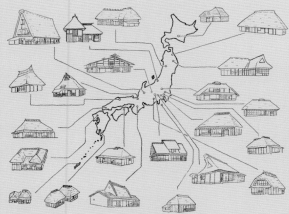

Above, figure 10 This map of regional *minka* styles illustrates the varied *minka* types found in Japan.
Right Tall dry-laid stone walls protect houses from the frequent strong typhoons that batter the village of Sotodomari on Uwajima Island.

Left After the autumn harvest, a farmer gathers and bundles rice straw, which will be dried and stored during the winter for use the following spring.
Above Woven reed *sudare* blinds hang from the eaves to shade the interior of the house in hot weather.

Vernacular Landscape Forms

Not only were *minka* constructed in correspondence to the local environment, the surrounding landscapes were transformed to work with the climate and topography. Most *minka* had little or no space for ornamental gardens because land was needed for agriculture more than for pleasure. However, land immediately adjacent to the *minka* often was utilized to aid in creating shelter and modifying the climate. In hot climates, trees shade the houses in summer, and in the open plains, high hedges help to shelter the houses from strong winter winds.

Villages developed in Shimane Prefecture, on the Japan Sea side of southern Honshū, for example, where every residential complex was protected by high hedges (figure 11). Two lines of hedges, trimmed to form high walls, were planted perpendicular to one another to create a corner. The hedges grew thick and blocked the cold winter wind. However, because they were on just two sides, the houses were open in the direction of the summer breezes on the other two sides. Beyond the hedges and around the house were agricultural fields. In this way, the land was altered to enhance the level of comfort provided by the *minka*, just as carefully as it was altered for agriculture.

Agriculture is the strongest reason for the transformation of the landscape in vernacular communities, especially in the terracing and berming of the land for wet rice farming. In many traditional communities in Japan, flat land is scarce, and therefore all land is used carefully and economically. Often rice paddies and other agricultural fields are built right up next to houses and spread out to cover all workable land, ending where the ground starts to slope steeply. Irrigation channels course through villages, with diversions and reservoirs to provide ample water to each field and each household. Resources and infrastructure are shared and maintained by the members of the community.

Water typically is not scarce in Japan, but it must be controlled for agricultural uses, especially rice farming. Therefore, the transformation of the land based on water use is an important aspect of the vernacular landscape.

As snow melts and water streams down the mountainsides, it is diverted into channels that lead into and through the villages. Berms at the edges of the rice paddies hold the water, and systems of channels and locks, taking advantage of gravity, are used to control the amount and flow of the water into the rice paddies.

These ways of working the land to create places of agriculture, as well as places of shelter, take different forms throughout Japan. The various ways of transforming the land, just like the varied forms of the *minka*, developed due to differences in topography, climate, and available materials, together with local ways of life.

Traditional Community Forms

The great variety of regional differences in vernacular dwellings and landscapes can be seen in the following examples of four very different traditional communities. Two are island communities—one a small island off the southwest coast of Shikoku Island, Okinoshima, and the other a small island in the Ryūkyū Island chain, Taketomishima. Another community, the fishing village of Ine-cho, also is focused toward the ocean but is located on the Japan Sea coast of the main island of Honshū. The fourth, Shirakawago, is a mountain village in the Hida region of central Honshū.

The siting of the buildings, the architectural forms, and the communal life of each of these villages developed very closely with the climate and environment. The villages have been well documented and studied as fine examples of traditional communities in Japan.[23] Although they have changed over time and certainly now show the influence of contemporary conveniences, still today they basically stay true to their original forms and continue many of the traditional communal ways of life.

Okinoshima, also known as Hahajima, is a small mountainous island in the Pacific Ocean, between the islands of Shikoku and Kyūshū. The steep slopes of the mountain face strong winds during much of the year, and the few trees growing on the rocky slopes do not get very large. Because of the sloping land, the strong wind, and the lack of plentiful lumber,

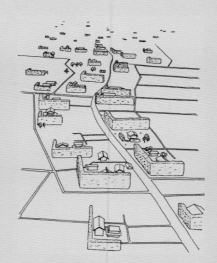

Above left Bundles of rice straw hang on a bamboo frame, drying in the sun, after the rice has been harvested from the rice paddies.
Left Simple stone figures grace the top of the sacred Ogahana Point, which offers an expansive view of the surrounding mountains.
Above, figure 11 Tall hedges block the winter wind while defining the private residential space.
Right Utility buildings, like this tool shed, follow the time-tested form of *minka* of the region, with walls faced in wood from the plentiful forests and roofs covered with a thick thatch of rice straw to protect against the winter snows.

the forms of the buildings on Okinoshima developed in response to these particular conditions. The houses are terraced into the land, with narrow walkways and channels of coursing water between them. The houses fill the lower part of the hill, following the water channels down to the port full of fishing boats at the water's edge, while agricultural fields are terraced into the land above the village. The single-story houses have low roofs covered with heavy ceramic tiles to battle the wind. Each property has a small flat work area in the front, facing the sea, and a narrow passage between the house and the adjacent high stone retaining wall in the back. Communal walks and stairs are terraced into the slopes between the properties. Since the houses are sited on many different levels, the villagers avoided closing off the houses from one another by building bamboo decks that expand the flat

areas in front of the houses and often extend over the communal walkways. The decks provide a place for neighboring families to gather on summer evenings to enjoy the cool ocean breezes.

Taketomishima is in a very different setting, with a distinctly different climate, and the architectural forms express that local climate and culture. The island is flat and tropical, with frequent strong winds, seasonal typhoons, and continuous hot sun. There are some wooded areas, but they are not widespread, and the trees tend to be small. The houses are built using this small-dimension lumber as economically as possible. The single-story dwellings have low heavy ceramic tiled roofs to protect against the typhoons and the sun—the red tiles are held together with light-colored mortar in the typical Okinawan style. Most exterior walls can be opened to

allow the winds to naturally ventilate the house. Residential compounds typically consist of the house, a separate kitchen building, and one or two small auxiliary structures. The perimeter of the property is enclosed with walls of dry-laid coral stone, a prevalent local material. Members of the community sweep the streets in front of their houses each morning and use that time to exchange news and make conversation.

A fishing village built along a thin strip of coastline, Ine-cho is on the eastern edge of the Tango Peninsula in the Kinki region of Honshū. Isolated from neighboring villages by the mountainous topography, Ine-cho developed a distinctive building form that is closely related to the local way of life. With little flat land available, fields for agriculture were cleared near the tops of the mountains, and the village was built right on the coast,

Right In the historic neighborhoods of the mountain town of Takayama, carefully crafted two-story wood structures are expressive of the high level of the forestry and carpentry professions in the region.

Below left Once famous for the iron ore mined in the area, the houses in Fukiya feature walls covered with plaster tinted with *bengara*, soil containing iron oxide.

Below center Temples traditionally were places of learning as well as important community spiritual centers. The seventh-century Hōryūji Temple complex displays the appropriate symbolic presence.

Below right Ceramic roof tiles were introduced to Japan from China and Korea with the advent of Buddhism in the sixth century CE. The houses in the Okinawa Islands take advantage of the weight of the roofs to protect against the sun and the wind.

where the mountains meet the sea. Wood-paneled buildings line both sides of the single road that parallels the coastline. Properties on the ocean side are long and narrow, fronting both the street and the sea, while the properties on the mountain side of the street typically have a wider street frontage but are not as deep. The two-story buildings on the ocean side are built over the water, and the first floor serves as a garage for the family's fishing boat, with storage for fishing equipment on the upper floor. The boat-garage, as well as the narrow walkways between the buildings and any space in front of the houses, are used to hang trays of fish and fishing nets to dry. The families live in the houses across the street—which, before the advent of cars, was a garden space, where the villagers would sit in front of their houses, mending nets and sharing with each other news of the day's catch.

Shirakawago is a small village in the middle of the high mountains of the Hida region in central Honshū. Like Ine-cho, the mountainous terrain isolates Shirakawago from other villages. However, unlike Ine-cho, Shirakawago is landlocked, far from the ocean. Built along a river that is a constant source of water and a seasonal source of food, the village is located in a narrow valley within a heavily forested area. The inhabitants traditionally have depended on agriculture and forestry for their livelihood. Rice paddies and vegetable patches are planted right up next to the grand three or more story *gasshō-zukuri* houses. With lumber readily available, the houses feature heavy timber framing and wood-paneled walls. Several generations live together, and in the past the families often would use the upper story to raise silkworms in the winter, when the snows were too high for outdoor work.

The thickly thatched roofs utilize rice straw, which is saved and dried for use in replacing or repairing the thatch on houses or the local temple. The thatch is replaced on two buildings each year. Traditionally, the thatching is done by the community, with everyone helping with the work and joining in the festival-like atmosphere. The thatching activity brings people together in a common task and provides the opportunity for the villagers to exchange information and share stories.

These four examples clearly show how traditional communities are tied closely to the local culture, climate, and natural environment. From the way land is transformed to the way buildings are constructed and maintained, the people of these villages design the land and the buildings to act together to support and enhance the local lifestyle and promote a sense of community.

Chapter 6
Tools and techniques

The act of building requires several inter-dependent factors: the functional need for shelter or some other purpose, the builder's creative urge, a place to build, the materials for construction, and the tools to work the materials. The need, place, and materials provide the context and basis for building, but the builder and the tools are the core of the act of construction. The tool serves as an extension of the builder's body, allowing the hands to complete what is in the mind.

The traditional Japanese craftsman treats his tools with the utmost care and respect, for without his tools he has no craft. It has been said that "the tool is the soul of the Japanese carpenter just as the sword was the soul of the samurai."[24] Each tool is carefully tuned to fit the craftsman's body, precisely adjusted to each day's specific atmospheric conditions and particular construction material, and meticulously maintained to assure its continued good use and long life.

The History of Tools in Japan

Although many architectural forms found in Japan originated in China, most of the major tools needed to construct the first Buddhist temples in Japan had already been developed before Chinese and Korean craftsmen were brought to Japan to build the temples in the sixth century. The tools already in use included the chisel, ax, adze, gimlet, mallet, wedge, and spear-head plane or planing knife.[25] Initially, tools were made of stone with wood handles, and many of the stone blades may have been imported from the Asian continent, but from about 250 CE iron blades became dominant.[26] Despite the greater sophistication of the forms of Chinese Buddhist architecture, only the

Opposite Carpenters work together to lift and join heavy timber framing in a reproduction of an Edo-period wood-block print used as an image on a temporary construction wall in downtown Tokyo.
Above Hands and tool act as one—a master carpenter guides his chisel to smooth the surface of a joint in a *hinoki* cypress roof beam.
Right The patina from years of devoted use ornaments the rich wood handles and tempered steel blades of the carpenter's carefully maintained chisels and plane.

crosscut push saw (*yokobiki-noko*) and the ink pot and snap line (*sumitsubo*) were introduced with the new architecture.[27]

Over the 700 years until the start of the Edo period, other important tools that were introduced from China were the two-man frame ripsaw (*oga*) in the fifteenth century and the single-blade push plane (*dai-ganna*) in the sixteenth century. Tools that developed in Japan during this time include the carpenter's square with square root scale (*sashigane* with *urame*) and the leaf-shaped crosscut push saw (*konohagata-noko*) in the twelfth century and the one-man ripsaw (*maebiki-oga*) in the sixteenth century.[28] As with the architectural forms, the tools that were introduced from China at first were copied and used exactly as they had been in China. However, over time some tools (especially push saws and push planes) were altered and adapted to the Japanese way of working, eventually changing so radically that they are now quite different from their original Chinese counterparts.

Two tools that developed very differently in Japan from those in China and other parts of the world are the saw (*noko-giri*) and the plane (*kanna*). In China, as well as in other Asian countries and in the West, the saw and the plane cut on the push stroke. In contrast, in Japan these tools cut on the pull stroke. The development of the pull-action plane in Japan may be based on indigenous ways of working, such as sitting on the ground to do certain kinds of work. Planing wood by pushing rather than pulling may seem like a small difference, but cutting wood with a saw by pulling is very different from cutting wood on the push stroke. Pushing puts the blade under compressive pressure and may cause it to bend, while pulling puts the saw in tension and keeps the blade straight. The leaf-shaped crosscut saw was developed into a pull action saw by the early fourteenth century, and later all Japanese saws were converted to cut on the pull stroke.[29] By the late sixteenth or early seventeenth century, the Japanese had transformed the

earlier single-blade block plane that cut with a pushing action into a handle-less block plane that cut by pulling.[30] Tools evolved further in the Edo period and even in the early Meiji period when two important advances were made—the tenon or back saw (*dōtsuki-noko*) and the double-bladed plane (a block plane with an added chip breaker) were developed.[31]

Toolmaking in Japan also advanced greatly after two significant developments in metal smithing. First, by the sixteenth century, Japanese blacksmiths had developed a method for melting iron sand into an iron bloom and then forging and working the iron until it acquired the appropriate amount of carbon to become carbon steel, which could be laminated to create high-quality blades for knives, saws, chisels, and planes. The second important development was steel blades for chisels and planes with a high carbon tip on an iron core. The softer steel is easier to work, while the harder carbon steel is more brittle but keeps a sharp edge. The steel-tipped blades are more

Left A carpenter pulls a block plane along the surface of the wood, giving it a smooth, flat finish.
Below left The primary structure of a traditional Japanese building is fabricated in a workshop rather than at the construction site, like these members with completed joints, which will be moved to the site for quick assembly.
Right Planes and chisels are used to finish the surface of a wood joint.

durable and hold their edge longer than earlier wrought-iron blades, and the iron core gives the tools flexibility.[32]

Traditional Japanese buildings are renowned for the fine craftsmanship of the timber structure and wood details, especially the complex joinery. Concurrent with the improvement in the technology of toolmaking and the quality of tools was the advancement of the skill and ingenuity of the carpenter. The quality and variety of tools enhances the master carpenter's ability and knowledge. At the height of wood construction at the beginning of the Edo period, a master carpenter had an extensive collection of tools. As recently as 1949, a survey indicated that a traditional Japanese carpenter typically required as many as 179 tools to complete his work. Of these tools, there were 49 different chisels, 40 planes, 26 gimlets, 12 saws, as well as squares, *sumitsubo*, marking gauges, nail pincers and claws, hammers and mallets, an adze, an ax, whetstones, and files.[33] Each tool had a specific purpose and technique for use. In general, traditional Japanese carpentry tools can be divided into two types—tools that are used for measuring and marking, which architectural historian William Coaldrake aptly calls "instruments of the mind," and tools that are used for cutting and finishing, Coaldrake's "tools of the hand."[34]

Carpentry Tools for Measuring and Marking

The types of tools used for measuring and marking include the carpenter's square (*sashigane* or *kanejaku*), the measuring rod (*shaku-zue* or *kenzao*), the plan board (*ita-zu* or *ezu-ita*), the ink pot and snap line (*sumitsubo*), the bamboo pen (*sumisashi*), measuring gauges (*jōgi*), marking gauges (*kebiki*), and the plumb line (*sagefuri*).[35] The carpenter's square is especially unique—it is marked with several different measuring scales that allow the carpenter to calculate angles and curves as well as to easily complete mathematical tasks such as determining the dimensions of a square post to be cut from a round trunk. All scales use the traditional measurement system, which is based on the distance of one

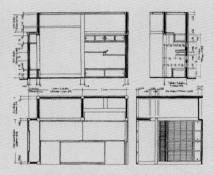

Above The carpenter's *sumitsubo* (ink pot) is a valued tool and often is ornately carved by the carpenter to fit his hand.
Left A craftsman uses a carpenter's square and a bamboo pen to measure and mark a joint that is under way.
Right, figure 12 The *kiwari* proportional system is the basis for measurements used in traditional Japanese architecture.

structural bay (*ken*, equal to 180 centimeters or about 6 feet), which is divided into 6 *shaku* (1 *shaku* is 30 centimeters or about 1 foot). Each *shaku* is divided into 10 *sun* (each equal to about 3 centimeters or just over 1 inch), and each *sun* is divided into 10 *bu*, which are further divided into 10 *rin*. The *sashigane* is now fabricated out of metal, usually with metric units, but originally it was made of bamboo, with the front side (*omoteme*) marked in increments of *sun* and *bu*, and the back side (*urame*) marked with two separate scales. One is increments of *sun* multiplied by the square root of 2 (*kakume*), and the other is *sun* multiplied by the multiplicative inverse of pi, or $1/3.1416$ (*marume*). The development of the *kakume* scale in the twelfth century made previously complex calculations simple,

and thus the *sashigane* became indispensable for any carpenter.

The *shaku-zue* is a long wood pole, typically 10 *shaku* (1 *jō*) or 6 *shaku* (1 *ken*) high, marked with the important heights to be used in the construction of a specific building. The heights are based on a proportional system called *kiwari* (literally "wood divide"), which allows the determination of proportional height and width relationships of different elements (figure 12). The *kiwari* system is based on the unit of the *ken*, which differed from region to region and was not standardized until the late nineteenth century. One *ken* is the length of one bay (the distance from the center of one column to the center of the next column (*kyō-ma*) or the distance between columns (*inaka-ma*), depending on the locale). Typically, the height of a residential building from the top of the foundation to the top of the major structural beam (at the roof eave) is 2 *ken*.[36] The division of the *ken* into 6 *shaku* allows for flexibility within the system. For example, the size of a *tatami* mat, which eventually became the module for determining the size of a room, is 6 *shaku* in length by 3 *shaku* in width. All the elements of a particular building are based on this established system of proportional relationships, and the specific dimensions are shown on the *shaku-zue*.

In addition to the *shaku-zue*, one other traditional means of recording the measurements of the building is used. The carpenter draws the basic floor plan of the building on a thin wood board, known as an *ita-zu* or *ezu-ita*. Again, based on the *kiwari* proportional system, the location of the major structural columns as well as the heights of important members are noted on the board. Traditionally, the *ezu-ita* serves as the single design drawing used to construct the building. Because the design of buildings historically was based on the *kiwari* system, which was familiar to all the craftsmen from the different trades, and the construction was overseen by one person (the *tōryō*, literally "ridge pole" or chief master carpenter), the *ezu-ita* provided sufficient information for the builders.

The *sumitsubo* or ink pot and snap line (similar to a chalk line) is perhaps the most distinctive of the traditional Japanese carpentry tools, for the carpenter himself typically fashions the ink pot from a block of wood, often zelkova. He makes the ink pot in a size and shape that fits his hand and may embellish it with ornate carving. In different eras, different designs were popular and had symbolic associations—a heart shape represents the shape of a leaf from the Bodhi tree, the tree under which Gautama Buddha sat when he gained enlightenment. Late nineteenth-century designs included cranes and tortoises, which are symbolic of longevity and have long been part of Japanese mythology.[37]

The *sumitsubo* is carved so that it can be held comfortably in the palm of one hand. An indentation in the center holds a wad of silk batting that is doused with black or red ink.

The black ink is mixed with seawood glue to make it insoluble in water, but the red ink is made from pigment mixed with water and is used in places where the marks are visible and therefore must be easily removable. A length of silk string, attached with a pin to the piece of lumber to be marked, is drawn through the inked silk batting. The string is held taut and then snapped, so that it strikes the lumber and leaves an ink mark in a straight line.

When a carpenter needs to draw a line or write a label, he uses a simple pen which he carves out of bamboo, the *sumisashi*. The *sumisashi* is fashioned with one flat angled end and one pointed end, allowing the carpenter to make different kinds of marks. The flat end is used for lines and tick marks, while the pointed end is used to write numbers and *kanji* pictographic characters. The carpenter applies ink to the *sumisashi* by dipping it in the ink pot and then uses it to mark the wood as needed. The kinds of markings that carpenters make include lines and tick marks that denote how the wood is be cut or finished and characters and numbers which show where different members join into each other and where they are located in the main plan. The marks that indicate how pieces fit together usually are characters, which are also used to denote the directions up, down, cardinal directions, and other means of showing the proper placement of the piece.

Tools for Cutting and Finishing

While the tools used for marking and measuring are utilized throughout the construction process, the tools used for cutting and finishing have very specialized functions and are utilized only at specific times. Axes and adzes, saws, chisels, planes, gimlets, and hammers and mallets come in many different sizes and styles to meet the needs of the craftsmen during the various phases of construction.

Using traditional methods, timber cutters cut down trees in the forest using chopping axes (*kiri-yoki*) and single-edged crosscut saws (such as the rounded-nose roughing saw or *hanamaru-noko*). The branches are removed and the tree trunks are then brought down the mountain on sleds. Often the lumber is floated

down a river to the lumber yard where it is cut and dried. The traditional method of cutting the lumber into boards uses a frame saw (*oga*), typically handled by two sawyers, or a wide-bladed ripsaw (*maebiki-oga*) used by one person. Columns and beams also are cut from tree trunks with a frame saw or a single-person wide-bladed ripsaw. Before the introduction of the two-person frame saw from China in the fifteenth century, carpenters did the work of splitting and sawing the logs. The introduction of the frame saw created a niche for sawyers (*kobiki*).[38] Now, it is typical for boards, beams, and columns to be stacked to dry at a lumber yard until they are ready for use and purchased by a carpenter. In the past and even now in the case of special buildings, such as temples or teahouses, carpenters go into the forest and choose the particular trees they want to use in the building's construction.

The carpenter cuts the lumber to the desired length using various types of saws that have differing configurations of teeth to cut across or with the wood grain and to make a cleaner or rougher cut. A crosscut saw (*yokobiki-noko*) cuts across the grain, whereas a rip saw (*maebiki-noko*) cuts along the grain (figure 13). Both types of saws are made in a wide range of sizes, with teeth of different widths and lengths. Once the members are cut to size, they are finished using an assortment of tools depending on their shape and the desired surface finish. Round columns are finished with a spear-head plane (*yari-ganna*), which can be used to make a smooth finish on a curved surface. Flat surfaces are finished with a block plane (*kanna*) to achieve an extremely smooth even surface, while both round and flat surfaces can be finished with an adze (*chōna*), which gives a textured surface.

The intricate joinery for which Japanese carpentry is so well known is constructed primarily using saws, chisels, hammers, and planes. Chisels (*nomi*) are used to cut notches and holes (small holes are cut with a gimlet or *kiri*) as well as to smooth some surfaces. The different uses of the chisel resulted in two distinct types. Chisels for cutting (*tataki-nomi*) are used with hammers and have a metal band around the top of the handle to keep the wood

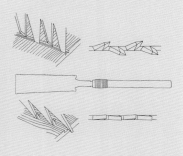

Top A specially constructed chest holds dozens of carpentry tools in a carpenter's workshop.
Above, figure 13 The detail of a cross-cut saw blade (above) shows how the teeth are angled in two directions to cut through the grain of the wood in contrast to the teeth of the ripsaw blade (below), which cut parallel to the grain.
Above left For each hammer, the size and shape of the metal head lends itself to specific uses.
Center left Axes and adzes are utilized to roughly finish wood but are only rarely used to give the final finish surface.
Below left Many different types of saws are used throughout the process of felling trees, splitting lumber, and cutting wood members to size.

from splitting. Chisels for finishing surfaces or mortise holes (*shiage-nomi* or *tsuki-nomi*) typically have long handles and no metal bands, since they are used only with the force of the hand to shave surfaces where planes will not fit.

Hammers (*kanazuchi* or *gennō*) are used with chisels to cut and form wood but also are employed to pound nails. The head of the hammer is expressive of its particular application. The head of a *gennō* is double-sided, one side is flat and the other convex. The flat head is used to strike a chisel or a nail, while the slightly rounded head is used to flatten wood surfaces or for the final tap of the nail. The curvature of the head assures that the nail is pounded in completely without the surrounding material being damaged by the force of the hammer. Similarly, the slightly pointed head of the *kanazuchi* is used primarily to finish pounding nails after they have been driven in part way with its flat-headed side. When structural members are joined, wood mallets (*kizuchi*) are used to pound the joints together and to fix the wood draw pins (*komisen*), keys (*shachi*), dowels (*dabo*), or wedges (*kusabi*) that secure some of the joints. A wood mallet is less likely to dent the lumber than a metal mallet.

Planes come in a number of sizes and can be made to be used for flat or curved surfaces. The craftsman chooses the proper plane based on the part of the wood that is being planed and the desired degree of smoothness. The typical Japanese smoothing plane (*hira-ganna*) consists of a block of wood (usually oak) and one or two blades held together by a small metal rod. If two blades are used, the outer blade is a chip breaker or capping iron (*osae-ba*), which smoothes the irregularities of the wood before it is planed by the inner blade (*kanna-mi*). Carpenters very carefully sharpen the blades after using them and constantly adjust them to make sure the cutting thickness is correct, which can vary depending on a number of factors, including the type of wood, its size and density, the climate (especially the amount of humidity and the air temperature), and the required quality of craftsmanship of the finished product.

Left Lacquer craftsman Hiraki Yasaburo chooses the correct brush to put the finishing touches on a finely lacquered wood *butsudan* cabinet.
Above Tools must be carefully maintained to function properly. Carpenters regularly clean and sharpen the laminated blades of their tools, such as the plane blade shown here.

As noted earlier, carpenters must maintain their tools meticulously, treating them with both care and reverence to ensure that the tools remain in good condition and will last for as long as they are required. Carpenters therefore require other tools for this purpose. Typical maintenance tools include rasps and files (*yasuri*) to sharpen saw teeth and whetstones (*to-ishi*) to sharpen chisels and plane blades. A carpenter possesses a number of different sizes of files and grits of whetstone. Typically, at the end of each day, the carpenter cleans and maintains his tools before carefully storing them for the next day's work.

Tools for Other Trades

While the tools discussed in the previous pages are the major groups of tools that traditionally are used by carpenters in the construction of Japanese buildings, other craftsmen, especially those involved in construction, use some of the same tools as well as some very different tools that are specific to their trades. The other major trades involved in the construction of the primary elements of traditional buildings are stonemasons (*ishi-ya*), plaster craftsmen (*sakan-ya*), door and screen carpenters (*tategu-ya*), and roofers (*yane-ya*).

Stone workers cut stone with chisels (*nomi*), wedges (*ya*), mallets (*tsuchi*), and sledge hammers (*gennō*); move stone with levers (*teko*), wheelbarrows (*nekoguruma*), logs for rolling (*shura*), pulleys (*rokuro*), and bellows (*fuigo*); and shape stone with chisels (*nomi*), double-headed mallets (*gundera*), bush hammers (*bishan*), and hammers (*tataki*).[39] Plaster craftsmen use wood palettes known as "hawks" (*kote-ita*) to hold the plaster, and metal trowels (*kote*) of innumerable sizes and shapes to apply and finish the plaster. *Tategu-ya*, carpenters who specialize in making doors, windows, and screen frames, use a special tool similar to a *sashigane* (carpenter's square), called a *maki-gane*, and a tool similar to a *sumisashi* (bamboo pen) but made of metal, called a *shiragaki*, as well as small marking knives (*kogatana*) for tasks requiring measuring and marking. For cutting and finishing, they use various types of saws (*noko-giri*), chisels (*nomi*), including *tsuba-nomi* and *kamakiri-nomi* (or *kama-nomi*), knives such as *kiridome-hōchō*, and other tools like clamps (*hatagane*) and long-handled cleaning chisels (*sokosarai-nomi*). Roofers use different tools depending on the type of roofing material. Cypress bark roofs (*hiwada-buki*) are attached using bamboo nails (*takekugi*) and require a hammer (*kanazuchi*) with a special short square head. Different types of knives (*hōchō*) are used, including the *hiwada-bōchō* used at the end of the process to trim the edges. Ceramic tile (*kawara*) roofs traditionally were attached with mud (now nails are used), and roofers used trowels (*kote*) and string (*ito*) rather than hammers.

Each trade developed the tools which are best suited for specific work. While some of the tools, such as the carpenter's ink pot and bamboo pen, are fabricated by the craftsmen themselves, most tools are made by specialized toolmakers, particularly in the case of metal tools. Saw blades, hammer heads, and chisel blades are carefully crafted by metalsmiths. Many craftsmen work directly with the metalsmiths to determine the desired qualities of the tool and assure the proper result. A relationship of mutual respect and trust between the craftsman and the toolmaker is imperative, as tools are the lifeblood of the craftsman.

Tools for Making Tools

The art of making high-quality tools, especially steel-tipped blades for saws, chisels, and planes, developed over centuries in Japan and resulted in some of the finest blades produced in the world. A well-crafted saw or chisel blade is very expensive but can be sharpened over and over and lasts for decades. A master craftsman understands the benefits of a well-crafted tool and may seek out a particular master metalsmith to make his tools, but the smith, too, requires tools for his work.

The primary tools used by the traditional Japanese *kaji-ya* (metalsmith) are the forge (*hokubo*), bellows (*fuigo*), and anvil (*kanashiki*). Iron ore is heated in the forge, with the bellows used to increase combustion and thus the heat. When the ore reaches the desired temperature (which the master smith understands from the color of the hot metal), it is removed with long pincers (*kajihibashi*). The master smith places the hot metal on the iron anvil, and apprentices pound the metal into a flat shape using heavy steel-headed hammers (*atebishi*). The metal is cut to its basic shape by marking with hits of the *tagane* (graver). As the metal takes shape, as many as three apprentices may strike in succession while the master controls the shape of the metal by flipping it over from side to side as the apprentices hammer it, at the same time manipulating the temperature by quenching the metal in water or returning it to the forge. The pounding is done in a rhythmic collaboration between master and apprentices.

At the end of the process, the temperature of the steel is lowered by immersing it in straw ash (*wara no hai*). Finally, the blade is placed on a special platform (*sentokodai*) and smoothed with a draw knife (*sen*) or first with a file (*yasuri*) and then with a whetstone (*to-ishi*). It is covered with coating of shavings from the sharpening process, mixed with water (*doro-nuri*), so that it will cool faster, then heated one more time and tempered by suddenly being quenched in water to cool (*yaki-ire*). After the blade has cooled, it is sharpened once again with a whetstone. This time-honored process results in very high-quality blades.

Left The apprentice daughter of a family of paper lantern makers with a 200-year history maintains the craft tradition as she applies paint to a decorative pattern on a lantern.
Above A wide brush is used to apply glue to the bamboo frame of a lantern that will be covered with *washi* paper.

List of Traditional Construction Trades:[40]

wood	kikori	woodcutter, lumberjack
	daiku	carpenter
	motokawa-shi	removes bark from cypress trees for *hiwada-buki*
	hiwadabuki-ya	Japanese cypress bark roof craftsman
	kibori-shi	woodcarver
	tategu-ya	screen and door carpenter
plants	tatami-ya	*tatami* maker
	washi shokunin	paper maker
	hyōgu-ya	paper mounter
	e-shi	ornamental painter
	urushi shokunin	lacquer craftsman
stone	ishi-ya	stonemason
earth	kawarabuki-ya	ceramic tile roofer
	oni-shi	*onigawara* ornamental tile craftsman
	sakan-ya	plaster craftsman
metal	imono-ya	cast metal craftsman
	kazari kanagu-ya	ornamental metal craftsman
	kirikane-shi	metal leaf craftsman

Chapter 7
Materials

Each of the major types of materials that are used in traditional building in Japan—wood, grasses and straws, stone, earth, and metal—require specific tools and construction techniques which vary depending on the particular nature of the material. Although similar tools may be used in different areas of the construction process by different craftsmen, the tools are not exactly the same, nor are the ways in which they are used the same. For example, stone workers, carpenters, and *tategu-ya* (screen and door makers) all use chisels, but the chisels are made and used differently because of the dissimilarity of working with stone versus wood, and also due to the size and precision of the work.

Because of the need for close collaboration between the trades as well as the similarities in some aspects of their work, most craftsmen employed in the building trades are familiar with many different tools, techniques, and materials, but the specialization of the trades requires them to be adept at their specific craft. In addition to the major trades of stone worker, lumberjack, carpenter, plasterer, roofer, and metalworker, a number of specialized trades also developed. These include screen and door makers (*tategu-ya*), paper makers (*washi shokunin*), tatami makers (*tatami-ya*), lacquer craftsmen (*urushi shokunin*), and metal leaf craftsmen (*kirikane-shi*). For each trade, the artisans study the materials to learn their unique qualities and the best methods for using them, and practice working the materials with the tools in order to learn the potential of the tools and become expert in their use.

Traditionally, construction trades are learned on the job. An apprentice carpenter works with a master for about ten years before becoming

independent. In those ten years, the apprentice learns by watching the master and practicing. For an apprentice carpenter, this means often spending days cleaning the construction site and moving materials and spending nights practicing his craft. Few lessons are directly taught—most are "stolen" from the master through the apprentice's keen observation. In this way, the traditional techniques and knowledge of the tools and materials are passed down from generation to generation.

Wood
Traditional Japanese buildings are well known for their highly refined yet at times powerfully rough uses of wood, especially sophisticated wood joinery (figure 14). Most of the Japanese

Above The structure of the Shōkintei Tea Pavilion at the Katsura Imperial Villa is expressive of the *sukiya* style. The rough bark remains on the columns and beams, which support the bamboo and reed roof structure.

Left The sweeping stair of the Garyūro Sleeping Dragon Corridor at the Eikandō Temple in Kyoto is an excellent example of the sophisticated use of wood found in Buddhist temple architecture.

Top The ends of the *engawa* wood floorboards show the marks of time and weather.

Center A round column joins neatly into a round beam, which holds up a long round beam supporting many roof rafters.

Above Only a hint of the complex joinery of multiple beams connecting into a single round column is visible from the ends of the beams that extend through the column.

islands are heavily forested, so builders have access to mature trees of many varieties. Wood is chosen for its strength, its color and grain, even its unusual shape—and it is worked and used in ways which best take advantage of its inherent structural qualities and beauty.

Traditional Japanese carpenters well understand trees, how they grow and how the manner and place in which they grow affects their structural strength and dictates how they should be used. Trees that grow near the top of a mountain slope tend to grow straight and strong, and it is these trees that carpenters choose for a building's primary structural elements—the columns and beams. Trees that grow in the lower mid-mountain slope are straight but thin, so they are not as strong as those that grow at the higher elevation. However, they still are useful for exposed elements because they tend to have few knots and fine surfaces. Trees that grow in the valleys between mountains are understood to be structurally weak and have a high moisture content, which makes them suitable only for non-structural uses.[41] Some trees that grow on steep slopes or in windy areas are curved or bent, and skillful carpenters can "weave" them into a fabric-like structure of beams (figure 36). Smaller dimension trees with curves, bends, and twists can be used as beautiful decorative columns, such as the *tokobashira* at the edge of the *tokonoma* decorative alcove.

When used as columns, the timbers are always positioned as they grow in the forest, with the root side down and the canopy side up. Trees that grow on north-facing slopes are best used on the north side of buildings, and trees that grow on south-facing slopes work best where they get southern exposure. A carpenter can look at a piece of lumber and understand through its markings and warping tendencies just how it grew in the forest. The carpenter also understands that the way the tree grew affects the forces that occur naturally within the wood, and therefore employs the wood in ways that make the most of those naturally occurring forces. For example, when joining two timbers to create a long beam, the root ends of the timbers are never joined together because the natural forces following the upward growth of the tree tend to pull the timbers apart. However, joining the canopy ends together takes advantage of those forces that will push the timbers toward each other, locking the joint. Joining one root end to one canopy end is also satisfactory, as the forces run in the same direction. Similarly, when joining two timbers to use vertically as a column, carpenters typically join the canopy end of the lower timber to the root end of the upper timber, allowing the natural stresses to continue in a single direction.

Large diameter trees can be sliced into boards or cut into dimensional lumber for use as secondary structure, framing for openings, floorboards, or paneling on wall or ceiling surfaces. The stresses in the wood play an important role in the way in which the lumber is cut, as the wood has natural tendencies to warp in one direction or the other, depending on the grain and the temperature and moisture content of the air. For boards in which the expression of the grain of the wood is important, the way in which the boards are sawed creates the pattern of the grain. Boards that are cut perpendicular to the tree rings have tight, even straight-line grains, and those that are cut tangent to the tree rings have more expressive grain patterns.

Because of its malleability, wood can easily be cut into myriad sizes and shapes, including thinly sliced strips that can be woven into ceiling panels (typically Sawara cypress is used for this). Wood can be carved into complex forms, such as those found in transoms (*ranma*), and the surface can be finished many different ways. An adze can be used to give a wavy *honchōna* finish; a plane can be used to give a silky smooth finish; or the surface of the wood can be charred to a dark black *yakisugi* finish to repel insects and add durability against rain and snow. Even the bark of certain trees is used in construction, such as the layers of cypress bark used for roofing (*hiwada-buki*) and the inner bark of the paper mulberry tree (*kōzo*) that is used to make traditional *washi* paper. Master carpenters choose the wood and the methods of cutting and finishing based on the desired architectural effect and structural needs.

Different varieties of wood have distinctive grains and differing structural strengths. Traditional carpenters categorize woods as *shinyōju* (needle-leafed trees, softwoods) and *kōyōju* (broad-leafed trees, hardwoods). The *shinyōju* woods typically used in the construction of traditional Japanese buildings before the *sukiya* style became popular include *akamatsu* (red pine), *asunarō* (a hatchet-leafed arborvitae—an evergreen of the pine family), *hiba* (a type of Japanese cypress), *hinoki* (Japanese cypress), *kuromatsu* (black pine), *matsu* (pine), *nezuko* (white cedar), *sawara* (a type of Japanese cypress known as Sawara cypress), *sugi* (Japanese cedar or cryptomeria),

and *tsuga* (hemlock-spruce). The *kōyōju* woods used include *kashi* (oak), *keyaki* (zelkova), and *sakura* (cherry).[42]

Sukiya-style architecture is renowned for its integration of many different types of woods in building construction, and each wood is chosen for its particular qualities and used in a way that best expresses those natural characteristics. *Sukiya* buildings utilize many of the same softwoods as the earlier traditional buildings, including *akamatsu*, *asunarō*, *nezuko*, *sawara*, and *sugi*, but many more varieties of hardwoods are incorporated into *sukiya* designs. The hardwoods include *ichō* (gingko), *kiri* (paulownia), *kokutan* (ebony or blackwood), *kuri* (chestnut), *kurokaki* (black persimmon), *kurumi* (walnut), *kusu* (camphor), *kuwa* (mulberry), *momi* (white fir), *nara* (Japanese oak), *sarusuberi* (crape myrtle), *shioji* (ash), *shitan* (red sandalwood or rosewood), *tagayasan* (Indian ironwood), *tochi* (horse chestnut), *tsubaki* (camellia), *tsutsuji* (azalea), *ume* (plum), and others.

Traditionally, the wood that is used most commonly for the primary structural elements of Japanese buildings is Japanese cypress (*hinoki*), which is easy to work yet structurally strong. *Hinoki* has a straight fine grain, an attractive even color, and a pleasant scent. Japanese cedar (*sugi*) is also frequently used in building construction. It has similar characteristics to *hinoki* but is softer and therefore is more suitable for sliding wood panel doors (*amado*) and cabinetry. Japanese cypress and Japanese cedar both grow widely throughout Japan and are rot-resistant and durable.

The wood of the zelkova tree (*keyaki*) is prized for its strength and size and is popular also for use in residential architecture as the *daikokubashira*, literally the "god of fortune column" or central column. The beautiful grain and coloration of zelkova wood enhance the power and strength apparent in its size and form. Zelkova is a hardwood, which makes it more difficult to work, but it is very durable and more elastic than *hinoki*. Zelkova typically is not used for all the primary structural elements in a house but only for certain important ones, like the *daikokubashira*. In addition, zelkova is a favored wood for cabinetry.

Pine trees, especially red pine (*akamatsu*) and black pine (*kuromatsu*), also grow widely and are used in both buildings and gardens. Pine is a softwood and therefore easy to work, but it often grows bent or twisted. Pine has a more figured grain than cedar or cypress—sometimes expressively uneven with waves and knots. Red pine, especially, can be used structurally for roof beams and other members that do not need to be completely straight, and it is sometimes used for decorative elements like the *tokobashira* (alcove column). Often it is used in exterior applications because the resin in the pine wood acts to preserve it.

Cherry trees (*sakura*) are revered in Japan for their beautiful clouds of blossoms in the early spring, but cherry wood is an uncommon material in traditional Japanese buildings and primarily is used for ornamental rather than structural purposes. The reddish color and attractive grain are distinguishing characteristics of the wood, and the mottled red-brown bark of the tree is prized for its unique markings. Cherry wood columns with the bark left intact frequently are employed as *tokobashira* and for other decorative uses.

Paulownia wood (*kiri*) is valued for its consistent grain and creamy color. *Kiri* is a hardwood, but it is light and soft, making it easy to work. Although sometimes used in *sukiya*-style buildings, *kiri* most frequently is utilized for furniture, especially *tansu* chests used for storing *kimono*, as the wood is resistant to moisture and strong yet flexible.

Wood of the mulberry tree (*kuwa*) is used only occasionally as a construction material in *sukiya* buildings, but the paper mulberry (*kōzo*) is commonly used to make *washi*, the paper that covers *shōji* and *fusuma* screens.

To make *washi*, branches of *kōzo* are steamed in large wooden tubs (*koshiki*) to loosen the outer bark, which is removed, and then the inner bark is peeled off. This fibrous inner bark is the material for the paper. The fibers make the paper strong, but the inner bark must be dried, washed, cleaned, and then boiled with alkali (*sōda*) for several hours to break down the fibers. The boiled fibers are pounded into a pulp with a wood stick (*bai*) and then mixed into a vat of water with *tororo* (the pounded root of the *Hibiscus manihot*) or some other glutinous vegetable material (*neri*), which serves to slow the drainage of water from the pulp mixture during the unique *nageshi-suki* papermaking process. After the pulp is well combined, a bamboo screen (*su*) is placed in a removable wood frame (*sakuketa*), and the frame is dipped deeply into the vat to pick up the pulp mixture. After the initial dip, the pulp is poured off, and the screen is dipped again. This time the screen is shaken back and forth in alternating directions, from side to side and from front to back. Once the water has seeped through the screen, the process is repeated to build up layers of fibers running in different directions to give the paper strength and thickness. Once the desired thickness is attained, the screen is removed from the frame, and the wet paper is peeled off the screen and laid on a flat board. After many sheets of paper have been layered atop each other on the board, the water is pressed out of the paper. The sheets are then removed one by one and brushed onto a flat gingko wood board to dry.

Washi also can be made with fibers from the uncommon and slow-growing gampi shrub, known in Japan as *gampi* or *kaminoki* (literally "paper tree"), or the *mitsumata* shrub (paperbush or giant leaf paper plant), as well as grasses and straws such as bamboo, hemp, rice, and wheat.

Another tree that is important in traditional construction but is not used for its wood is the Japanese lacquer tree (*urushi*). Lacquer is used as a protective and decorative coating, typically applied to wood, such as the frames of *shōji* or *fusuma* screens.

Lacquer is harvested by cutting incisions in the bark of the lacquer tree and allowing the sap to collect in containers. The sap is aged for three to five years before it is refined. It may be colored with pigment or have an adhesive (such as glue made from *nori* seaweed) added to it before it is applied with a brush. Depending on the size and style, *urushi* brushes are made from animal hair (horse and weasel are common) or human hair (traditionally from Japanese girls).

The careful processes of making paper and lacquer demonstrate the same care and art that go into the craft of traditional Japanese carpentry. The manner in which a material or a joint is expressed may appear straightforward and simple, but often the outward simplicity hides the inner complexity.

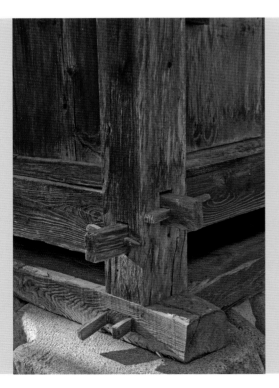

Left Pin-jointed connections between the vertical and horizontal structural members are expressed in exaggerated fashion, with the elements intersecting each other and the joints held together with wood wedges.
Above right, figure 14 A gooseneck mortise-and-tenon joint splices together two timbers.
Below right A carpenter uses a heavy wood mallet to pound a pin to permanently splice together two roof beams.

Typical Wood and Plant Materials Used in Traditional Japanese Carpentry

shinyōju: needle-leafed trees, softwoods (*also used in sukiya)

akamatsu*	red pine	Pinus densiflora
asunarō*	false arborvitae, hiba arborvitae	Thujopsis dolabrata
hiba	a type of Japanese cypress	Thujopsis dolabrata
hinoki	Japanese cypress	Chamaecyparis obtusa
kuromatsu	black pine	Pinus thumbergii
matsu	pine	Pinus densiflora
nezuko*	white cedar	Thuja standishii
sawara*	Sawara cypress	Chamaecyparis pisifera
sugi*	Japanese cedar	Cryptomeria japonica
tsuga	hemlock-spruce	Tsuga siekoldii

kōyōju: broad-leafed trees, hardwoods (*also used in sukiya; **used only in sukiya)

ichō**	gingko or maidenhair	Gingko biloba
kashi	oak	Quercus serrata
keyaki	zelkova	Zelkova acuminata
kiri**	paulownia	Paulownia imperialis
kokutan**	ebony, blackwood	Diospyros ebenum
kuri**	chestnut	Castanea crenata
kurobe**	Japanese arbor vitae	Thuja standishii
kurokaki**	black persimmon	Diospyros nitida Merr.
kurumi**	walnut	Juglans ailantifolia
kusu**	camphor	Cinnamomum camphora
kuwa**	mulberry	Broussonetia papyrifera
mitsuba tsutsuji**	azalea	Rhododendron dilatatum
momi**	white fir or Japanese fir	Abies firma
nara**	Japanese oak	Quercus crispula
sakura	cherry	Prunus japonica
sarusuberi**	crape myrtle	Lagerstroemia indica
shioji**	ash	Fraxinus spaethiana Lingelsh
shitan**	red sandalwood, rosewood	Dalbergia latifolia Roxb.
tagayasan**	Indian ironwood	Mesua ferrea L.
tochi**	horse chestnut	Aesculus turbinata
tsubaki**	camellia	Camellia japonica
tsutsuji**	azalea	Rhododendron indicum
ume	plum	Prunus mume
urushi, urushi-no-ki	Japanese lacquer tree	Toxicodendron verniciflum (formerly Rhus verniciflua)

grasses, reeds, rushes, shrubs, and straws

gampi or kaminoki	gampi shrub	Wikstroemia sikokiana
hachiku	Henon bamboo	Phyllostachys nigra f. henonis
igusa	a type of rush	Juncus alatus
kaya**	miscanthus, Japanese torreya	Torreya nucifera
kuro-chiku	black bamboo	Phyllostachys nigra
madake	madake bamboo	Phyllostachys bambusoides
medake	simon bamboo	Pleioblastus simonii
mitsumata	paperbush or giant leaf paper plant	Edgeworthia papyrifera
mōsō-chiku	Moso bamboo	Phyllostachys heterocycla f. pubensis
sasa (kuma-zasa)	(kuma) bamboo grass	Sasa veitchii
wara	rice straw	Oryza sativa var. japonica
yoshi	ditch reed	Phragmites australis

Grasses, Reeds, Rushes, and Straws

Various grasses, reeds, rushes, and straws grow in the wild and also are cultivated in Japan. The generally temperate climate and relatively high humidity create an excellent environment, and these plants are abundant and fast-growing. They are easy to harvest and transport, as well as simple to work and very versatile. Grasses, reeds, rushes, and straws are used in traditional Japanese architecture for many different purposes, from structural members to delicate ornamental screens. Most applications require that the materials be dried carefully before they are used, but in a few cases living reeds or bamboo are utilized for fences.

The most common and by far the most versatile grass used in Japanese architecture—and the only one used structurally—is bamboo (take). Many different kinds of bamboo are grown in Japan (over 100 species, of which 84 are indigenous), but the most commonly used in construction are madake (a long-jointed bamboo used for rafters, gutters, fences, sudare screens and lath), mōsō-chiku (the largest bamboo in Japan, used for roofs and tokobashira), and hachiku (a light-colored bamboo that is easy to split, used for rafters, fences, lath, and nails).[43] Bamboo grows very quickly—some species in Japan can grow 1.2 meters (almost four feet) in one year. Bamboo has a net-like root structure of runners or clumps that sends up shoots, which are edible and considered a seasonal delicacy in Japan. Bamboo can be very invasive, however, and often is considered a weed; although the bamboo culms are easy to cut with a saw or a heavy knife, the roots are very difficult to remove.

Bamboo has sturdy, thick-walled, hollow culms with solid joints (fushi) at intervals along the stalk. It is flexible and light in weight yet durable and structurally sound. Large poles of bamboo can be used as building structure, most commonly for roof rafters or secondary roof structure. Because bamboo is both round and hollow, typical wood joinery methods do not work. Bamboo usually is connected to other members by binding with rope, which is generally made from rice straw.

Bamboo poles in unusual shapes, which may grow naturally (such as kikkō-chiku, "tortoise

Above Light filters through a forest of bamboo at the Rakusei Bamboo Park in Kyoto.
Near right Bamboo poles are tied together with black rope to create a uniform bamboo fence.
Center right Thin strips of bamboo woven into a *sudare* matchstick blind provide shade from the hot Okinawa sun.
Far right Stacked bamboo poles show both the hollow core and the solid joints that occur at intervals as the bamboo grows.

shell bamboo," in which the joints are on alternating diagonals, giving the stalk a variegated or tortoiseshell appearance) or may be trained while growing to be square or twisted, often are used as *tokobashira* or for other similar ornamental purposes. Bamboo poles in small to medium diameters are used for floor and ceiling surfaces. Lined up one beside the other, the play of light on the round bamboo poles is beautiful, but the surface is hardly comfortable for sitting and normally is covered with woven rush *tatami* mats or cushions.

In the Japanese garden, small diameter bamboo poles are frequently used for fences and gates or in pavilion construction for the exposed roof structure or ornamental lattice window openings (*shitajimado*). Live bamboo or *sasa* (bamboo grass) sometimes is planted in a line and lashed together with thin horizontal bamboo poles to form a living fence.

Bamboo is split into halves, quarters, or strips and used for a variety of non-structural purposes, both in gardens and inside buildings. Bamboo strips are tied together in a grid pattern to make the lath for a wall, known as *komai*, on which mud plaster is applied (figure 26). Thin horizontal strips of bamboo are woven with hemp string or silk thread (in the case of special *misu* blinds used at shrines, temples, palaces, and aristocratic residences) to create screens called *sudare*, which are hung from the ends of roof eaves to block the sun. Thin strips also are used to form decorative patterns in sliding screens or transoms. In the garden, bamboo strips of various widths are bent or woven into delicate fences and gates, or they are bundled and tied by cords and vines to create dense fences.

Bamboo is cut even smaller to make thin sharp nails that are used to attach layers of cypress bark (*hiwada-buki*) or thin wood shingles (*kokerabuki*) to roofs. Roofers, who carve the nails themselves, developed an unusual way of using them. Sitting on the roof, they put small handfuls of bamboo nails in their mouths, use their tongues to line up one nail with the point facing toward the lips, and then spit the nail toward the roof, catching it and simultaneously pounding it in with a hammer in one fluid motion.

Left Easily manufactured and replaced, a hollowed-out length of bamboo serves as a simple water spout. A bamboo pole is split in half and the solid joints are removed to create a channel through which water can flow. The sight or sound of dripping water reminds the viewer of the essential role of water in the garden.

Another common and versatile material is rice straw (*wara*). After the rice has been harvested, the straw is dried thoroughly. Traditionally, rice straw is used for everything from clothing, including woven straw sandals (*waraji*) and raincoats (*mino*), to construction materials, such as rough woven floor mats (*komo*) and thatched roofs (*warabuki*)—in both cases similarly underfoot and overhead.

The most obvious architectural use for rice straw is as roof thatch, especially for *minka* (figure 15). Such roofs are known as *warabuki*, literally "straw cover." Dried straw is tied into bundles, which then are tied to the roof structure, with the upper bundles overlapping the lower bundles to protect the roof from rain and snow. The thick thatch also provides insulation for the building and is kept dry and free from insects by the smoke from the ever-burning fire in the hearth. Rice straw similarly is used on the sides of buildings in some cold areas—the bundles are tied to a wood frame that is attached to the building—to protect it from snow and provide a bit of insulation.

The rope that is used to tie bundles of thatch or bamboo poles typically is made from rice straw, which is braided or twisted into various thickness and lengths. The *shimenawa*, the rope that separates the sacred space of a *shintō* shrine from the profane space of the everyday, is perhaps the best example of the beauty and usefulness of rice straw rope. A *shimenawa* can be very thin and simple or very thick and imposing, such as the wonderfully overscaled *shimenawa* at the Izumo Shrine.

Wara also commonly is used as a cushion material—for the inner cushion in *tatami* mats or woven into seat cushions, like the circular *enza*, for use on wood or bamboo floors. For *tatami* mats, the straw is bundled and tied into a thick tight layer, creating a dense yet spongy cushion that is covered with a mat of woven rush (*igusa*).

Igusa is a thin rush that can be tightly woven into a fabric-like mat. As mentioned above, sheets of woven *igusa* are used for the covering of *tatami* mats, edged with strips of colored fabric. When a *tatami* mat is first made, the *igusa* is light green in color, but over time it fades into a yellowish beige. Thin woven *igusa*

Above A bamboo frame supports a fabric of woven reeds to shade the *engawa* veranda at the Kotōin Subtemple of Daitokuji Temple in Kyoto.
Below left A heavy tassel weights a thick rope of twisted rice straw, which is used to sound a bell to draw the attention of the *shintō* deities at the Wakamei Shrine in Akiya.

Below right The sandals used by a craftsman when working inside have a surface similar to a *tatami* mat.

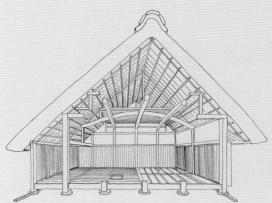

Above A craftsman carefully places *tatami* mats over the wood subfloor.

Left, figure 15 A section drawing shows the raised floors, wood-paneled walls, and thickly thatched roof typical of a *minka* farmhouse found in a mountainous area.

Below left Expressively grained wood boards are intermixed with thin bamboo poles for a refined wall surface.

Below center A detailed view of the corner of a thatched roof shows the thickness and density of the rice straw.

Below right Rice straw twisted into a rough *shimenawa* decorated with folded paper *shide* and fern leaves.

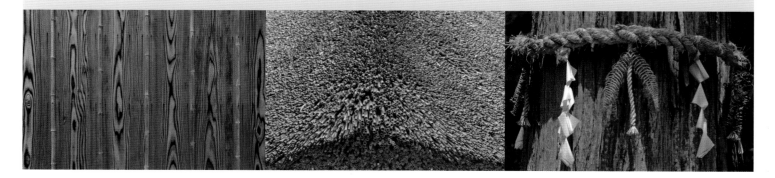

mats also are used alone, hung like *sudare* as blinds to block the sunlight or used as temporary floor coverings. These mats, known as *goza*, are lightweight and easily rolled up for storage.

As discussed previously, *sudare* blinds can be made from bamboo strips or *goza*, but usually they are made from *yoshi*, a kind of fine reed which looks like thin bamboo and also can be used for thatch or in screens (*fusuma*). The thin stalks of *yoshi* are laid horizontally and woven with hemp string to create the mats for the *sudare*. For *fusuma* screens, the *yoshi* typically is positioned vertically and held in place with horizontal battens of thin bamboo or wood. To use for thatching roofs, bundles of *yoshi* are tied to the roof structure, utilizing the same methods as rice straw thatch. Roofs thatched with *yoshi* are much less common than the *warabuki* roofs thatched with rice straw but are more durable. Also more durable than *warabuki* are *kayabuki* roofs thatched with miscanthus grass (*kaya*), which are used primarily for small *sukiya*-style buildings such as teahouses.

Stone

Of all the materials used in traditional Japanese architecture, stone is the most permanent—it is durable, strong, heavy, and rough. But it also can be light, smooth, and delicate. In traditional Japanese buildings and gardens, all these qualities of stone are used to show its particular character and the vast possibilities of its expression. As a permanent, durable material, stone is used as the foundation under a column or wall or as a retaining wall for a garden or terraced rice paddy. As a light, delicate material, stone is used to represent moving water in gardens or to give texture and pattern to tamped earth floors (*tataki*) and mud plaster walls. Each stone is carefully chosen by the builder or garden designer for its specific use based on its particular qualities and characteristics.

A number of varieties of stone that are useful in construction occur naturally in Japan. Because of their compositions and sizes, some types of stone work better as structural elements than others. Stone like granite (an igneous rock formed by intense heat such as

volcanic activity) that is dense and has a uniform composition works well structurally but can be difficult to shape. Softer stone like Oya tuff (*oya-ishi*, a porous stone formed by rhyolitic volcanic ash deposited in the deep sea) is less dense and has an inconsistent composition and therefore is weaker structurally but easier to cut and form. This kind of stone is better suited for ornamental rather than structural use in buildings.

Granite is the most commonly used stone in traditional Japanese buildings and gardens. There are many different names for granite in Japanese, including *honmikage*, *ikoma-ishi*, *kakōgan*, *kaji-ishi*, *mikage-ishi*, *okushū-mikage*, *ōshima-ishi*—the names reflect the different qualities or localities of the particular granite. Although its density makes granite difficult to cut and shape, it is an excellent construction material and is the preferred choice for foundations and retaining walls (figure 16). Granite is found in different sizes, sometimes as small or medium-sized stones that can be used as is, but often it occurs in large masses. Because of its size and weight, most granite must be quarried and cut into smaller pieces before it can be used architecturally. Granite is employed both in its rough form and cut into clean geometric shapes. The surface can be polished smooth or given a chiseled texture.

Oya-ishi (Oya stone or Oya tuff), named after the town of Oya (north of Tokyo) where it is most prevalent, is another stone commonly used in construction in Japan. It is lightly colored and often flecked with rust-colored specks of zeolites (hydrated aluminosilicate minerals). Over time, the zeolites leach out, leaving holes in the surface of the stone. Because of its porous composition, *oya-ishi* rarely is used for structural purposes but most frequently for exterior retaining walls (including walls in burial mounds from 1,500 years ago) and decorative stonework (such as in Frank Lloyd Wright's famous Imperial Hotel in Tokyo from 1923).

Like granite, Oya stone must be quarried. However, it is much lighter and softer than granite, making it easier to cut and form as well as to transport and to work with in construction. Oya stone generally is cut into

Above Horizontal planes of stone progress through the landscape of the Chionin Temple as a sequence of different levels separated by wide stone stairs.
Near right Slabs of granite give a sense of permanence to the stairs of the Higashi Ōtemon Main Gate at the Nijō Castle in Kyoto.
Center right A stone walking surface is constructed as a pattern of shifting geometries.
Far right Exhibiting subtle wit, the columns of the Hōnenin Temple gate are spliced with the lower part made of stone and the upper part of wood. Metal bands reinforce the joint.

Top The Reitaikyō Bridge is one of several finely constructed stone bridges in Kumamoto Prefecture. **Above** The curve of the carved base stones gives a sense of lightness to the heavy wood columns of the Sanmon Main Gate at Nanzenji Temple. Metal bands reinforce the bottom of the columns.

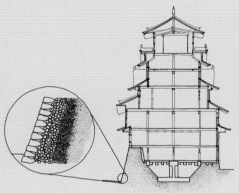

Above River rocks are used to create the Suhama Stone Shore at the South Pond of the Sentō Imperial Palace in Kyoto.

Top right The donjon tower of the Kumamoto Castle is raised high above the ground on the curving Niyō-no-Ishigaki stone foundation walls.

Right A dry-laid wall of variously shaped stones follows the topography to create a boundary at the Nakijin Castle ruins in Okinawa.

Top In the center of downtown Tokyo, the stone Nijūbashi Bridge crosses the moat surrounding the Imperial Palace grounds.

Above, figure 16 A section sketch shows the method used to construct a typical castle foundation.

regular shapes and finished with either a slightly textured or a completely smooth surface.

Marble, called *dairi-seki* ("Dàli stone") in Japanese after the Chinese city of Dàli, which is famous for the high quality of its marble, is a common construction material in many countries. However, although it does occur naturally in Japan, it is uncommon and rarely used architecturally. Instead, pieces of marble traditionally were displayed as decorative objects. Only in one area of Yamaguchi Prefecture, in far west Honshū, was marble historically used for *torii* gates, lanterns, retaining and garden walls, and the like. The Yamaguchi marble is white when it is first quarried, but as it ages it discolors to resemble granite. For this reason, it never became popular outside of the local area.[44]

Another stone that has been used architecturally but only rarely is *teppei-seki* ("flat iron stone," pyroxene andesite). *Teppei-seki* is a slate-like stone that served as a roofing material from the late Edo period through the start of the Meiji era in the Suwa region in Japan. It is composed of layers, which makes it easy to split into board-like pieces that can be used as roof shingles or for similar purposes.

The types of stone found in traditional Japanese gardens and landscapes include those like granite and Oya tuff that are used architecturally, as well as a number of other kinds of rock that are rarely or never used in buildings. Stone is utilized for many different elements in traditional landscapes—retaining walls, borders, bridges, paths, stepping stones, courtyards, ornamental and symbolic groupings, and decorative objects such as basins and lanterns. Because of its durability and prevalence, granite is most commonly used for retaining walls, borders, bridges, paths, and stepping stones, while other types of stone are found as surfaces in courtyards and in ornamental groupings.

Ornamental and symbolic rock groupings are a major feature of traditional Japanese gardens. The rocks are chosen for their size, shape, and markings. Groups of rocks may include only one type, or they may highlight several different kinds. Common types of rock that are used in gardens in this way include various kinds of granite (*kakōgan* and others), tuff (*gyōkaigan*, including *oya-ishi*), Sado red stone (*sado-akadama-ishi*), limestone (*sekkaigan*), sandstone (*sagan*), and andesite (*anzangan*), and other types of igneous rock (*kaseigan*), such as basalt (*genbugan*) and dolerite (also known as diabase, *kiryokugan*), as well as crystalline schist (*kesshōhengan*) and slate (*ita-ishi* or *surēto*). Historically, rocks with good proportions and fine markings were highly prized, and when they were found in nature, they were often shipped great distances for use in future gardens.[45]

Sand (*suna*), often a course sand known as *masago* or *shirakawa-suna* ("White River sand"),[46] or fine gravel (*jari*) made from crushed granite is used in many gardens to cover flat areas of the ground as a representation of a body of water. The light-colored sand or gravel can be mounded to create three-dimensional forms (*sunamori*), such as cones or platforms, or it can cover the ground plane and be raked to express movement, from ripples to heavy waves. Although gravel often is used to cover large areas, the different sizes of the crushed stone and the ways it is raked to produce texture and movement create a level of detail that captures and holds the viewer's attention. The expanses of sand and gravel also reflect sunlight, sending soft light under the eaves of buildings into the far reaches of the interior.

River rocks, fist-sized softly rounded pieces of granite, sandstone, or flint, known in Japanese as *tama-ishi* (literally "ball stone"), often are used in gardens to cover low areas next to water to symbolize beaches (*ishihama*), as in the garden at the Sentō Gosho Imperial Palace in Kyoto. They have also been used to represent moving water in meandering rivers, such as in the Shinnyoin garden in Kyoto. River rocks are valued for their soft quality and evenness of size and color.

Earth

The use of earth as a building material is prevalent in many cultures around the world. Earth is readily available—always at one's feet—and very versatile. Earth is a good insulator and is strong against wind and, depending on how it is used, even rain. It can be mixed with other materials to increase its strength and durability and to add texture and color.

The first use of earth in architecture in Japan was as the floor material in ancient dwellings. The pit dwellings were dug about one meter into the ground, and the earth was tamped to create a smooth hard floor surface. This act of tamping the earth to make a floor continued even when houses began to be built on top of the ground, with the earthen-floored every-day entry and work space known as the *doma* (literally "earth space").

Minka farmhouses in many regions of Japan have these large earthen-floored areas (*doma*), which serve as the entry, kitchen, and general work space of the house. The surface of the *doma*, the smooth and hard *tataki*, is made by tamping the earth with water and bittern (a by-product of the process of making salt from seawater). The bittern helps to harden the earth and its use may be associated with *shintō* purification rites. "Bittern is added to a *tataki* much the same way that salt is scattered over a *sumo* [traditional wrestling] ring: it purifies the earth that has been drawn into the living space."[47]

Earth also can be tamped to make walls, usually using wooden formwork to create the shape of the wall with layers of earth tamped within the forms to the desired height. This kind of rammed earth (*hanchiku*) wall is rare in Japan, ostensibly because it is not strong in earthquakes, and much stronger materials like wood are readily available. None the less, there are some beautiful examples of rammed earth walls in Japan, such as those used to surround the subtemple grounds in the Buddhist temple compound of Hōryūji in Nara.

One of the most common uses of earth in traditional Japanese architecture, which can be found in the simplest *minka* and the most refined *sukiya*-style villa, is in mud plaster walls (*tsuchikabe*, literally "mud wall"). Japanese craftsmen developed hundreds of differ-ent mixes and finishes for mud plasters. Most mud plasters are a combination of different soils to get the necessary amount of clay and the desired color and texture. At a minimum, sand, straw, and water are added to the soil

mixture to bind it and make it workable. Some plasters also contain glue traditionally made from seaweed (red algae, *tsunomata*) as a binder. The mud plaster is thoroughly mixed and applied to a lath on a wall (typically con-structed from a grid of bamboo strips, called *komai*, figure 26) using a trowel (*kote*) to pick up the plaster from a wood hawk (*kote-ita*) and coat the lath.

Walls are plastered in layers, with the first coat called *arakabe*, literally "rough wall," expressing the surface texture needed for subsequent coats to adhere well. The *arakabe* is made with a thick plaster containing long strips of straw as a binder and a good amount of sand for texture. The next coat of plaster, called *nakanuri* or "middle coating," is still rough, though not as rough as the *arakabe*, and contains smaller lengths of straw and finer sand. The final coat, *shiage*, literally "finish," can be any number of different textures and colors, from a slightly finer version of the *nakanuri* to the smoothly polished and highly reflective *haitsuchi migaki* finish, which uses pulverized straw and seaweed or casein glue to bind finely ground dried earth and requires constant troweling by the plaster craftsman until the surface dries.

In many Buddhist temples and *shinden*- and *shoin*-style residences, the final plaster coat is a thin layer of lime plaster (*shikkui*) rather than mud plaster. Lime plaster dries to a smooth, hard, bright white finish and is made from a mixture of lime (calcium carbonate from limestone or sea shells), pulverized straw or other similar plant, seaweed glue, and water.

The use of mud plaster on walls in Japan developed into a highly skilled craft from a simple act of using a common material to create a weathertight surface. The finest mud plaster walls use earth from specific regions renowned for their beautiful color or have pigment, such as iron oxide (*bengara*), added and may be finished smoothly, brushed for a slight roughness, or even ribbed to catch the light. The combinations of color and texture are innumerable.

Mud plaster also is used as the finish for the *kamado* cook stove typically located in the *doma*. The basic form of the *kamado* is made

Top Straw acts as a binder and gives texture to a coarse mud plaster wall.
Center Smoothly finished earthen plaster is used for this unusual *ro* (hearth) in the Shōkatei Tea Pavilion in the garden of the Katsura Imperial Villa.
Above Graffiti and peeling plaster give character to a garden wall.
Below Hand-formed balls of mud plaster are pre-pared for use in repairing a wall.

Left Refined earthen plaster walls form infill between thin wood columns at the Rakushiken Middle Villa of the Shūgakuin Imperial Villa.
Right, figure 17 An early nineteenth-century illustration shows craftsmen going through the process of making ceramic tiles, from mixing the clay to forming the tiles.
Below The roof tiles of the eleventh-century Byōdōin Temple express the inconsistencies in color and shape that are typical of old hand-formed ceramic tiles.

86

from pieces of stone or broken tile, which are covered with mud plaster to give a smooth sculptural surface. A portable version of the *kamado* is the *shichirin*, which is a small cooking stove that normally is made from baked clay tile, mud plaster, or *keisodo* (diatomaceous earth, a lightweight but water-repellant sedimentary rock made from silica skeletons of plankton and algae that is quarried from areas that once were covered by oceans). *Keisodo* is quarried in blocks and ground to a fine powder that can be used in a plaster mix, giving a smooth surface similar to a lime plaster but with a pink hue.

A very different method of using earth in architecture requires that the earth be mixed with water and molded into shapes that then are baked in an oven to harden. The most widespread baked-earth material in Japan is the roof tile (*kawara*). Roof tiles were first brought to Japan from China with the Buddhist temple architecture of the sixth century. Soon after, Japanese craftsmen began making *kawara* themselves (figure 17), and the use of roof tiles spread from temples to aristocratic residences and eventually to some *minka*. Although *kawara* always have been symbolic of high social status and wealth, during the Edo period *kawara* were utilized as a fireproof material for commoners' houses in the cramped city of Edo, after the city experienced devastating fires.

Kawara tiles are made by mixing several types of dried pulverized earth together to achieve the proper clay content, adding water, and mixing to get a stiff but malleable wet clay. The wet clay traditionally is formed by hand on wooden molds to obtain the desired shape and size. Wood paddles are used to smooth the surface of the clay before it is left to air-dry for several days. After being air-dried, the tiles are stacked in a kiln and baked until they have hardened. The typical gray Japanese roof tiles, *ibushi-kawara* ("smoked tile"), which get their color from the carbon in the firing process, are not glazed. However, tiles with glazes (*yūyaku*) also are manufactured in Japan but are not as widespread.

Roof tiles are made in many different shapes, the most typical being wave-shaped pieces that overlap each other, half-cylinders that are used

Left The patina of age is apparent on the ceramic roof tiles of the Jōrenji Temple.
Center left A wave-like trowel pattern creates shadow and texture on a lime plaster wall.
Below left Flat square ceramic tiles with exaggerated lime plaster joints create a fireproof *namako-kabe* wall surface.
Below Time and weather have given character to the striated rammed earth walls that surround the dry garden at the Ryōanji Temple in Kyoto.

Above left A circular opening in an earthen plaster wall reveals a grid of bamboo and straw rope suggesting the continuation of the bamboo lath on which the plaster is applied.
Above Plaster craftsmen apply a final coat of lime plaster to a wall.
Left A smooth surface of mud plaster imparts an abstract sculptural quality to a *kamado* cook stove.

in pairs (one facing up, the other facing down), and flat square tiles. Flat tiles can be used on roofs or on walls as part of a *namako-kabe* finish (in which the tiles, typically set in a diagonal grid pattern, are nailed through holes in their corners to the exterior surface of a wall, and the joints between them are filled in with lime plaster to create a fireproof finish). End tiles often are more intricate, embossed with family crests or carved into elaborate forms. The large ornamental tiles used at the ends of roof ridges, called *onigawara* or "demon tiles," can be very elaborate and take many different forms, such as demons, fish, or geometric patterns, which may include a family crest and often mimic natural shapes. A well-known example of fine *onigawara* are the *shachi-gawara* (grampus dolphin-shaped roof tiles) gracing the top of the many-layered Himeji Castle roof. Although *kawara* primarily are used as a roofing material, many attain a second life creating pattern and texture in mud plaster walls or in garden paths.

Metal

One of the earliest uses for metal in traditional Japanese architecture remains its most important—that of being the primary material for making tools. Because Japanese buildings developed within a culture of wood, metal initially was not used as a building material. Traditionally, all joints, connections, and bracing are constructed using wood and other plant materials, which are readily available and easier to work than metal, but metal tools made the work possible.

Metal is durable yet malleable, and this is the quality that makes it unique compared with the other materials used in traditional Japanese architecture. Stone is durable, but it is hardly malleable—it is difficult to form and does not perform well under tensile forces. Wood can be formed easily and is somewhat elastic, so it works reasonably well in both tension and compression, but its strength is dependent on its size and shape, with only large members able to function structurally. Large timbers can last for centuries but must be protected from the weather. Other plant materials, such as bamboo and straw, are very

malleable but not very durable, nor are they useful for most structural purposes. Earth is malleable and can be durable, especially when baked (and no longer malleable), but it is difficult to use structurally as it is weak in both tension and compression. With both the qualities of durability and malleability, metal offers many opportunities that other materials do not. However, the amount of effort required to work metal ore into a form that can be used in building historically made the material too difficult for many applications, more so as wood was prevalent and much easier to work.

Metal working is generally understood to have been introduced from China and Korea in the Yayoi period (300 BCE–300 CE). Iron ore, which is used to make steel tools, occurs naturally in many areas in Japan, though not in abundance. The process of refining the mined ore starts with smelting in a bloomery furnace to form "blooms" (*kaimentetsu*), sponge-like masses of iron and slag that also contain some carbon. Blooms with too little iron are weak

due to their high glass content, while blooms with too much iron turn into cast iron, which is too brittle to be formed into tools. The blooms are formed into basic shapes, for example, in the case of tools, for saw blades, hammer heads, and chisel and plane blades, through a series of poundings, heatings, and quenchings.

This process of making tools in Japan developed using two different strengths of steel—a high carbon tip on a softer core, which is a hallmark of Japanese metalwork. The core is more flexible, while the harder high carbon steel holds its sharp edge longer. Because of this combination of metals, together with the unique process of laminating steel that developed in Japan, the country is known for producing very high quality tools. Since the tool is an extension of the craftsman's body, these first-rate tools made it possible for craftsmen to hone their remarkably fine skills, and thus the tool is an important part of the development of traditional Japanese architecture.

In addition to its use for making tools, metal—especially bronze (a copper alloy)—was utilized in Japanese buildings after the introduction of the Buddhist temple architecture from China. Chinese temple buildings incorporate metal in ways that are both decorative and functional. For example, starting from the early Buddhist architecture, the exposed ends of wood rafters sometimes were capped with decorative metal (typically bronze) plates (*koguchi kanagu* or *koguchi kanamono*). These caps help to keep the end grain of the wood from absorbing water, thereby adding to its lifespan, as well as enhance the ornamental quality of the roof. From the same time, heavy wood-paneled doors incorporating decorated bronze straps (*sankarado*) were hung with pivot hinges (*jikuzuri*) in metal sockets (*waraza*). The hinges and straps often are embossed with geometric patterns or images of leaves or flowers. Metalwork on the bottom of pillars also illustrates the attention to detail that is typical of many traditional buildings.

Far left A thick metal strap reinforces the base of a heavy wood column. **Center left** Ornamental metalwork covers rafter ends and joints at the Ninomaru Palace in Nijō Castle in Kyoto. **Left, figure 18** Finely crafted copper sculptures of phoenixes adorn both ends of the ceramic tile roof ridge of the Hōōdō Phoenix Hall at the Byōdōin Temple.

Metal, especially bronze, also is used for sculpture that accompanies the architecture—or in some cases, such as the eighth-century Daibutsuden Hall of the Tōdaiji Temple complex in Nara, housing sculpture is the reason the building was constructed. The enormous 15-meter-high (more than 49 feet) gilt bronze Buddha statue at Tōdaiji required an equally enormous building to contain the statue. When the building was rebuilt in 1709 following a fire, the length of the building was shortened by one-third, but the original height was maintained in order to accommodate the Buddha statue. Despite its diminished size, the Daibutsuden remains the largest wood building in the world.[48]

As the Chinese Buddhist temple forms transitioned into *shinden*-style complexes, the use of metal in the buildings did not change significantly. Metal continued to be utilized primarily for hardware, hinges, and fittings that enhance the use of the building, but which also add a decorative element. Metal rods and hooks (*tsuri-kanamono*) used to hold wood lattice shutters that hinge upward, called *shitomido*, first appeared in *shinden*-style architecture and also were used in *shoin* buildings. Metal continued to be used for sculpture contained within the buildings as well as some on the exterior. The famous Hōōdō Phoenix Hall of the Byōdōin *shinden* complex in Uji features two highly ornamental phoenix sculptures placed on either end of the roof ridge (figure 18). Fabricated from copper plate, the delicate sculptures seem ready for flight and enhance the quality of lightness in the building.

During the transition to the *shoin* style and the later *sukiya* style of architecture, decorative metal fittings (*kazari kanamono*) continued to be used in upper-class dwellings as well as temples and shrines. Various metals, such as iron, gilt bronze, and copper, began to be used for joint covers and door pulls, which were both practical and decorative. An ornamental nail cover or *kugikakushi* (literally "nail hider") is placed over the head of a metal nail used to connect a head beam (*nageshi*) to a column. Because the covers are clearly visible, often at a height near eye level, it is logical that they would be ornamented in some way. Typical ornamentation for a *kugikakushi* in a *sukiya*-style building is a half-sphere or a flower with four, six, or eight petals. *Kugikakushi* also are used to cover nail heads on wood-paneled doors.

Similarly, door pulls (*hikite*) for sliding doors, primarily *fusuma*, as well as some hinged doors, started to be fabricated from metal rather than wood, which is not as durable. Ornamental door pulls were used in *shoin*-style buildings and became more elaborate in *sukiya* architecture. Some metal door pulls are simple rectangles, but others take the form of stylized flowers or leaves—sometimes in the same motif as the *kugikakushi*, reflecting the connection to nature that is ubiquitous in the materials and ornamentation of *sukiya* buildings.

PART 3
Architecture

雪ふるよ
障子の穴を
見てあれば

正岡 子規

Snow's falling!
I see it through
a hole in the shōji screen....[1]

MASAOKA SHIKI (1867–1902)

Chapter 8
Roofs

In a traditional Japanese building, the roof is the most visually dominant architectural element. Often tall and large with long overhanging eaves that have a gentle upward curve, the roof is a strong symbol of shelter and social status—the larger the roof, the greater the wealth and therefore the power of the owner. The need for a roof as a sheltering element is obvious, and the roof has had a straightforward development from the early flat-land houses and pit dwellings to the stately roofs of *shoin*- and *sukiya*-style imperial villas. The roof of the flat-land house sat directly on the ground, serving as both roof and wall, as did the pithouse roof, with rafters reaching the ground and leaning against beams raised above the ground on columns. The roof was designed purely for function; it enclosed space, sheltered inhabitants from the weather, and was just large enough to allow for daily life activities to take place under it. As dwellings developed, the roof was detached from the ground and lifted atop a wooden frame of columns and beams with infill walls. The size of the roof and the long extension of the eaves create a strong visual connection between the interior and exterior.

Roofs grew as dwellings were enlarged to accommodate additional activities within the interior space of the house. Roof forms, especially those of *minka* (houses of the common people), historically are adapted to the local climate and reflect the types of building materials that are available locally (figures 10 and 19). Houses in cold snowy climates have tall steep roofs covered with rice straw thatch which enclosed two-, three-, or four-story spaces. Houses in windy warmer climates had long low roofs sheltering single-floor spaces; the roofs often were covered with

wood shingles or planks weighted down with stones. A unique roof form, such as the *kabuto* or "helmet" style, which developed in the central area of the main island, became a distinctive regional symbol, emblematic of the wealth and creativity of the people of that area.

Since the primary purpose of a roof is to provide shelter from the elements (sun, wind, rain, and snow) and from nature (animals, insects, and other living creatures) the basic form of the roof reflects that purpose. The roof is sized to contain all the necessary functions of daily life, while also eventually incorporating a long eave to shade and keep the rain off the open-sided veranda (*engawa*) that extends from the floor plane. The combination of the veranda and long eave serves as a horizontal framing device for viewing the garden from inside the building.

The slope of the roof is designed to repel rain, snow, and wind, and aid in the ventilation of the building. Smoke gathers at the highest point of the tall roofs in cold climates. In warm climates, wind passes through the open walls and under the gently sloped roofs. The planes of roofs initially were constructed flat and

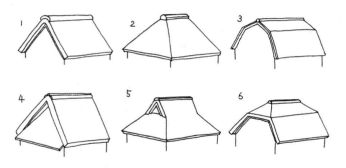

Pages 90–1 The serene Takayama Jinya at Takayama, Gifu Prefecture.
Opposite Layers of ceramic tile roofs on the grand Himeji Castle.
Top The expansive shingled roof of the Shōrinin Temple *hiwada-buki*.
Above Layers of thin cedar shingles create the smooth curve of a roof of the Shōdaibu-no-Ma at the Kyoto Imperial Palace.
Left, figure 19 Typical *minka* roofs include gable (1), hipped (2), mansard (3), and combination (4–6).

Top A combination of expensive permanent materials (the lower ceramic tile roofs) and more economical but more transitory materials (the upper roof of thatch).
Above Stones weigh down battens which hold wood shakes in place on a *minka* roof.
Below A ceramic *shīsā* guardian lion-dog watches over the house from the rooftop of this eighteenth-century Okinawan home.

straight, without an exaggerated curve, for ease of construction. The inclusion of the curving eave was a result of the influence of the Chinese-style Buddhist architecture that entered Japan in the sixth century. Used initially in the Buddhist temples, the curving roof became popular for the houses of the aristocrats as well. Over time, the curve fell out of favor, and most roofs were constructed with straight slopes, although a combination of straight, curved, and cusped roofs can be found in some examples of aristocratic dwellings, such as at the entrance of the Ōmiya Palace of the Sentō Imperial Palace in Kyoto (originally built in the seventeenth century and reconstructed after a fire in 1854). The cusped roof (*nokikarahafu*, figure 47) was introduced from China in the Heian period and was adopted for use in temples, gates, and aristocratic dwellings, especially as a way to mark the main entrance.[2]

The materials used to cover roofs varied from region to region, reflecting what was available locally. Thatch, wood shakes, and wood planks with stone weights were common early roof materials. Over time, of course, rough materials became more refined, such as the cypress bark shingles (*hiwada-buki*) and thin wood shingles (*kokerabuki*) that add an air of elegance to temples, shrines, and aristocratic residences. Roof materials also reflected outside influences, especially with the advent

of Chinese-style Buddhist architecture. The Chinese and Korean carpenters who built the first Buddhist temples in Japan, brought with them a new roof material—ceramic tile. This heavy, durable, and long-lasting material is well designed for the Japanese climate, and the ceramic tile roof has become the quintessential example of a traditional Japanese roof and still is in use today.

Roof construction and design went through many changes over the centuries but came almost full circle with the spaces designed for the *wabi* style of tea starting from the sixteenth century. These teahouses look to the "primitive" architecture and materials of the *minka* and hermit's hut in the woods for inspiration for their form and construction. The small buildings often feature beautifully constructed roofs of thatch, perhaps with the ridge reinforced with extra bundles of thatch held in place with simple poles of bamboo. The idea of using such "primitive" materials is that of rustic elegance, a return to the simplicity of life in close connection with nature. Yet the careful craft and refined rusticity of the finishes place this architecture in an entirely different realm.

Structure

The first structures designed to hold up the roofs of permanent buildings in Japan were only slightly more advanced than simple lean-to structures. The pithouses (*tateana jūkyo*) incorporated a straightforward post-and-beam system with four columns driven into the ground in the center of a circular or oblong pit (figure 3). The columns marked the corners of a square or rectangle and supported four beams. Rafters rested on the ground and leaned up against the beams. The primary rafters formed gable ends and may have supported a ridge pole. Secondary rafters created a skirt around the building and provided structure to attach bundles of thatch. As houses developed and grew larger, floors and roofs were lifted off the ground, and a more complex system of structural support became necessary. Buildings still were based on a post-and-beam wall system, but the roof structure developed into a variety of distinctive truss systems that took advantage of the ready supply of wood in Japan.

Above The interior of the Yoshijima house in Takayama reveals sophisticated layers of structure and hidden joinery in the enormous beams and columns.
Top right An unusual umbrella-like wooden ceiling of a garden pavilion in the Saimyōji Temple complex.
Above center A curved beam at the Kōrinin Subtemple in the Daitokuji complex.
Above right Layers of brackets support the extended roof eaves of a building at the Great South Gate of the Tōdaiji Temple in Nara.
Right, figure 20 Typical *minka* truss systems range from simple column-and-beam structures to complex *wagoya* trusses.

The two most common forms of roof structures, used especially in *minka*, are the "inverted U" and the "rising beam"[3] (figure 20). For the inverted U structure, two columns (*hashira*) hold up one beam (*hari*), thereby creating a frame in the shape of an upside-down U, and a series of frames are attached to each other with additional beams. Each inverted U frame supports smaller columnar elements, struts (*tsuka*), which are tallest at the center point of the beam where they support the roof ridge pole and are increasingly shorter as they move toward the edge of the structure. The struts support purlins (*keta*), which run the horizontal length of the structure, connecting the frames and supporting the rafters (*taruki*). The rafters, in turn, support the substructure of the roof.

In the "rising beam" roof structure, two columns are connected by a beam at ceiling height, forming a frame. The columns extend above the beam and support a line of beams or girders which run the perimeter of the

structure and connect all the frames. These horizontal beams support rising beams (*noboribari*), which extend from the beam at the top of each column to rest on an inner ridge pole (*jimune*) supported by tall columns at the gable ends of the building. The rising beams support struts and purlins that hold up the rafters and ridge pole (*munagi*).

In the more complex *wagoya* roof structure, trusses with tiers of struts and purlins support rafters. The lower struts carry intermediate purlins, which in turn carry additional struts. The wood members of these truss systems are joined without the use of hardware, creating flexible structures that resist the forces of the wind and snow and allow flexibility during seismic activity.

An unusual roof structure can be found in many *kura* storage buildings. Built to be fireproof, *kura* often have a double roof with air space between the two roofs. Both roofs are constructed of timber, but the lower or inner roof is completely covered with plaster on the

exterior for fireproofing. The outer roof shades the plaster roof and is covered with ceramic roof tiles, wood shingles, or thatch. In the event of fire, the wood structure of the outer roof might burn, but the inner roof would remain intact. The shade provided by the outer roof and the ventilating air space between the roofs (as well as the thickly plastered walls) keep the interior of the building cool.

Construction

As noted previously, in the typical image of a traditional Japanese building, the roof is covered with ceramic tile. Tile roofs indeed have been common since the introduction of ceramic tile from China, and the durability of tile made it popular (alone or in combination with other materials) for many different building types—aristocratic dwellings and storehouses, temples and shrines, castles and teahouses. Initially, tile was too expensive for commoners to use—and later Edo-period sumptuary edicts reinforced the idea of

privilege associated with roof tile by prohibiting its use on many building types. However, many other materials are used to cover roofs, and each material has unique qualities.

For *minka*, a common roof surface material is thatch made from rice straw (*wara*) or occasionally from miscanthus (*kaya*). The straw is bundled and tied into place using rope (also made from rice straw). It is layered to a thickness of up to 60 centimeters or more (about 2 feet) for insulation and protection from the elements. Historically, the act of thatching the roof of a building was an important event in a community, as the whole community worked together to collect and dry the rice straw and then to thatch several buildings each year. Thatching days had a festival-like atmosphere and were an opportunity for the villagers to exchange information. Thatch on a roof typically lasts about twenty years, so the community rotated through its buildings, ensuring that every building had the thatched roof replaced when needed.

Other roof materials that are used frequently include wood shingles and shakes (shingles are sawn, shakes are split), which usually are crafted from *hinoki* cypress (sometimes cedar or persimmon wood is used) and held in place with bamboo nails. In a less refined fashion, wood shakes can be held down by wood or bamboo battens which are weighted down by stones. The same method of weighting with stones is used with wood boards (figure 21). They are set parallel to the edge of the roof and overlap one another, as they are layered up the slope of the roof. An even more refined version of a shingled roof uses layers of cypress bark (*hiwada-buki*). The bark is carefully harvested from the living tree, applied to the roof in thick layers (up to about 18 centimeters or 7 inches),[4] and attached using bamboo nails. The cedar bark lasts much longer than thatch, and because of its multiple layers it is much denser than shingles. The layers of bark have a soft sculptural quality that enhances curving eaves.

Often roof surfaces are constructed using a combination of materials, especially at the ridge of the roof, which is the weakest point against the weather. If a family had the resources, the ridge of their thatch roof might

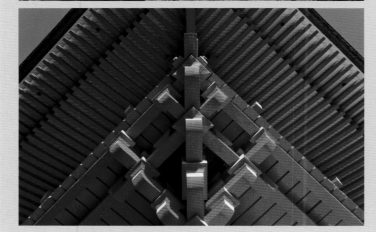

Above Smooth cylindrical tiles emphasize the ridge and joints of the Meditation Hall at Tenryūji Temple in Kyoto.
Center The soaring roofs of the Daibutsuden Great Buddha Hall of Tōdaiji Temple seem to float above the treetops.
Below Intricate brackets support layers of closely spaced rafters bearing the load of the long eaves of the Rōmon Tower Gate at Kiyomizu Temple in Kyoto.
Bottom, figure 21 An unusual *minka* roof utilizes the weight of stones to keep the wood battens and shakes in place.

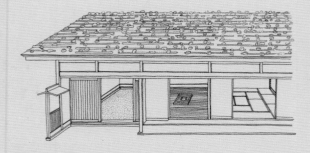

be reinforced with ceramic tile, held in place with mortar. Roofs covered with shingles, shakes, or bark also might have a ridge reinforced with ceramic tile. Thatch roofs might have a ridge reinforced with extra bundles of thatch held in place with bamboo poles or wooden boards, or even plants (*shibamune*), such as the Japanese Roof Iris (*Iris tectorum*). Planted on the ridge perhaps to ward off evil spirits or disease,[5] the flower got its name after being found growing on *minka* roofs. The thick layer of soil and roots of the plants absorb rainwater but prevent it from penetrating the roof.

Main roofs may be covered with one material (bark or tile, for instance) and smaller secondary roofs might be covered in another (wood plank or, later, metal). Metal, specifically copper formed into shingles, was used as a roofing material from the early Edo period, and initially was utilized for castles, shrines, aristocratic residences, and the like, often in combination with other materials. Combining materials adds to the building's visual interest, especially in the case of the teahouse, where several different roofing materials may be combined to express the hierarchy of spaces within the building.

Openings

Because the roof is the primary element that keeps the weather out of a building, making openings in a roof intrinsically undermines its purpose. Although it is beneficial to have openings for ventilation and light, there is always a risk of water leaks and the possibility of compromising the durability of the roof. Because of this, and despite the fact that in the past many traditional Japanese buildings, especially *minka*, constantly had a fire going inside, openings in the roof to ventilate smoke are often lacking. Some *minka* have no openings in the roof, so smoke gathers inside under the ridge of the roof. This has some advantages, since the smoke keeps insects out of the thatch and built-up carbon helps to protect the wood structure, but the air in these *minka* is always smoky. Other houses incorporate grills high in the walls at the gable ends of the buildings or just below the ridge in a combination hip-and-

gable (*irimoya*) roof. On occasion, a dormer provides ventilation, usually placed along the center of the roof ridge. However, the smoke openings are often small, and in warm weather it is more likely for ventilation to occur horizontally through the wall openings than vertically through a roof opening.

Roof openings made especially for letting light in are even less common than openings for ventilation. In fact, in his comprehensive late nineteenth-century study of traditional Japanese houses, Edward S. Morse offers a thoughtful analysis of "smoke-outlets" but does not mention a single instance of a roof opening for light.[6] Instead, light enters traditional Japanese buildings from the sides, through openings in the walls. Some buildings are designed with courtyards, sometimes even very small interior courtyards called *tsuboniwa*. These courtyards are not roofed, so light and air can enter into the adjacent spaces. Courtyards like this are a common feature in *machiya* townhouses, which are often long and narrow and constructed immediately adjacent to one another, with little space for openings in the long side walls.

One instance of a skylight is in the Yoshijima house and shop in Hida Takayama. A fine example of a high-class urban merchant's house, the Yoshijima house was remodeled after a fire in 1905,[7] and the interior features a tall space with an incredible exposed timber structure. The skylight, placed high up on a wall just below the roof rather than cut into the roof itself, is covered with a simple shutter,

which opens using a rope and pulley system. When the shutter is lowered, the light from the skylight gently plays off the layers of struts and purlins, expressing and enhancing the surprisingly high space.

Some traditional teahouses do have skylight openings in the roof. These small skylights are covered on the exterior by tight-fitting wooden shutters that hinge up to allow light to pass through an oiled paper screen (*aburashōji* or *amashōji*). Occasionally, teahouses, such as the Shōkintei at Katsura Rikyū Imperial Villa in Kyoto, have two such skylights to allow filtered light into the inward-facing space.

Chapter 9
Foundations

The foundations of many ancient buildings in Japan were constructed simply using the most basic material at hand—soil. The floors of the *tateana jūkyo* pit dwellings were sunken into the ground, with supporting wood columns driven directly into the earth. Some Yayoi-era dwellings may have been built without a sunken floor but with columns set into the ground and the addition of a low wall of rammed earth as a foundation for the perimeter walls.[8] Elevated storehouses (*takakura*) of the Yayoi era had wood floors lifted high above the ground supported by columns driven into the earth. Similar construction is used for the Ise Shrine on the Kii Peninsula in Mie Prefecture, which dates originally from the late third century. As construction progressed, such columns were driven into the ground with a primitive pile driver, after first digging a hole and preparing a base of rocks.

With the advent of Buddhism and its accompanying architecture in the sixth century CE, a new type of foundation came into use. A podium of stone (*danjōzumi kidan*, figure 22) serves as a base to raise the wood structure off the ground. The height and solidity of the podium add to the monumentality of the building. Although the podium is the major foundation element in such a building, it is not the only type of foundation used in traditional Japanese buildings. Most residential buildings have wood columns set on separate stone bases (*soseki*, figure 23) and walls formed on wood sills (*dodai*) placed on continuous stone footings (*renzoku-kiso*, figure 24). After their introduction in Japan, these three types of stone foundations began to be used either separately or in combination for almost every type of building.

Podia

Japanese buildings which are derived from Chinese forms, especially important Buddhist temples such as those of Hōryūji and Yakushi-ji in Nara, typically are built upon stone podia (figure 22). This type of large raised platform supported by stone walls, which serves as the foundation for a building, is the earliest type of stone foundation used in Japan.[9] Stone walls, usually consisting of large stones closely fit together without mortar, are built up from the ground, often to a height of several steps or sometimes even 2 or more meters (over 6 feet), and define the perimeter of the foundation. Initially, the area inside the stone walls was excavated and then filled with tamped earth to the top of the stone walls. However, in the next stage of development, during the Nara period (mid-seventh to late eighth century), the area within the stone walls was not excavated but simply filled in with layers of tamped sand and clay. It then was topped with a layer of tamped earth containing lime to give it a

Opposite The bark-covered columns of the Bashōan Teahouse at Konpukuji Temple in Kyoto rest on variously shaped rocks.
Top A single base stone set into the tamped earthen *doma* floor supports a rough wood column.
Above The lower rails for sliding partitions sit on rows of small stones, creating a continuous foundation as well as a threshold between the lower and higher floor levels.
Left A *dodai* sill plate is carved to fit precisely on rounded foundation stones.

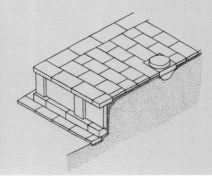

Left The Daikodō Great Hall at Hōryūji Temple is raised off the ground on a stone podium foundation, with centrally placed stairs, as is typical of a Buddhist temple building.
Below left Heavy timber columns are supported by carved round base stones set atop the stone podium.
Below center A simple round base stone lifts the wood column above the surface of the foundation.
Below right, figure 22 The section drawing of a stone podium foundation shows the mounded earth retained by stone walls and covered by a stone floor surface with a base stone set into it.
Opposite A combination of large blocks of stone and small infill stones are dry laid in an upward-sweeping curve to create the foundation of the donjon tower at Kumamoto Castle.

hard surface or finished with a surface of stone or square *kawara* tiles.[10]

Raising the buildings above the ground on podia is useful in the humid Japanese climate, since this removes the wood structures from direct contact with the damp ground.[11] Visually, the size of the podium helps to balance the perceived weight of the roof, creating a pleasantly proportioned building. The podium adds to the monumentality and feeling of power expressed by a great timber frame structure like a Buddhist temple. The podium lifts the building above the level of the ground and requires worshippers to ascend a set of stairs to reach the temple entrance. The act of ascension serves to emphasize the separation of the worshipper from the interior of the building. The height of the podium reinforces the hierarchy of buildings and spaces within the entire temple complex, as the various buildings within a complex often have foundations of different heights, expressing their relative importance. Generally, the building with the highest foundation podium is the

kondō (literally "golden hall"), the centrally located main hall which houses an image of the Buddha.

Stone podia often are quite large and require the use of a great amount of stone, which must be carefully worked to create tight-fitting joints and perfectly shaped side walls and top surfaces. Because of the large size—and therefore heavy weight—of the buildings, most temples also incorporate stone bases (*soseki*) set within the podium for each of the major columns, as well as continuous stone footings (*renzoku-kiso*) under all the walls. In these situations the podium acts both as the general foundation for the building and as a second ground level, reinforcing worshippers' awareness of having left the everyday world and moved to a sacred place. Structurally, the weight of the columns is concentrated on the *soseki* and the weight of the walls on the *renzoku-kiso*.

As Japanese architecture developed from the Chinese-influenced Buddhist forms to the less monumental but still formal *shinden* style, the stone podium foundation also changed. It

did not immediately disappear, but it began to play a less obvious role in the aesthetics of the building. In the intermediate *shinden* style, the height of the podia decreased, often to just a few steps above the ground. Moreover, not every building in a *shinden* complex was constructed on a podium. This allowed a stronger connection between the interior and the exterior, as the interior spaces were much closer to the ground, and a person inside the building could easily see and converse with a person outside.

The use of stone podium foundations declined significantly in the *shoin* style, with the height of the podia decreasing to just above (or at) ground level. In some *shoin* buildings, podia are eliminated altogether, and the visual emphasis is instead on the raised wood floors. In the later *sukiya*-style buildings, the stone podium all but disappeared, and other types of foundations were used.

In the late sixteenth and early seventeenth centuries, Japanese castle builders took the concept of the stone podium foundation and

used it in an exaggerated way that greatly increases the height and enhances the sense of centrality of power of the castle complex (figure 16). Japanese castles are multistory constructions built on a hill; alternately, a high area was specially constructed for the castle. Since the castles were built by the feudal lords (*daimyō*) as a display of power and wealth as much as—or sometimes even more than—for defensive purposes, the high foundations played an important role both in physically elevating the buildings and in adding to the overall perceived sense of height.

Stone podium castle foundations typically are constructed with a slight curve to the steep sides, which creates a beautiful transition from the ground to the building itself. Although constructed from many different sizes and shapes of stones, the stones are fit together very tightly, and the sides of the castle foundations are effectively impossible to climb. The foundations are built to great heights—as much as 15 meters (more than 49 feet) in the case of Himeji Castle[12]—and are often designed to enclose intricate paths with dead ends and gooseneck turns to trick invaders. Because the foundation walls are too steep to be scaled, invading troops had to follow the paths delineated by the walls to enter into the central compound of the castle. This allowed the defending army to know exactly how the invaders would move and when they would reach the points which were easily defensible. Although only a few original castle buildings exist (most were destroyed by fire or war), the stone foundations remain as testimony to the incredible skill of the craftspeople who built them.

Base Stones

The foundation system using base stones (*soseki*, literally "foundation stone," figure 23) directly supporting columns, is the most usual type of foundation system used for traditional Japanese dwellings and was first developed in the seventh century CE.[13] In many buildings, base stones are used in combination with continuous stone footings, and some temple, shrines and similar buildings use base stones set into the top of a podium foundation. Granite (*kakōgan*), because of its strength and durability, is most commonly used for foundation stones, although other types of stone, notably andesite (*anzangan*) and a kind of tufa know as *gyōkaigan*,[14] also are used.

The base stone foundation works quite simply—each major structural column rests on a separate stone base. The stone base often appears to be a single stone set onto or into the ground, but typically the base stone is set upon a bed of small stones within a deep hole in the ground. The wood columns are connected to the stones with simple mortise-and-tenon joints. Typically, the mortise (*hozoana*, the hole to receive the tenon) is carved into the base stone and the tenon (*hozo*, the pin-like projection) is carved from the bottom of the column, although the reverse is also found. Because of the frequent seismic activity in Japan, columns which are not constructed with an attachment to the base may become detached during an earthquake. The mortise-and-tenon allow structural flexibility, at the same time maintaining the close connection between the column and the base.

Depending on the level of formality of a building, stone bases can take on many different shapes. In formal buildings, such as temples and shrines, the stone bases may be pure geometric shapes—squares or circles carefully carved with straight or curving sides, with the perfectly rounded or squared columns set directly on the centers of the bases. In the eighth century, the shapes of the base stones were quite formal, but by the sixteenth century both very ornately carved geometric shapes and naturalistic forms were common. Such carved stones are used in formal buildings like temples, while in the less formal *sukiya*-style architecture base stones have a much more natural appearance. For *sukiya* buildings, stones often are used as they are found in nature, asymmetrical and roughly textured, and the bottom edge of each wood column is carved to match the top surface of the stone base. This small detail shows the unique skill of the traditional Japanese carpenter and emphasizes the natural qualities of the materials.

The construction of a traditional building in Japan begins with the placement of the foundation stones, after which the primary structural framework of columns and beams is assembled on them. With the columns resting on separate stone bases, it is easy to attach the floor structure above the ground level, as is typical in traditional Japanese architecture. The beams which support the floor system (sleepers, *ōbiki*) are connected to the columns above the base stones. Raising the floor off the ground allows for natural ventilation below the floor and keeps the living space above the damp ground and away from rodents and insects. Once floors began to be raised off the ground from the late eighth century, most column bases were no longer visible, and the forms of the bases were simplified.[15] From the interior spaces, where the floor surfaces extend to the outside with a veranda-like *engawa*, the floors simply seem to float above the ground. From outside, the landscape appears to continue uninterrupted underneath the *engawa*, which gives the impression of the building sitting very gently

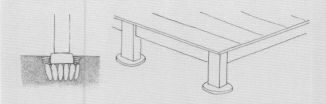

Top, figure 23 Section and axonometric drawings show the base stone foundation system.
Center Emerging from the ground, a rounded base stone lifts a wood column above the ground level, protecting it from the damp soil.
Below At the *sukiya*-style Shōkintei Tea Pavilion at Katsura Imperial Villa, the base stone for a teahouse column is set within a group of stones with similarly irregular shapes.
Bottom A coral stone serves as the base for a square wood column on Taketomi Island.

on the land. With the other foundation systems—the continuous stone footing and podium—the relationship of the building to the land tends to be much more obvious, as the walls of the building directly meet the surface of the ground (or the constructed ground in the case of podia), and the foundation is not hidden by an *engawa*.

Continuous Footings

The continuous footing foundation (*renzoku-kiso*, figure 24) is constructed with many medium-sized stones (*hazama-ishi*) or several long pieces of dressed (cut) stone (*nuno-ishi*) placed in a line and slightly recessed into the ground to form the foundation for a wall. Generally, a horizontal wood member (*jifuku*) or sill plate (*dodai*) is placed directly on top of the foundation stones. In some cases, the lath for a plaster wall may be built directly on the continuous stone footing, and the plaster covers the wall to the top of the stones. Continuous footing foundations are used for freestanding garden walls or in small to medium-sized buildings, where they often are used in combination with a base stone foundation and support tie beams (*jifuku*), which connect and stabilize the columns.

A major difference between this foundation and the base stone and podium foundation systems is that the walls of the building are brought down almost to ground level, rather than stopped well above the ground. However, in this case, like the others, the actual floor of the building is raised above the ground, with the floor structure attached to the columns at a level above the sill plate. In this way, the benefits of raising the floor above the damp ground are realized, but at the same time the building appears to have a connection to the ground.

Many *minka* or "people's houses" utilize this type of foundation system, often incorporating larger base stones within the row of footing stones to carry the weight of the columns. Since the villagers who lived in the *minka* often did much of the construction themselves, this foundation system could be built using tools and methods easily available and familiar to them. The construction of the foundation system is quite straightforward.

A shallow trench is dug into the ground, and the stones are placed in a row within it. Earth is filled in around the base of the stones to hold them in place. The major structural columns sit on the base stones and the wood sill plates then are set directly on top of the continuous footing stones between the columns.

One disadvantage of this type of foundation system that is not present with the base stone and podium systems is the possibility of water damage to the walls due to their proximity to the ground. Often the walls are covered with mud or lime plaster, which is troweled to a smooth finish and can repel a certain amount of water. However, when a wall is close to the ground, it is not unusual for water to splash in a heavy rain and eventually to be absorbed into the surface of the wall. Over time, this can cause damage to the plaster on the wall as well as to a wood sill plate. For this reason, areas which get frequent snows or heavy rain often protect the lower part of these walls with permanent wood panels or layers of tree bark. Sometimes, temporary skirts made of bundled thatch are placed against the exterior of the walls seasonally.

Above A row of low stones creates a continuous footing, which supports wide wood beams and is punctuated by a larger stone bearing the weight of a structural column.
Left, figure 24 Section and axonometric drawings illustrate how columns and sill plates are supported by continuous footings.
Below Rough stones with slight gaps between them form the foundation for a *minka*.
Bottom Smooth rectangular stones are placed adjacent to one another to create a continuous footing in a temple.

Chapter 10
Walls

Traditional Japanese buildings are well known for their use of exposed heavy timber framing (figure 25). In this construction system, the composition of the building structure is clearly expressed, with the major columns and beams visible and solid walls or walls of movable partitions filling the spaces between them. The expression of the structure often adds to the monumentality of the building, as in the case of great Buddhist temples like Hōryūji and Yakushiji. It also can add to the aesthetic based on nature, which is apparent in the *sukiya*-style architecture of traditional teahouses and imperial villas such as Katsura Rikyū or Shūgakuin Rikyū. Thus, the exposed skeleton of the building acts both as the structure and the aesthetic.

Because Japan is a heavily forested country, timber frame construction is used extensively and developed into a very fine art. *Minka* often incorporate timbers which are roughly hewn, unlike the finely finished timbers typically used in Buddhist temples and *shoin*- and *sukiya*-style buildings. The timbers in the *minka* both express the strength and power of the structure and showcase the natural beauty and life-force of the tree. Large *minka* often have quite complex structural systems to support three stories of living spaces and to hold up the large roofs. Skilled carpenters create complex truss systems, often incorporating timbers that have natural curves and bends, and utilizing them in ways that take advantage of the natural stresses in them (figure 36).

Early buildings like the inner and outer shrines at Ise (Naiku and Geku, respectively) also show a clean expression of the timber frame skeleton in their designs. The finely finished Japanese cypress (*hinoki*) columns and beams age gracefully to a silvery gray during the twenty-year life of the shrine buildings. One unusual feature of the buildings at Ise is that the primary structural columns holding up the roof ridge beam do not sit on stone foundations, as is common in most traditional Japanese buildings. Instead, the columns are set directly into the ground. This detail—which harks back to the early foundation systems of the pit dwellings and elevated storehouses—works fine at Ise, because the shrine buildings are reconstructed completely every twenty years, and the amount of deterioration of the columns is minimal. However, because the columns are subject to constant changes in dampness at the point at which they enter the ground, they would remain in better condition if they were separated from the damp soil atop stone foundations.

Although timber frame construction existed in Japan before the Chinese Buddhist temples forms were brought into the country, the temple construction dictated major changes from previous construction techniques and helped to elevate the level of carpentry skill. The construction techniques that the Chinese and Korean carpenters used in the first temples

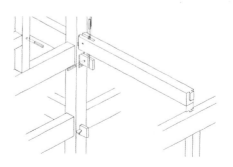

Opposite Columns and beams form a grid of structure that frames expanses of earthen plaster walls and supports top and bottom rails for sliding partitions, including the hanging column holding up the top rail at the far left.
Left, figure 25 A typical column-and-beam structure incorporates many different types of connections, which may be fixed by the form of the joint or with the use of a wood pin.
Right A view through a private residence reveals layers of expressed structure.

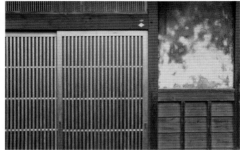

Top left Beautifully figured wood boards are set off by the regularity of the structural framework.

Top right Walls are carefully considered compositions of material, color, and texture. Here, sliding wood lattice doors, *shitami-ita* clapboard siding, and earthen plaster walls express the beauty of the patina that comes with age and use.

Center left Twisted and bent tree trunks become the structure for a *minka*. Rough mud plaster over a woven

bamboo lath and coarse wood boards fill the spaces between structural elements.

Center right White lime plaster walls are set off by the deep tones of the wood structure. Wood plank *amado* shutters are stored away during the day to reveal translucent sliding *shōji* screens and refined interior spaces.

Above *Shōji* screens slide in tracks and can be removed completely to open up the interior space to framed views of the adjacent garden.

in Japan allowed the Japanese carpenters to start building at a much larger scale than previously had been done in Japan.[16] These massive buildings feature huge timbers that give the impression of power and strength, as was appropriate for buildings designed to show the concentration of power of Buddhism.

Columns normally are round and finished with a spear plane to give a smooth surface to the wood. Beams, usually rectangular, are joined into the columns at various points. Tie beams connect the columns near the foundation for stabilization. Sleepers connect between the columns above the tie beams and support the floor system. Mid-wall tie beams connect between the columns as well as serve as headers for framed openings. Head tie beams penetrate through the tops of the columns and support the roof assembly. All these major columns and beams are left exposed, and walls and openings are placed between them.

As the architecture of Japan slowly changed over the centuries, the scale and shape of the columns also changed. In the *shinden* and *shoin* styles, columns often are square in section and finished with a block plane rather than the more primitive spear plane, which is used on columns with round surfaces. The *shinden* and *shoin* buildings tend to be less massive than the Buddhist temples and therefore require slightly smaller timbers. The smaller scale of the buildings, together with a decrease in the size of the foundation podia, led to buildings that maintained a high level of formality but were less monumental. However, like the Buddhist temples, these buildings use the expression of the structure as an aesthetic language.

The idea of structure as aesthetic expression is most clear in the *sukiya* style. Villas and teahouses built in this style are designed to show off the natural qualities of all materials used in the construction, and the timber structure is an essential part of that language. Columns frequently are used with the bark intact or with only the bark removed but the uneven surface of the column exposed. Other times trees are carefully pruned while living to create a pleasingly rough surface and curved form that adds to the expression of naturalness when used in a

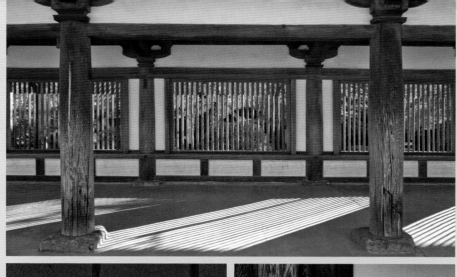

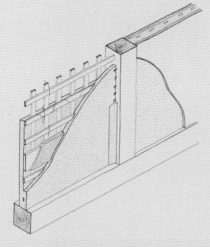

Above left Early morning light filters through the wood lattice screen and accentuates the autumnal colors of the garden beyond this corridor in the Hōryūji Temple.
Above, figure 26 Bamboo strips tied together with rope made from rice straw form the core of a traditional plaster wall. Layers of mud plaster are applied to the lath. Each successive layer is more refined than the last.
Far left A farmhouse wall is built for shelter not show, with thick plaster walls between uneven wood columns.
Left The color of a refined plaster wall melds with beautifully figured wood paneling in a Kyoto residence.

building. The use of textured timbers in *sukiya*-style buildings is highly influenced by the natural quality of the lumber used in *minka*.

The beauty of the columns and beams is especially apparent in the most significant columns—the *daikokubashira* central column of a house, the *tokobashira* main column of the *tokonoma* decorative alcove, and the *nakabashira* center column near the hearth in a tea ceremony room. The *daikokubashira* is overscaled and often made of a wood that is different from other structural columns to set it off. *Tokobashira* and *nakabashira* frequently have a slight bend or a beautiful texture that makes them focal points in the space and imparts an elemental sense of nature.

Infill Walls

The expression of the exposed structure of traditional Japanese buildings is enhanced by the color and texture of the solid walls that fill in the spaces between the column and beam structure. This type of wall is built up of layers of mud plaster troweled onto a lath made of bamboo. The final coat is lime plaster or a mud plaster that reflects the red, yellow, or green hues of the earth of the area where the building is located. These finely finished walls also can

express subtle textures and surface qualities that the plaster craftsmen use to further connect the building to the site and to show off their highly skilled craft.

The bamboo lath (*komai*) is constructed by the plasterers using strips of bamboo tied together with rope. The mud plaster, a mixture of soil, sand, straw, and water, is applied in layers (typically three but sometimes more), with each successive layer using a finer mix, resulting in a smoother finish (figure 26). The first layer or scratch coat (*ara-nuri*, "rough coat") is applied to the bamboo lath so that it fills in all the gaps and provides a heavily textured initial surface for the successive coats of plaster. The *ara-nuri* typically has large pieces of straw or other fibers that bind the mud and straw together and give the plaster a rough texture. After the first coat dries, a second or brown coat (*nakanuri*, "middle coat"), using the same ingredients but with a slightly less rough texture, is troweled on top of the rough coat. The final coat (*uwanuri* or *shiagenuri*, "finish coat") is applied to the first two (or more) layers and is used by the plasterer to express a desired aesthetic.

The final coat might include *bengara*, a red pigment made from iron oxide which occurs

naturally in Japan, especially in the Sanin Valley area north of Okayama. *Bengara* is said to have been named from the iron oxide pigment that was brought to Japan from the Bengal region of India in the sixteenth century.[17] Special walls also are given distinctive color by using soil from areas well known for having beautiful hues. Historically, these finishes were used only by those who could afford it, as most people had to be content with the color and texture of the earth from the area where their building was located.

Lime plaster often is used as the final coat for walls. It has a very hard texture and bright white color, which create a strong contrast with the exposed wood structure. Lime plaster gives a very fine smooth finish to a wall, whereas mud plasters allow a variation of finishes from smooth and refined to rough and textured, depending on the desired aesthetic and the plasterer's skill. Many *sukiya*-style villas and teahouses feature carefully crafted mud plaster walls that show off the color of the earth and the texture of the straw and the sand in the plaster mixture. In some cases, the final coat is designed to mimic the highly textured rough coat, giving a mottled appearance and a texture that catches the light as it plays over the wall.

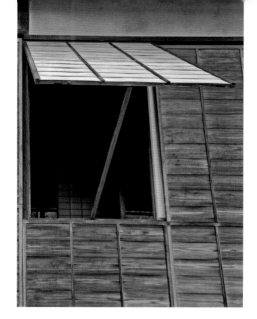

Mud and lime plaster walls are an important fireproof element within traditional Japanese buildings, as the wood structures are highly flammable, and historically fires were prevalent. Because of this, certain buildings, such as *kura* storehouses, were completely covered with plaster to protect a family's important possessions in the event of a fire. Many of these buildings have an unusual double roof structure, with the lower roof and walls—even the door and window shutters—entirely covered in plaster, and the upper roof structure left exposed so that only the upper roof would burn in a fire.

The placement of the solid plaster-covered walls within the overall structure of a building is important both for structural purposes and for privacy. Structurally, the walls help to brace the timber frame and support the structure against lateral wind and seismic loads. For privacy, the plaster walls often are among the few non-movable walls within the structure, as most interior walls and many exterior walls of traditional Japanese buildings, especially *sukiya*-style buildings, are designed to slide or be completely removed.

Although most infill walls are made from plaster, there are examples of infill walls constructed from wood panels, particularly in *minka* in areas where wood is abundant. There also are cases of wood and plaster being used together, for example with plaster used on the interior and wood on the exterior to help protect the plaster from the effects of the weather. A typical method of constructing exterior wood paneling is called *shitami-ita*

("see-below board", figure 48) Overlapping horizontal planks of wood attached to the building structure with thin vertical wood rails, similar to board-and-batten siding found in the United States and Europe, except that board-and-batten planks are laid vertically.

Another method of creating a solid unmovable fireproof wall is *namako-kabe* or "sea slug wall." Typical of *kura* storehouses, this method is utilized extensively in western Japan, especially in the Kurashiki region. *Namako-kabe* uses a combination of square tiles (made in the same manner as *kawara* roof tiles) and lime plaster. The tiles normally are used on the diagonal, with the plaster joints between the tiles bulging out in a smooth curve to create a vibrant diagonal grid pattern. The curved shape of the plaster joint, suggestive of a sea slug, gives the style of wall its name.

Openings

Openings in walls in traditional Japanese buildings take many different forms, and the forms often reflect the particular style of architecture in fashion at the time the building was constructed. Windows generally are built for sitting height (with viewers sitting on the floor), rather than chair or standing height as in Western architecture. Most windows are rectangular, but they also can be square or round, or take on a familiar form, such as a moon or a fan. Windows have both practical and symbolic functions. They provide light and ventilation as well as allow views out of and into a building. Symbolically, an opening can

suggest a connection to a world beyond, and—as in the case of the *nijiri-guchi* ("crawl-in entrance") of a *sukiya*-style teahouse—can induce a certain frame of mind, as both a physical and symbolic threshold. When windows take on ornamental form, as is often the case in teahouses, they represent a connection to nature through that form.

Windows in *minka* tend to be very utilitarian, since *minka* were built with shelter as the primary focus. Only when a family is wealthy can ideas of *asobi*, or "play," be incorporated into the house. Because glass was not used architecturally in Japan until the seventeenth and eighteenth centuries, windows open to the air and are permeable to the weather. In most *minka*, especially in urban areas, the windows on both the lower and upper levels generally have wood slats or bars on the exterior as protection. Some windows have wood-paneled shutters (*amado*) that slide in tracks to cover them; others have *shōji* (sliding wood lattice screens faced with paper) to filter the light. Window openings tend to be small and are used in places where a larger opening with sliding doors and screens does not fit or is not desired.

In the Chinese-influenced Buddhist temple architecture, there are very few windows. Most openings are large and at the level of the stone podium foundation. These openings utilize removable sliding partitions, although some incorporate heavy wood-paneled doors on hinges. Rather than only using the hinges vertically as is typical of doors in the West,

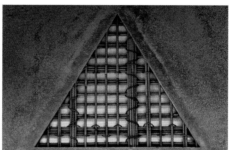

many doors hinge upward and hook onto metal rods, which hold them in place as horizontal planes. The few openings in the walls typically have wood grilles set into the frames of the openings and can be closed off using wood-paneled shutters. In a well-known example of a symbolically important wall opening, the Tōdaiji Temple in Nara has a window high in the front wall, which can be opened so that the face of the enormous Buddha statue inside the temple is visible. Similarly, in the later *shinden*-style Hōōdō at Byōdōin in Uji, a high window allows a view of that much smaller Buddha statue. Like the early Buddhist architecture, the *shinden*-style architecture has few openings in the walls except for those with movable partitions at the ground level.

This began to change as Japanese architecture evolved from these early styles to the later *shoin* and *sukiya* styles. *Shoin*-style buildings incorporate many of the elements of the earlier styles but also begin to adapt those elements to a more Japanese taste. The *sukiya*-style buildings take this further by incorporating decorative elements into the window openings. The primary permanent wall opening in a *shoin*-style building is the window above the *tsukeshoin* or writing desk. The window often is made in an ornamental shape, perhaps with a cusped arch, and can be closed from the interior with paper screens (*shōji*) that slide on tracks built into the wall. When one is sitting at the writing desk, the *shōji* can be opened for a view of the garden or closed to filter the sunlight and the view.

In the *sukiya* style, the *shoin* desk and window remain important elements in the *shoin* study room, and the form and style of the

window changed only slightly. However, other windows in *sukiya*-style buildings, especially in teahouses and buildings that were built for entertainment, like the Sumiya *ageya* (elegant entertainment house) in Kyoto, are much more decorative. Some windows in Sumiya have fanciful forms, such as quarter-circles, gourds, and fans. Others are constructed to appear as though the lath for the mud plaster wall simply was left unplastered to make the opening. In this case, a special ornamental lath is framed into the wall to achieve this effect. When the enclosing *shōji* screens are moved into place in front of the opening, it creates a beautiful layering of pattern and shadow.

Movable Walls

Traditional Japanese buildings are well known for their movable wall partitions, especially the translucent paper-covered wood lattice *shōji* screens and the opaque paper-covered *fusuma*, which are often embellished with ink paintings. These partitions are set in wood tracks above (*kamoi*) and below (*shikii*) between the structural columns, allowing them to slide and also be lifted out of the tracks completely. The tracks are constructed so that the screens can slide all to one side, or half the screens can slide to one side and the other half to the other side, or they can be closed and used to separate two spaces. Because of their lightweight construction, *shōji* and *fusuma* serve only as visual barriers and are not effective for sound privacy.

Movable partitions were used as early as the ninth century in Japan. Constructed of wood panels (*ita-shōji*) or covered with fabric (*tsuitate-shōji*), these screens were freestanding or fixed to columns.[18] They provided visual separation between spaces when needed but also allowed for interior spaces to be opened up to one another. This flexibility was important, because many rooms served multiple functions and had to be adjusted for large and small gatherings. When a large public function took place, all the partitions could be completely removed, and only a few columns would remain within the space. The shift to sliding partitions was a logical way to provide spatial flexibility with partitions that were lighter in weight and therefore easier to move.

Opposite Many different systems are used to enclose wall openings, including overscaled wood doors on hinges at a Buddhist temple (left), a small fireproof plastered door in a *kura* storehouse (center), and a top-hinged wood shutter in a teahouse (right).
Left, top to bottom Wall openings take many different shapes. Some are representational, such as the gourd-shaped opening (top), while others are abstract, taking the shape of a triangle or circle. Still others display a refined ornamentation, such as the cusped openings shown here (bottom).

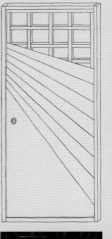

Top, figure 27 *Fusuma* partitions have a wood lattice core, which is covered on both sides by multiple layers of *washi* paper.
Below Sliding partitions can be removed to open up space or to be cleaned.
Right Screens slide open to reveal and frame a view of the Anrakuji Temple garden in Kyoto.
Opposite Sliding partitions filter or block light and views. They can be ornamental through their construction as simple wood lattices, solid wood planks, checkerboards of colored *washi* paper, or with the addition of painted scenes.

These sliding *fusuma* and *shōji* screens are important elements in the later *shoin-* and *sukiya*-style buildings. The need to open up spaces for public functions was prevalent in formal buildings, such as *shoin*-style palaces like the Nijō Palace in Kyoto and *sukiya*-style imperial villas like Katsura Rikyū and Shūgakuin Rikyū in Kyoto. As the sliding partitions came into common use in aristocratic residences, they also began to be used in the less formal *machiya* urban townhouses and the countryside *minka*. Traditionally, ceremonies such as wedding feasts and funerals take place in the *minka*, and the partitions are removed to allow many guests to sit in one continuous space.

Shōji screens typically are constructed of a lightweight wood lattice grid set within a wood frame and covered on one side with *washi* paper. The paper is attached to the frame with glue, which customarily is made from rice. *Shōji* are used at the perimeter of a room, where exterior light can filter through the paper into the interior spaces. They often are used to separate an interior space and an *engawa* (veranda) at the edge of a building. The *engawa* is a roofed space, although usually it has no exterior wall, so the *shōji* is protected from the weather. Traditionally, the *washi* paper on the screens is replaced once a year. If it is damaged, a hole can be repaired by covering it with a small piece of *washi*, often cut in a decorative shape.

The size of a typical *shōji* or *fusuma* relates to the traditional *kiwari* proportioning system (figure 12) and is approximately the same size as a *tatami* mat (90 centimeters wide and 180 centimeters tall, roughly 3 feet by 6 feet). The spacing of the wood strips in the lattice of a *shōji* screen is sized to fit both the overall size of the screen and the width of the *washi* paper. The paper is produced in rolls with a width of 9 *sun* (27.9 centimeters or 11 inches) and is applied to the screen horizontally, starting from the bottom, with each successive row of paper slightly overlapping the previous one. Applied in this way, even if the paper becomes loose from the frame, it still keeps out the dust.[19]

Although the usual construction of the wood lattice of a *shōji* screen is based on a rectangular grid (and the rectangles may be oriented either horizontally or vertically), there are many variations. In Edo-period *sukiya*-style buildings, such as the Sumiya *ageya* in Kyoto, the *tategu-ya* (screen and door carpenter) considered the building's function as an elegant place for entertainment and expressed his creativity, skill, and sense of *asobi* ("play") by constructing *shōji* screens with unusual latticework designs. Some lattices are shifted so that the grid runs diagonal to the frame; other grids are on the diagonal but the wood strips are set in sharp zigzags rather than remaining parallel to each other. Still others have the strips running parallel to each other but spaced unevenly. Other *shōji* from the same period use unconventional dimensions for the lattice grids or have the *washi* paper applied partly on one side and partly on the other, again as a way to show the idea of *asobi*.

In many *shōji* screens, the paper-covered wood lattice runs the full height of the screen, but some *shōji* have thin wood paneling at the base. Other types incorporate sliding sections on tracks set within the frame of the screen. *Yukimi shōji* ("snow-viewing" *shōji*) are specially designed so that the lower half of the screen can be raised up over the upper part of the screen, allowing for a view of the falling snow when

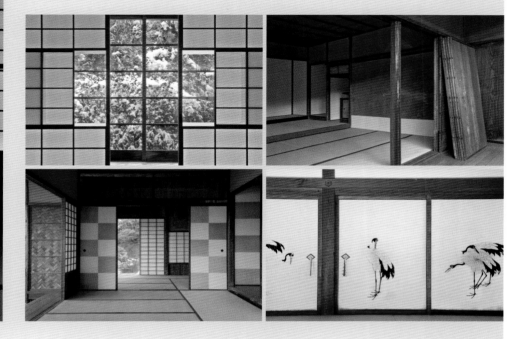

sitting inside a room. Contemporary versions of *yukimi shōji* incorporate glass into the lower portion of the screen to keep the weather out.

Fusuma are used similarly to *shōji* except that they are found mostly between interior rooms. Since they are opaque, and movement is not visible through them, they provide slightly more visual privacy than *shōji*. For the *fusuma*, many layers of *washi* paper (as many as ten or twelve,[20] figure 27) are applied to both sides of a lightweight wood frame. Unlike *shōji*, which have two different sides (one with the wood frame expressed and the other with paper covering the frame), *fusuma* have the same material on both sides and often are decorated with paintings—ink washes are usual, although colored pigments, sparkling mica dust, gold or silver leaf, etc., also are used. *Fusuma* typically have a thin wood frame, often finished in glossy black lacquer, around the perimeter of the screen, which helps to protect the paper. Small handles, usually made of metal or wood, are set into the door, allowing the screens to be slid open and closed without the hand ever touching the surface of the paper. These door pulls often are cleverly

designed in the form of a recognizable object. For example, at the *sukiya*-style Katsura Imperial Villa, some of the door pulls are in the shape of oars—a reference to boating on the pond in the garden just outside the villa.

Both *shōji* and *fusuma* fit into the space between the columns, floor, and the lintel (*magusa*) or tie beam (*nageshi*). Sometimes the area above the sliding screens (between the lintel or tie beam and the ceiling) is filled in with plaster but often it is used as a transom (*ranma*) for ventilation and light. *Ranma* can be constructed just like *shōji* and *fusuma*, complete with tracks above and below to slide open and close. Opaque paper-covered *ranma* may be painted to match the *fusuma* or left unembellished. Many *ranma* are fixed panels intricately carved out of wood, often depicting scenes from nature—cranes in flight, floating clouds, or flowers or trees in bloom—sometimes sumptuously colored with paint or lacquer. Others are geometric lattice patterns constructed from wood or reeds with the material left in its natural state. These *ranma* filter the light and let the air (and sound) pass from space to space, even if the *fusuma* or *shōji* below are closed.

In addition to *shōji* and *fusuma*, other types of removable partitions are found in traditional Japanese architecture, such as *amado* and *sudare*. *Amado* are sliding wood-paneled shutters that are used to close off a building at night or in bad weather. The single track for the *amado* usually is located at the outermost edge of a building or just on the inside of the *engawa* (veranda). The *amado* may run in a track which is adjacent and parallel to the tracks for the *shōji* at the interior edge of the *engawa*. In other cases, the track for the *amado* is pulled away from the *shōji* tracks. Because the *amado* shutters run in a single track, they butt up next to one another when they are all in use, and simple wood locks keep them in place. When not in use, the *amado* fit into a wood box (*tobukuro*, "door container") that is attached to the building. The box normally is constructed so the panels can be pushed into the box as each one is slid in. In addition to the *tobukuro*, a clever design device utilized to enhance the use of the *amado* is a simple wood pole. The pole is placed just outside of the *amado* tracks at a corner, and the tracks stop short of it. The shutters can be removed from the *tobukuro*, slid along the track, swung around the inside edge of the pole, and slid back into the track on the other side, thus making a 90-degree turn and eliminating the need for a second *tobukuro*.

Sudare are loosely woven blinds made from thin strips of bamboo, reeds, or other material, which are used to block views or filter hot sunlight. Unlike *amado*, *fusuma*, and *shōji*, which are used all year round, *sudare* tend to be used in summer—as temporary devices to keep the sun out of the interior of a building. *Sudare* are hung from hooks at the edge of the roof eave or from the bottom of the *nageshi* (tiebeams) that run between the columns at head height. (The upper tracks for *shōji* and *fusuma* are attached to the underside of the *nageshi*.) In many homes, *shōji* screens historically were replaced with *sudare-shōji* in the summer, which use *sudare* in place of *washi* paper, allowing more air to pass through the partitions. *Sudare* add another layer of privacy and filtered light to the multilayered interiors of traditional Japanese buildings.

Chapter 11
Floors

In the earliest Japanese dwellings (flat-land and pithouses), floors were earthen, merely tamped to make a firm surface. Although simple to construct, the floors were damp all year round and cold in the winter and—since life took place on the ground and not above the ground on chairs—provided no protection from vermin or insects.

As these early dwellings developed into what we now know as *minka*, the earthen floor remained in a part of the house, and a raised floor was added to separate spaces having different functions. The composition and construction of the earthen floor changed to produce a more durable surface. Bittern and water were mixed with the top layers of soil, and the soil was tamped to create a smooth floor. The bittern helps the earth mixture cure and dry with a hard surface, which becomes mostly impermeable to water and easy to clean.

The area with the tamped earthen floor (*tataki*) is known as the *doma* ("earth space") and accommodates functions that in the past took place outdoors—cooking, milling rice, and housing animals (in stalls). The daily entry leads into the *doma*, and in many ways it is treated as an extension of the outside. Shoes (typically wooden sandals called *geta*) always are worn in the *doma* but never in the raised floor areas of the house, however, as these areas are considered to be entirely inside rather than extensions of outside.

Lifting the floor above the ground was a major advance in the development of comfort in Japanese dwellings. The raised-floor living spaces could be kept cleaner, and the air under the floor helps to ventilate the house in the summer and keeps the inhabitants away from the cold damp ground in the winter.

Above left A long wood *engawa* creates a transitional space between the *tatami*-floored interior and the outside of a traditional building. *Shōji* screens slide in tracks at the edges of the *engawa* and can be adjusted to provide enclosure, frame a view to the garden, or filter the light from outside.
Below left Simple rectangular stones provide clear points of pause when entering or leaving a building. Inside the building, the stone is set into a well-worn tamped earth *tataki* floor. Outside, the stone contrasts with the irregularly shaped stones which create a walking surface.
Right A Buddhist monk's sandals rest on a stone floor, one step below the level of the wood *engawa* veranda. The sandals are turned away from the building, making it easy to step down from the *engawa* right into them.

Even when floors were built above ground level, the initial interior entry space, the *genkan*, remained *tataki*, and footwear used outside was left in this space as one stepped up to the raised floor. The *genkan* started as an entry porch for a residential hall at a Zen temple. It transformed over time to be a porch-like projection on a guardhouse and later to a formal entry space of an aristocratic residence. Eventually, the *genkan* became entirely internal to the building, initially in *machiya* townhouses.[21] Up until today the *genkan* remains an important element of the entry sequence to a residence, as most houses maintain the *genkan* as an interior space with the floor just above ground level, where shoes are removed before stepping up into the raised floor living areas of the house.

Above the Earth
Raised floors are made of various materials but initially were constructed quite simply out of small dimension bamboo poles (about 2.5 centimeters or 1 inch in diameter) laid one next to the other. The bamboo was not comfortable for sitting, so floor mats of roughly woven straw (*komo*) were placed on the bamboo. These mats are the precursors to the refined woven rush-covered *tatami* mats that first came into use as single mats for seating in the Heian period and were used to completely cover the floors of small rooms by the fifteenth century[22]—and still are used widely today.

When a family had the financial means or when lumber was readily available, wood planks were used for the raised floor. The planks provided a much more even surface and were more durable and longer lasting than bamboo, although they required a great deal more preparation for construction and were more costly. Therefore, a house with wood plank floors would show that the family had a certain amount of wealth or social standing. Originally, raised wood floors were a sign of nobility, as only the high-ranking *tenjōbito* ("person on the palace floor") were allowed access to such floors.[23]

Tatami floors, too, were a sign of aristocracy, and as families got wealthier they could afford to use *tatami* mats for floor surfaces. Initially, a house might have only one *tatami*-matted room, with the other rooms having wood plank floors. However, having more rooms with *tatami* floors indicated a higher social status.

Tatami mats are made with a thin covering of tightly woven rush (*igusa*) over a thick core of bundled rice straw. The straw core makes the mat rigid, while still allowing for a certain amount of softness. The *igusa* covering gives a smooth surface that is relatively easy to keep clean. *Tatami* mats are turned over

periodically to ensure that both sides are used evenly, and the *igusa* is replaced when worn. The edges of the mats can be made with the *igusa* simply folded over the sides, but typically the edges are finished with strips of fabric. The color and type of fabric—as well as the thickness of the *tatami* mat—can be used to denote a family's social standing. For example, dark colored fabric (blue, black, and brown) is commonly used for the edging on mats, but high-class houses may have *tatami* edged in fabric woven with colored silk or gold or silver threads.[24]

When *tatami* mats first developed, the size of the mats was based on the size of the room where they were used, and there were no consistent dimensions. However, over time the mats began to be made to standard dimensions, but the standards varied in different geographic regions. In the Muromachi period (1392–1568), two standard sizes of *tatami* mat developed—one with dimensions favored in the then-capital of Kyoto and the other in the countryside. The Kyoto-style mats (*kyōmadatami*) were sized to fit from the center of one column to the center of the next column (about 6.5 *shaku* or 197 centimeters (almost 6¹/₂ feet), with a width of about 98.5 centimeters or 3 feet 2¹/₂ inches), while the countryside mats (*inakadatami*) were dimensioned to fit between the columns, thus having a length of 6 *shaku* or 181.8 centimeters (almost 6 feet) and a width of 90.9 centimeters (nearly 3 feet). These dissimilar ways of measuring *tatami* mats demonstrate different ways of thinking about building construction and design. In the *kyōma* method, the layout of the structure is not dependent on the center line of the columns but on the standard size of the *tatami*, whereas with the *inaka-ma* method, the dimensions of the structure are based on the center lines

of the columns, and the *tatami* sizes are adjusted to the structural grid. Eventually, the dimensions of *tatami* mats were standardized throughout Japan at 182 centimeters by 91 centimeters (almost 6 feet by 3 feet), making the determination of proportions for an entire building much simpler but limiting flexibility in the sizes of rooms.[25]

The different floor surfaces used in a traditional house designate different functions as well as varied levels of significance. The most expensive floor covering, *tatami*, can be found in the most formal rooms, those that are used to receive important guests or serve as living and sleeping spaces for the head of the household. Wooden floors are used in utilitarian areas, such as the space adjacent to or surrounding the *irori* sunken hearth,

corridors, and toilet rooms, and in spaces for communication, like the *engawa* veranda at the perimeter of a building. *Doma*, or earthen floors, are used for work spaces, including the kitchen. It is typical to move up from the *doma* onto a wood step or floor before entering a room with a *tatami* floor (figure 28).

These three types of floors are used in various kinds of buildings. It is most typical of residential architecture, however, that a combination of all three occurs in the one building. Temples and shrines primarily have wooden plank floors, although *tatami* is utilized in living and sleeping spaces. Castles, too, have mostly wood floors but incorporate *tatami* in the living spaces. Theaters for traditional dramas of *nō* and *kabuki* also include wood floors in the performance and

back-of-house spaces, as well as the tiered side seating, but originally had earthen floored *doma* for the seating immediately in front of the stage, which was not covered by a roof. After the space was roofed, the *doma* areas were covered over with wood floors.

A room or independent building used for traditional tea ceremony, known as a *chashitsu* or "tearoom," almost always has a *tatami* mat floor, although if a *chashitsu* has an *engawa* (veranda), the *engawa* is constructed of wood. Not only are *tatami* mats essential for sitting comfortably during the tea ceremony, they are the means by which the size of the room is described and understood. Because the dimensions of the *tatami* mat are standardized, describing a room as *rokujō* or *yojōhan* ("six mats" or "four and a half mats") gives a

very clear image of the size of the room (figure 37). A typical tea ceremony room is four and a half mats in size (approximately 2.7 meters by 2.7 meters or about 9 feet by 9 feet), but others may be larger (six mats) or smaller (three mats), including the famous two-mat Taian teahouse designed by Sen no Rikyū in the late sixteenth century.

Today, many homes in Japan still use floors covered with *tatami* mats, although normally only for one or two rooms. These rooms are known as *washitsu* ("Japanese-style rooms") and are considered differently than other living rooms in the house, which are generally called *ima* ("living space") or *yōma* ("Western-style space"). Often *washitsu* are very traditional in character, with *fusuma* and/or *shōji* sliding partitions used to separate them from

other spaces. Frequently, a *tokonoma* decorative alcove is featured within one wall of the room, and the family ancestral Buddhist altar (*butsudan*) may be kept within another alcove.

As with other rooms in traditional Japanese houses, *washitsu* today also are used for multiple functions. The *washitsu* is both a living space and a guest room. Often guests are brought first to the *washitsu*, where they can pay their respects to the family at the ancestral altar, before they are taken to a Western-style living room, although in some houses the *washitsu* is used for all social activity. If guests stay overnight, sleeping mats (*futon*) are placed on the *tatami* in the *washitsu*, and the room is used as a guest room. Often there is a special deep closet within one of the walls of the *washitsu* to store the *futon*.

Opposite An eight-mat *tatami* room connects to an *engawa* made of wide wood boards, which extends the space of the room into the garden.
Left Thin bamboo poles were tied together to make the floor surface of this *minka*.
Below left A thick wood plank creates a narrow *engawa* veranda in this *minka* farmhouse.
Right, figure 28 A section drawing shows the changes in floor level from the low earthen *doma* floor up one step to the higher *tatami* mat floor of the living spaces.
Below right Wood bottom rails for sliding *shōji* screens separate the *engawa* from the *tatami* floor.

Chapter 12
Ceilings

The early Japanese pit dwellings were simple houses constructed using materials as economically as possible. Each element of the structure had a very specific function that was integral to the building as a whole. Ceilings were regarded as a useless and unnecessary luxury. Instead, the underside of the roof structure was left exposed, and the roofing materials served the role of ceiling.

As houses developed from the simple pit dwellings, which had living spaces sunken into the ground with thatched roofs constructed over the space, to buildings with multiple spaces having both ground level and raised floors, the roof structure continued to be exposed in many spaces, but ceilings also began to be used. In many *minka* ("people's houses") the living spaces are all on a single level, enclosed by one great roof (similar to a pit dwelling but on a much larger scale). In these houses, the ceilings customarily are not separate built elements, but rather the underside of the roof is left exposed and acts as the ceiling for the space.

The structure of the roof—the primary structure of wood timbers and the secondary structure of wood or bamboo poles—gives rhythm to the spaces and expresses the power of the heavy timber construction. Because the structure frequently is left exposed, it also can incorporate an aspect of design. Carpenters may choose timbers for the beams that are curved and join them in ways that show off their unusual forms as well as take advantage of the naturally occurring stresses in them (figure 36). In this way, the beams act as a decorative ceiling element, although they do not serve to enclose the space in the same way a ceiling does. The actual enclosure of the space is created by the sub-roof material, which ranges from wood planks or bamboo poles laid out lengthwise, side by side in rows, to simply showing the underside of the bundles of rice straw thatch which cover the roof.

In *minka* that are more than a single story high, the ceilings often are simply the underside of the floor above, which generally is constructed of wide wood planks. In this case, too, the wood structure holding up the floor is left exposed and gives a rhythm to the spaces below. This simple construction also allows the heat and smoke from the fire on the ground level to filter up to the upper levels of the house. In some *minka*, families in the past raised silkworms during the winter, and the heat helped to keep the worms warm. The smoke from the fire is an integral element in *minka* with thatched roofs, as it helps to keep insects out of the thatch, while the carbon in the smoke protects the wood structure.

Exposing the building structure and the underside of the floor above is the simplest, most practical, and most economical use of construction materials, but it gives little opportunity for the ceiling to become a decorative element or a symbol of social status, wealth, or power. Thus, some *minka* utilize ceilings in select spaces. These ceilings typically are found only in spaces that have special purposes, for example a room where honored guests are received, such as a formal *washitsu* reception room. Because these spaces are special, the materials for the ceilings are more refined than in other areas of the house. Carefully planed wood planks or rows of bamboo poles all chosen for their same color and dimension express the care and skill that go into creating such a ceiling, and appropriately display the family's social and financial standing.

Temples, Shrines, and Shinden
Traditional buildings that serve the public, primarily Buddhist temples and *shintō* shrines, often incorporate quite complex ceilings into the designs of their major spaces. The lavish construction and ornament of the ceilings reflect the role of the buildings as either important public monuments or, in some cases, private displays of piety and/or wealth.

The forms of many of the temple and shrine buildings reflect the style of Buddhist temple architecture initially brought over from China and Korea in the sixth century CE, in which the ceilings step up in height from the perimeter spaces to the central interior spaces to emphasize the hierarchical relationship of those spaces. However, as the Buddhist religion developed and changed over time, from the opulence of early Mahayana Buddhism from the sixth

Left The wood board and batten ceiling and the *tatami* mat floor create a sense of interior when the *shōji* screens are removed and the interior space feels connected to the garden.

Above Acting as a vertical extension of the walls, the lime plaster ceiling follows the slope of the roof to create a soaring space.

century and Pure Land Buddhism (*jōdoshū*) from the eighth to twelfth centuries, to the disciplined simplicity of Zen in the twelfth to fourteenth centuries, architectural taste changed, and ceilings varied in relationship to the changes in roof styles.

Early temple buildings such as those at Hōryūji and Tōdaiji in Nara have ceilings constructed of wood boards at multiple levels to reflect the hierarchy of spaces inside. For example, in the *kondō* ("golden hall") at Hōryūji, low flat ceilings cover the spaces around the perimeter of the building, which serve as the entry spaces. A line of structural columns separates this space from the adjacent more interior space where, although the floor level remains the same, the ceiling height increases. The ceilings in the outer spaces are flat, but over the innermost space, which is defined by a perimeter of primary structural columns and a raised floor level, the ceiling is not only higher than the preceding ceilings, it also has pyramidal sides which slope up to a central flat ceiling. The ceilings hide the tall structure of the building, yet they reinforce the formal and perceived hierarchy of the spaces.

In the eleventh century Byōdōin Hōōdō, the small interior space has a single-level floor of simple wood planks, but the multilevel ceilings are highly ornate—painted with intricate and colorful patterns and utilizing

decorative metalwork to cover important joints (figure 29). The ceilings are further enhanced by the use of a hanging element—four panels of intricately carved wood covered with lacquer and gold leaf are hung in a square around the top of the statue of Amidha Buddha, which is the obvious focal point of the space.

Later temple and shrine buildings also utilize ceilings to reflect the formal and symbolic hierarchy of the spaces. However, the buildings sometimes are simpler in form than earlier buildings, with only one roof rather than multiple layers of roofs, as in the Hōryūji example, which has three layers of roofs. One instance of this is the Saikokuji *kondō* in Hiroshima from the fourteenth century, when Zen Buddhism was the norm. The Saikokuji *kondō* has a relatively simple form, with only one main floor level raised slightly above the *engawa* and a single hip-and-gable roof. However, the ceiling over the main floor is divided into multiple sections at different heights—even within the space of a single room—to emphasize the most important area.

Shoin Ceilings

Just as the ceilings in earlier temple, shrine, and *shinden*-style buildings reinforce the strict formal hierarchy of spaces, so too do the ceilings of the architectural style which followed, the *shoin* style. Many features of the *shoin* style initially developed in *shinden* buildings and in the residential quarters of Zen monasteries.[26] The most important room in a *shoin*-style residence, which itself is called the *shoin*, features a coved and/or coffered ceiling constructed entirely of wood (figure 30). Wood panels are inset into a lattice of wood battens and curve as they change from horizontal to

vertical where the ceiling meets the wall. The lattice and inset panels typically wrap down the wall to the height of one panel before ending at the *tenjō-nageshi* ceiling rail (a tie beam that runs the perimeter of the room, just below the ceiling). In this way, the ceiling serves to cap and contain the space of the room.

The inset panels are at times elaborately decorated with colorful patterns or pictures of natural objects, such as flowers or butterflies. Paint, lacquer in black, red, gold, or green, and even gold leaf are used to decorate the panels. In very elaborate rooms, the joints of the battens are covered with ornamental metalwork, often fabricated in gold. The beauty and intensity of the decoration emphasizes the high social standing of the house owner, as well as the desire to provide an appropriately formal and elegant room for guests.

Other ceilings in *shoin* buildings are less eye-catching, as the other rooms are not as formal or socially important as the *shoin* room. Nonetheless, the ceilings are constructed with care and a high level of craft, and although they might not be as highly decorated are no less beautiful in their construction. Interior rooms typically have flat ceilings using wide unornamented wood boards that appear to be supported by thinner battens although, as with the coved ceiling, they actually are suspended from above. The ceilings end at the top of the wall, rather than wrapping down the upper part of the wall. Often there is a horizontal plastered strip at the very top of the wall (below the ceiling and above the *tenjō-nageshi*) that gives the ceiling the sense of lightness or floating. This produces an effect of quiet, stately elegance, where the ceiling is not the visual focal point of the space but rather one element that helps to contain and define the space without overpowering other more decorative elements.

These ceilings are constructed of thin wood boards (about 3 millimeters or 1/8 inch thick), which overlap one another slightly and are nailed to the wood battens from above. Since the battens are not structural, the ceilings are hung in place. One method uses thicker wood battens attached to the hidden upper side of the wood boards and joined to wood poles which connect those battens to the roof structure.[27]

Right Wood ceilings with a grid of battens are typical of the *shoin* style.
Below, figure 29 The *shinden*-style Hōōdō Phoenix Hall of the Byōdōin Temple features layers of ornate ceilings that denote the hierarchy of the space.
Bottom The Hatto Dharma Hall at the Kenninji Temple in Kyoto has a ceiling covered with an elaborate dragon painting.

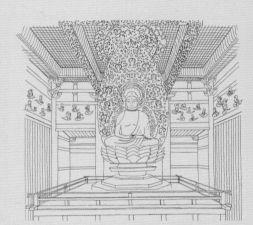

Engawa (veranda) spaces often have sloped ceilings, where the height of the ceiling next to the wall is the high point (and higher than the ceiling inside), and the ceiling slopes down toward the outside. The ceilings in this kind of veranda space are attached to the underside of the roof structure, as the roofs are designed to slope low over the *engawa*. The slope of the ceiling helps to guide the eye out to the landscape and create a strong connection to the garden outside. The edge of the roof serves as the top of the frame through which the garden can be viewed when the interior spaces are opened up to the outside.

Sukiya Ceilings

Developing from the more formal *shoin* style, the *sukiya* style is famous for its refined simplicity and strong connection to nature. This is evident in the ceiling as well as other architectural elements, especially in *sukiya*-style teahouses, where the ceiling plays an important function in the spatial hierarchy.

Even the smallest teahouses utilize the ceiling as a major design element, reinforcing the function and perception of the small space by dividing the ceiling into two or three sections, each made very differently (figure 31). Like earlier examples, *sukiya*-style ceilings are constructed of wood and utilize many of the same techniques. For instance, some of the ceilings in the main house at the Katsura Imperial Villa in Kyoto are constructed of thin wood boards running in one direction (along their length) and thin wood battens running in the opposite direction, ostensibly holding up the boards. (In reality, the boards are hung from above, as with the *shoin* ceilings.) Other ceilings, especially in the *sukiya-shoin* room and the *ichi-no-ma* ("first room") in the New Goten, are similar to the flat *shoin* ceilings constructed with a lattice of thin battens and thin wood boards. Also similar to many *shoin*-style buildings, the ceilings over the inner and outer verandas are sloped and are attached directly to the underside of the roof structure.

Where the *sukiya* style most obviously departs from the *shoin* style, however, is in the lack of applied decoration to the ceilings (figure 30). It is unusual for a *sukiya*-style ceiling to be

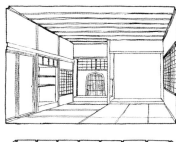

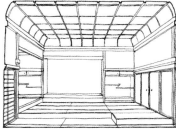

painted or lacquered or to include any ornamental metalwork, although some entertainment houses, like the Sumiya *ageya* in Kyoto, do have ornamented ceilings. Rather than add decoration, the beauty of the natural wood is the ornament for most *sukiya* ceilings. For example, a sliver of space can be left between the wood boards, revealing a dark shadow line that adds dimension to the ceiling; or the battens and the boards can be made from different woods, and the variation in the colors of the woods adds a decorative quality. Or in place of wood battens, bamboo poles might be used, and again the natural contrast of the materials acts as ornament.

The most creative ceilings, however, are found in teahouses. One of the most spectacular ceilings found in a *sukiya*-style teahouse is woven from very thinly sliced strips of cedar—about 12–15 centimeters (5–6 inches) wide by about 1 millimeter ($^1/_{16}$ inch) thick. Other teahouse ceilings are constructed to appear as though they are simply the underside of the roof, with thick bamboo poles like rafters holding up thinner bamboo poles running horizontally, which in turn support a ceiling of reeds. Other ceilings use the lattice battens in a decorative grid pattern, with every other batten shortened and turned in the opposite direction—or some battens are doubled or tripled to create a pleasing rhythm. In extreme cases, the ceilings may be divided by a sinuously curving length of bamboo, with two very different types of ceilings on either side of the curve—one a wide lattice grid of battens with boards of expressive wood grain, for example,

and the other a finer grid of battens with boards having a more continuous grain.[28] No matter how elaborate or simple the construction of the ceiling in a *sukiya* building is, the ceiling is designed and constructed to express the natural character of the building materials and to add another layer of rusticated yet refined sophistication to the architecture.

Above left, figure 30 The illustration compares two formal *shōin* reception rooms, one in the *sukiya* style (top) and the other in the *shoin* style (below).
Above The ceiling of the Kuroshoin reception room at the Nishi Honganji Temple uses wide wood battens to draw the eye through the connected spaces.

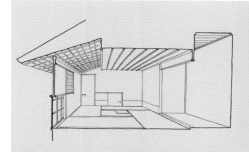

Above, figure 31 The section drawing shows the complex hierarchy of ceiling planes and types in a *sukiya*-style teahouse.
Above right The ceiling of the Shōkatei Tea Pavilion at the Katsura Imperial Villa is the exposed roof structure, a grid of bamboo rafters and purlins with a bark-covered beam at the ridge.
Right A ceiling of woven thin cedar strips marks the importance of a special space in a teahouse.

Chapter 13
Built-ins

Japanese buildings traditionally are designed to have flexible spaces, free of a great quantity of furniture and other objects that are permanently placed in a space. Instead, the necessary storage and fittings are built into or securely attached to the walls, floors, or ceilings. Although the spaces are multifunctional, these built-ins suggest specific uses that are more appropriate for certain spaces or parts of spaces. For example, in a room adjacent to the *doma*, an *irori* (sunken hearth) customarily is built into the floor. A fire always is going in the *irori*, not only to heat the house but also to keep the insects out of the thatched roof. A teakettle full of water is hung over the coals by a chain attached to the ceiling. Thus, hot water for tea is always available, and the space around the *irori* is a warm gathering place in cool weather.

Although most built-ins are practical in nature, some, like the *kamidana* and the *butsudan*, are inherently sacred, and others, like the *tokonoma* and *chigaidana*, serve more for aesthetic than practical purposes. Not every house or building necessarily includes examples of all the following built-ins, but many buildings do include most of them.

Sacred built-ins: Butsudan and Kamidana

A *butsudan* (ancestral Buddhist family altar) is a fixture in many traditional Japanese houses as well as temples, as is a *kamidana* ("deity shelf"), which is associated with *shintō*. Since Buddhism was introduced in Japan in such a way that it did not displace the vernacular religion of *shintō*, the two religions coexist, both in their specific roles in people's lives and also within physical spaces. Therefore, many homes have both a *butsudan* and a *kamidana*.

Left The *tokonoma* decorative alcove creates a place to hang a scroll painting on the wall and display an object on the raised floor. The adjacent staggered shelves and *tenbukuro* cabinets provide storage and additional display space.
Below, figure 32 A *kamidana* deity shelf typically is built in near the ceiling of the kitchen or living space and is a place for the family to make offerings to the *shintō* deities.

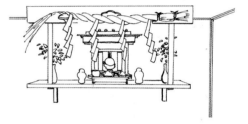

A *butsudan* is a cabinet which contains a Buddhist statue or other religious object as well as utensils used for making offerings or rituals, such as candlesticks, incense burners, a bell and drumstick, and trays to hold offerings. Typically, photos of the deceased and tablets listing the names of familial ancestors also are enclosed within the main space of the *butsudan*, which sits atop a base that usually consists of a set of drawers holding candles, incense, and other religious paraphernalia.

A *kamidana* is generally a simple wood shelf that is attached to the *nageshi* (tie beam that runs the perimeter of a room) or a lintel (*magusa*) on which are placed daily offerings (normally the first cup of tea and bowl of rice) for the tutelary deities of the house (figure 32). The *kamidana* often is found in the kitchen but also can be located in other spaces, such as a formal living space. In some cases, a house has more than one *kamidana*, and offerings are made at each.

Above A *butsudan* Buddhist ancestral altar is built into the wall of a house and includes cabinets and drawers to store associated utensils.
Right A slightly raised wood platform, a smooth *tokobashira* column, and an arched beam of bark-covered cherry wood denote the space of the *tokonoma* decorative alcove.

Decorative Alcove: Tokonoma

The *tokonoma* is a decorative alcove that can be found in traditional buildings of a certain social standing. The alcove is built within an interior wall of a room, usually a tearoom or reception space. It is the focal point of the room as it provides a place to hang a scroll and set an *ikebana* flower arrangement, *bonsai* miniaturized tree, or other decorative object (figure 5). Any scroll, flower arrangement, or other object on display is chosen to relate to the season and provide a strong connection to nature. Flowers often are picked from the garden or found nearby. In this way, although the *tokonoma* itself is very much part of the inside of the building, it has a strong relationship to the natural environment outside.

The *tokonoma* typically is located in a *tatami*-floored formal reception room (*zashiki*). The dimensions of the *tokonoma* follow the module of the *tatami* mat, but most *tokonoma* are not as deep as a *tatami* is wide. *Tokonoma* have slightly elevated floors made of wood, which often are particularly finely

crafted. The floor may be constructed from a single wide board or finished in an unusual way, as with the *honchōna* finish, in which an adze (*chōna*) is used to create an undulating surface. A large *tokonoma* may be especially deep and have a floor covered with a single *tatami* mat.

The ceiling of the *tokonoma* usually is flush with the ceiling of the room and finished in a similar way. The walls of the *tokonoma* often are finished with mud plaster, the same color and texture as the walls of the room or in a contrasting but complementary color. A striking feature of the *tokonoma* is the *tokobashira*, a wood column that separates the space of the *tokonoma* from that of the adjacent *chigaidana* (staggered shelves) or *oshiire* (storage closet). The *tokobashira* is usually a beautiful and at times unusual wood post, perhaps a thin tree trunk with the bark intact or a column with an unusual shape or texture. The *tokobashira* is an important element of the *tokonoma*, both as a focal point and as a symbolic connection to sacred *shintō* columns.

Decorative Shelves: Chigaidana

Initially, shelves and cabinets developed in dwellings for the practical function of holding personal belongings. However, as they became more popular in upper-class dwellings, especially in houses of the *shoin* style in the fifteenth and sixteenth centuries, *chigaidana*, or decorative shelves, were used to display objects of unusual function and beauty, such as tea bowls, incense burners, or boxes containing ink stones.[29]

The *chigaidana* are adjacent to the *tokonoma* but separated from it by the *tokobashira* and a partial wall (figure 5). *Chigaidana* typically feature an asymmetrical arrangement of shelves on different levels, from which the name derives, as *chigai* means "different" and *tana* means "shelf." The shelves are attached to the wall in a staggered composition, with thin vertical posts (*ebizuka*) connecting the horizontal boards. The top shelf incorporates an edge strip, called a *fudegaeshi* ("brush return"), with a decorative upward curve, ostensibly to keep a writing brush from rolling

Above A small side window illuminates a *tokonoma*.
Center left A simple *tokonoma* in a *minka* has a raised floor of thick wood planks and rough mud plaster walls.
Center right A *kamidana* deity shelf takes the form of a shrine building.
Below A scroll painting and a simple flower arrangement adorn a *tokonoma* with a long polished floor surface constructed from a single plank of wood.

off the edge. The form created by staggering the shelves is suggestive of the traditional pattern for a cloud, from which the shelves derive their second, less common name, *usu-kasumi-dana* or "thin mist shelf."[30]

A row of cabinets with doors usually is located just above the *chigaidana*. Known as *tenbukuro* ("heaven pouch"), they appear as though part of the ceiling, effectively lowering the height of the ceiling over the *chigaidana*. *Jibukuro* ("earth pouch") cabinets sometimes are placed below the shelves on the floor and have a top surface that can serve as a desk or counter (the *oshi-ita*). The doors of the cabinets often are covered with paper, like a *fusuma* opaque paper partition, and have small metal door handles. Generally in sets of two, the doors open by sliding one in front of the other. The floor level of the *chigaidana* area often is slightly lower than the *tokonoma* floor, although still higher than the adjacent floor of the room (however this varies), and the ceiling—when not hidden by the *tenbukuro*—is lower than that of the *tokonoma*.

Desks

Several kinds of built-in desks developed in traditional Japanese architecture. The *oshi-ita* or *toko-oshi-ita* often served as the top surface of the *jibukuro* cabinet, located below the *chigaidana*. Developed by the mid-fifteenth century, it became a permanent feature of formal *shoin* reception rooms.[31] The floor of the recess containing the *chigaidana* and *oshi-ita* is raised slightly above the level of the *tatami* (though not as high as the floor of the adjacent *tokonoma*), suggesting that the desk was not used for practical purposes such as writing but rather for displaying objects, a function similar to that of the *chigaidana*.

Another type of desk is the *tsukeshoin* predominantly found in the formal reception room (*shoin*) of a *shoin*-style building (figure 30). (It is the *tsukeshoin* desk which gave the name to the room and to the style.) The *tsuke-shoin* originated within the Buddhist temple residential quarters as a place where the abbot could sit and write. To take advantage of natural light, the desk normally is built into an exterior wall of a building and has a window

Above *Washi* paper covers the wall surface above the staggered shelves, while the wall below is coated with a rough earthen plaster with an unusual shaped opening exposing a bamboo grid lath.

Center left A candle lamp illuminates the space above built-in drawers, revealing the ceiling made from woven strips of cedar.

Below left The carved *fudegaeshi* lip on the top shelf is an ornamental embellishment to the simple lines of the *chigaidana* staggered shelves.

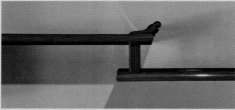

Right A single polished wood plank makes a simple desk in an alcove illuminated by an ornate window.

just above it. The desk often is constructed from a single plank of wood and finished with a smooth lacquer surface. Beneath the desk, which is used while sitting on the floor, are sliding doors hiding a small amount of storage. The doors can be slid open to make space for the writer's legs. Similarly, the adjacent window is covered with a *shōji* screen to filter the light, and the amount of light can be controlled by sliding the screen open and closed. Over time, this type of desk perhaps became more ornamental than functional, as it was a permanent element in formal *shoin* reception rooms and in later *sukiya*-style formal reception rooms as well.

Practical Storage

Since very little furniture is placed permanently in traditional Japanese rooms, it is necessary for storage to be designed into the buildings. Hidden behind simple wood-paneled doors or *fusuma* (opaque paper sliding doors), the *oshiire* are integrated well into the design of the entire building. The doors hide large closet-like spaces, often outfitted with shelves, which hold all the necessities of daily life, such as lacquer trays for serving meals, cushions for sitting on the floor, and *futon* for sleeping. Often *oshiire* are as deep or deeper than the width of a *tatami* mat, to accommodate the size of *futon* or other large objects. A house generally has a number of built-in storage closets, which also can be configured to help with temperature and sound insulation.

In the past, the stair in a multistory house or shop was combined with storage built beneath the risers and treads. Known as *kaidan-dansu* ("stair chest"), these stepped storage units feature a pleasing and practical arrangement of drawers, shelves, and cabinets used to store everyday necessities or shop goods. The quality of *kaidan-dansu* range from highly refined and finished in polished lacquer, as might be located in wealthy merchant houses, to those found in countryside *minka*, which might be roughly crafted and have stair treads worn to a concave surface expressing years of daily use.

Other built-in storage includes shelves and small closets to hold tea utensils in the kitchen area of a tea ceremony room or house. This area is used only to store objects needed for the tea ceremony and might be quite small or quite spacious, depending on the owner's wealth and interest in tea. Rather than being treated as "back of house," however, these storage areas are beautifully crafted, equally as refined as the teahouse itself, although perhaps more simple.

Hearths

In Japanese culture, as in many cultures worldwide, the hearth is an important element within the house. It is a place where people gather, where the actual and symbolic heart of the home is located. In traditional Japanese houses, there generally are two different hearths—the *irori*, which is set into a wood plank floor in a room adjacent to the earthen-floored *doma*, and the *kamado*, the cook stove located in the *doma*. A third type of hearth, the *ro*, is less common, and is used specifically to heat water for tea in tea ceremony rooms.

Left A *kaidan-dansu* stair chest provides access to an upper floor as well as drawers and cabinets for storage.
Right A sliding wood door encloses a deep closet space for storage of *futon* and bedding.

While the *irori* is a simple, usually rectangular pit for ashes and charcoal set flush with the floor, the *kamado* is a sculptural oven-like mound built on the *doma* floor. The *kamado* is practical—stone, tile, or other masonry material is used to create the basic shape at a comfortable working height and then is covered with mud plaster in a smooth sculptural finish. Low apertures (stoke holes) for wood to be burned and two or more openings on top for iron pots to be set into the *kamado* are basic features. While the *kamado* is found only in the kitchen area of the *doma* and is heated solely for cooking, the *irori* is more central within the house and is used for both heat and cooking. A fire is always kept burning in the *irori* (the smoke keeps insects out of thatched roofs and helps preserve the wood structure).

Historically, in cold weather a wood frame could be placed over the *irori* and a quilt thrown over the frame to trap the heat and warm people's feet. This became known as a *kotatsu* or *okigotatsu*, which eventually transformed into the movable *kotatsu* (figure 34, a table with a brazier attached under the top surface, usually with a quilt over the top) and the *horigotatsu* (a "dug out" *kotatsu*—a sunken space around the *irori* to allow people to sit on the floor as if sitting in a chair and have their legs warmed by the heat of the hearth).

The *ro* also is used for heating water but only for the occasion of a tea ceremony. Built into the floor of a tea ceremony room, the *ro* is a wooden box (*rodan*) with a thick clay liner that is filled with ash and burning charcoal. The box is about 40 centimeters on each side (16 inches) and 45 centimeters deep (18 inches). A metal stand is placed in the *ro* to support the teakettle. A typical *ro* is a small square in the corner of one *tatami* mat in the tearoom and can be covered with a similarly sized *tatami* when not in use. However, depending on the size and shape of the tearoom, the *ro* can take more unusual forms, being trapezoidal or even circular, and may be set into a wood plank floor rather than *tatami*.[32] Since the tea ceremony is a highly ritualized aesthetic pursuit, it is understandable that the form—but not the function—of the *ro* is ripe for aesthetic interpretation.

Above A metal *jizaikagi* kettle hanger is suspended from the ceiling, allowing the height of the teakettle to be easily adjusted.
Right A metal stand placed in the *irori* hearth supports a teakettle.
Below A carved wood fish on a rough rope is a simple but creative *jizaikagi*.

Kettle Hangers

A feature of most *irori* (sunken hearths) is the iron pot or kettle full of water that is kept over the coals. Although a pot or kettle can be placed on an iron tripod or four-legged stand within the hearth, quite often it is hung over the *irori* on a hook affixed to a metal chain or a thick rice straw rope. The chain or rope, in turn, is suspended from the building structure either by being directly attached to a beam or other structural member or, more often, by being connected to a vertical bamboo or wood pole which is joined to the structure. In some cases, the hook may be connected directly to a vertical or horizontal wood or bamboo pole rather than a chain.

An ingenious contraption, the *jizai* ("at one's will")[33] or *jizaikagi* (*kagi* means "hook") is used to adjust the height of the kettle. There are many variations of the *jizai*, but the concept behind it is the same for all—to use the weight of the kettle and the friction of one component (generally a wooden paddle attached with a metal rod) against another (the vertical bamboo or wood pole) to hold the kettle in place. In simple *minka*, *jizai* are equally simple, whereas in upper-class houses, *jizai* can be quite elaborate, incorporating

carved wooden fish or other symbolic forms or decorative metalwork.

In some dwellings, especially *minka*, a wood rack or panel called a *hidana* ("fire shelf") is suspended from the rafters. Most often constructed in the shape of a square with a hole cut in the middle for the kettle chain or rope, the rack is designed to keep the heat down close to the floor in cold weather. In addition, it can also be used for curing fish or meat with the smoke from the hearth. While the *hidana* works well to warm the area around the *irori* by keeping the heat close to the floor rather than escaping into the upper reaches of the space, it likewise blocks the smoke, making for a smoky interior environment.

Baths, Sinks, Toilets, and Urinals

Spaces for cleaning the body and eliminating waste traditionally are separated from the main part of a house or other building in Japan and located according to principles of *fūsui* (geomancy). A bath, or *furo*, is contained in its own space, separate from the room housing a toilet or urinal, and often is accessed from a corridor and tucked behind a corner of the house, usually on the north side to avoid direct sunlight. In some cases (especially the *goemonburo* described below), the bath is independent from the house, either in a separate small building just for that purpose or open-air with just a simple roof.

In Japan, bathing historically is a daily evening ritual in which the body, once clean, is immersed in a deep tub of hot water. The bathtub often is made out of wood planks, usually *hinoki* (Japanese cypress), which expands when wet and has a pleasant scent, and shaped into the form of a barrel or a box. The bath water is heated by a fire in an attached chamber or from coals in a compartment within the tub. In the case of the *goemonburo* (figure 33), the tub is a large iron cauldron filled with water and heated over a wood fire. The bather carefully steps on a wood pallet and sinks into the tub.

For washing the hands, simple basins of wood, copper, or perhaps ceramic historically served as sinks. Placed next to the sink, a container of water (with a wooden dipper) sits on a wood lattice or trough that allows the water to drain to the outside. The basin might be set on the floor or above the floor on a washstand. A sink used for kitchen tasks, placed in the *doma* or an adjacent space, often is a long trough carved out of wood with a gutter that takes the water outside.

Toilets and urinals are located in adjacent small rooms rather than together in one room. The rooms often are carefully constructed out of wood and attractively detailed, in a manner in keeping with the rest of the building. Such rooms perhaps include a small window with a view to a garden or to nature outside, as described by Tanizaki Jun'ichirō in his seminal essay on Japanese aesthetics, *In Praise of Shadows*. "The parlor may have its charms, but the Japanese toilet truly is a place of spiritual repose.... No words can describe that sensation as one sits in the dim light, basking in the faint glow reflected from the *shōji*, lost in meditation or gazing out at the garden."[34]

Left, figure 33 A section drawing of a *goemonburo* shows the iron cauldron supported by blocks of stone with space below for a fire. The bather sits on a wood pallet in the hot water to avoid contact with the metal.
Center A simple wood urinal is housed in a separate room with a window.
Below A basin carved from stone can serve as a place for washing hands.
Right A deep *hinoki* cypress wood bathtub is filled with water for soaking.

Chapter 14
Furniture

Furniture in traditional Japanese buildings, especially dwellings, typically is designed to be able to be moved around from room to room when necessary. Rooms are separated from one another by the use of sliding screens (*fusuma* and *shōji*), but spaces also are divided using portable standing or folding screens (*tsuitate* and *byōbu*). Historically, spatial hierarchy within a room, necessary for powerful lords to recognize honored guests as well as to show their own social position, was expressed using raised platforms covered with *tatami*. This created an additional vertical layer in the space that worked within the existing spatial hierarchy of the layers of floor and ceiling levels.

Because few rooms have only one permanent function but rather need to accommodate different numbers of people for different functions at different times, furniture tends to be sized more for the individual than for communal use. For example, since a single small room might be utilized for both sleeping and eating, with insufficient space for both activities to occur simultaneously, the furniture used for sleeping (a *futon*) and that required for sitting and eating (a *zabuton* cushion and a low table) have to be moved into place when needed and removed and stowed when not in use. Because life takes place on the floor (not above the floor on chairs and tables), furniture required for sitting, writing, and eating could be low to the ground and relatively small, making it easy to move and store.

Just as furniture needed for eating and sleeping is portable, so too the furniture necessary for lighting and heating is designed to be used by the individual and moved where needed. Rather than heating or lighting an

Opposite A circular straw *zabuton* cushion and a low writing desk are positioned on the wood floor with a view to the garden.
Above Fabric-covered *zabuton* cushions and a polished lacquer table are placed for quiet viewing of the garden at the Anrakuji Temple in Kyoto.
Center Bright fabric covers the cushion capping of a wood *makura* pillow.
Below A low table placed directly on the *tatami* mats easily can be moved or removed so the space can be used flexibly.

entire building or even a single room, heat and light are brought only to the places where they are needed. Candles, on stands or in lanterns, and later gas lamps provided light (as well as the beautiful "flickering and shimmering" ambience so poetically and nostalgically expressed by Tanizaki Jun'ichirō in his essay, *In Praise of Shadows*);[35] and *hibachi* ("fire box") braziers filled with burning charcoal provided heat.

Even in spaces designed and used only for one specific function, such as the tea ceremony room or the Buddhist temple *hondō* (main worship hall), most furniture is designed to fit the human body and be movable. In a tea ceremony room, a portable *ro* (brazier used to heat the water for tea), which sits on the *tatami* floor, is used during hot months in place of the *ro* built into the floor. Low tables and cushions used in temples by monks for their daily prayers, though generally left in place from day to day, easily can be removed for special ceremonies.

Space Dividers

Since the sliding partitions between rooms often are kept open, and may be removed altogether, many types of screens and curtains have been developed in Japan to provide privacy and to control the light. Standing screens, both those constructed of single solid panels of wood (*tsuitate*) as well as multiple panels that fold accordion-style (*byōbu*), are used to create separation and privacy within larger spaces. *Tsuitate* can be found in the *genkan* entrance hall of a house or inn to limit the view inside the building from the entryway. The screens also are used in restaurants and living spaces to give privacy and to adjust the space to a comfortable size for an individual or a small group of people. *Byōbu*—often beautifully painted or decorated—are used similarly to divide space. These devices stand on the floor and primarily block the view from a person's sitting height rather than standing height, as well as create physical barriers between spaces.

Hanging curtains and blinds, on the other hand, block views from a standing height without inhibiting movement between spaces. *Noren* curtains—hanging panels of fabric sewn together at the top and left separate for about the lower three-quarters—are hung on bamboo poles that attach to hooks at the top of a doorway. *Noren* are used especially at kitchen doorways in houses and at entrances to shops and restaurants, where the *noren* is hung only when the shop is open for business. (Some *noren* in residential use have the curtains attached to a movable wood stand,[36] but most are hung from doorways.) Thin strips of split bamboo or reeds are bound together to form hanging blinds known as *sudare*. These blinds usually are hung from the ends of the roof eaves to block sunlight from directly entering a room. The *sudare* filter the light coming into the interior of the building from the garden or exterior space, while extending the space of the interior to the edge of the veranda and eave.

Above right *Sudare* screens hung from the eaves shade a temple garden entrance.
Center right *Noren* curtains hang in a doorway, a sign that the shop is open for business.
Below right A *tsuitate* screen, made from a single piece of wood, divides the space of the entrance hall.
Far right A hinged *byōbu* screen can be moved to different spaces or stored as needed.

Life on the Floor

The activities of traditional Japanese daily life—eating, sitting, and sleeping—all take place on the floor and require a few specific pieces of furniture. Sitting on the floor was made more comfortable with a cushion, called a *zabuton*—a fabric case filled with wadding or, for warm weather, a thin cushion covered with woven grass (*goza*) similar to *tatami* covering. In imperial residences and some temples and shrines, throne-like chairs (known as *ishi*, *jōshō*, and *kyokuroku*) were sometimes used to raise the person of importance (the emperor or head priest) above the floor to a position of prestige. These "throne-seats" often are wide and deep—designed for sitting positions similar to being seated on the floor, and hence can be understood almost as a raised area of the floor rather than a chair in the Western sense.

Writing takes place on a small desk, a plank of wood usually supported by two side pieces with horizontal strips of wood at the bottom rather than legs which could damage the surface of the *tatami*. Sometimes a few drawers are built into the desk to hold writing utensils. Food is served on small footed lacquer trays, which raise the food above the level of the floor to a height from which bowls easily can be picked up and brought near the mouth, as is customary. The trays of food are prepared in the kitchen, with each type of food placed in a separate dish chosen to set off its color and texture, and brought out to the eating space. For special occasions, a small brazier, called a *shichirin*, is placed in front of each person for individually cooking food during the meal.

Sleeping occurs on a *futon*, a quilted mat made of wadding inside a fabric cover, usually about the same size as a *tatami* mat, which is placed directly on the floor, with a separate quilt on top. Traditional pillows (*makura*) are designed to keep the head raised above the floor when sleeping on the side—allowing air to flow under the neck and elaborate hairstyles to be kept in place. One type of traditional pillow was a wood box topped with a cylindrical cushion filled with buckwheat hulls and covered with a folded sheet of paper, which could be easily changed when dirty. Toiletries,

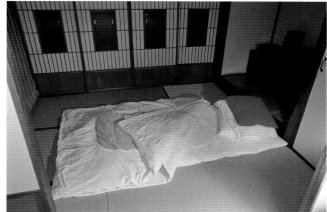

Above Woven grass *goza*, used as the surface for *tatami* mats, covers a simple summer *makura* pillow.
Left A thick *tatami* platform with a *zabuton* edged in colorful fabric denotes a place of honor.
Center A *futon* with a cover and pillow are laid out for the night, transforming a living room into a sleeping space.
Below An elaborate throne chair ornamented with dragons overlooks the opulent Seiden Main Hall in Shuri Castle.

such as combs and mirrors or other necessities could be stored in the box, which then could serve as a travel case. Edward Morse noted additional types of pillows—basketwork and ceramic, among others—and described that "[the foreigner's] first experience with it results in a stiff neck the next morning; and at intervals during the night he has the sensation that he is falling out of bed, for any freedom of movement of the head results in its downfall from the pillow."[37]

Articles of clothing are stored in *tansu* chests, although after a *kimono* is worn, traditionally it is aired on a special clothing rack called an *ikō*. Constructed of wood or bamboo poles, the *ikō* also are used to display beautiful *kimono*.

Heating and Lighting

Sources of heat and light (aside from some hearths, windows, and openings) are not built into traditional Japanese buildings. Rather, they are separate small elements used only when needed. They tend to be sized for a single person, providing just enough heat or light.

Candles, made of vegetable wax with paper wicks, initially were the only source of direct light at night and were set on metal stands that could be moved from room to room as needed. Candles also were placed in *washi* paper-covered wood-frame lanterns to create a glowing light. Vegetable (rapeseed) oil was used in early lamps, but after kerosene and oil were introduced in Japan in the Meiji period, kerosene and oil lamps became widely used.[38] The lamps take many forms, from simple metal dishes to elaborate lanterns made from ceramic or combinations of wood, paper, and metal. Some sit on a shelf or table, others are hung from above or stand on the floor.

Heating is provided in the form of a *hibachi* brazier filled with ash and charcoal. A metal or ceramic bowl often is used alone or perhaps placed inside a wood box having handles cut out of the sides for easy portability. A simple version is a metal pan on a wooden base. Long metal chopsticks are used to add or adjust the charcoal. The *hibachi* is a good source of heat but only warms what is nearby rather than an entire space. Large *hibachi* may include a metal stand (*gotoku*) to support a kettle to boil water for tea. A similar portable brazier, a *ro*, is utilized for the tea ceremony in warm weather, since it is cooler to use than the brazier built into the floor. The *ro* is placed on the floor, along with the other tea utensils. The *kotatsu* is a later development, where the brazier is placed under a table, and a quilt is thrown over the top of the table to keep the heat in (figure 34). This enables several people to share the heat of the *hibachi* by placing their legs under the table and covering their laps with the quilt. It is very effective for warming the legs and front half of the body.

Storage

Most storage is built into a building in the form of closets (*oshiire*) or occasionally a *kaidan-dansu* (chest built into a staircase), and some

Left A sunken *irori* hearth provides warmth to those adjacent to it as well as a place to heat water.
Below left, figure 34 A *kotatsu* table with a brazier of hot coals underneath and a thick quilt over the top creates a warm refuge from the winter chill.
Above right A simple wood candle holder with a metal bracket supporting the candle hooks onto the *nageshi* head beam.
Below right A cylindrical lamp contains a candle and can be moved around and attached to any *nageshi* head beam.
Far right A wood lantern with glass windows protects a traditional candle and has a handle and a flat base for use indoors or out.

Above Two chests, one with long drawers and low feet lifting it above the floor surface and the other sitting flat on the floor with many small drawers, fit into a corner of a room.

Above right A tall kitchen chest has cabinets and drawers to hold dishes and utensils.

Right Drawers and cabinets of multiple sizes and shapes utilize metal hinges, handles, pulls, and locks, which are both functional and ornamental.

Far right A small portable *tansu* chest has a metal carrying handle and two fabric straps, which hold the drawers in place when carried.

small amounts of storage are built into other objects, such as the base of the *makura* (pillow). However, one important piece of furniture used for storage that is not built in and is designed to be movable is the *tansu* chest. Many *tansu* are small enough to be carried, but some large *tansu*, if they are meant to be moved frequently, are outfitted with wheels.

These chests may include only drawers or be a combination of drawers and cabinets. *Tansu* are constructed from wood, and fine *tansu* use woods that inhibit insects and humidity, such as paulownia (*kiri*) or cedar (*sugi*). Cypress (*hinoki*), chestnut (*kuri*), and

yezo spruce (*ezo-matsu*), among other woods, also are used and may be covered with *urushi* (lacquer) or stained with *kaki-shibu* (persimmon tannin), *bengara* (iron oxide), or other pigment. *Tansu* can be constructed entirely from wood, but many incorporate metal hardware for door pulls and reinforcement on the corners of the drawers and the chest. The metalwork often is engraved and very ornamental, expressing the high social standing associated with a finely crafted *tansu*.

Tansu are built in many different sizes and serve various functions. In the Edo period, *tansu* were used by *samurai* (members of the aristocratic warrior class) for many purposes.

Typical types of *tansu* that reflect the lifestyle of the time include *sho-dansu* used to store books, *katana-dansu* for sword blades, *cha-dansu* for tea ceremony utensils, and *ishō-dansu* for clothing.[39] Some *tansu* are used as kitchen cupboards (*mizuya kasane-dansu*) to hold other everyday items or for merchant wares (*chōba-dansu*). Still other *tansu* are designed for specific objects, such as *kimono*, and the size and shape of the drawers reflect the use. In many regions, brides took a trousseau chest with them to their new home, perhaps an *ishō-dansu* filled with clothing and a smaller *temoto-dansu* for personal objects, such as hair ornaments and cosmetics.

Chapter 15
Decorative objects

Most of the decoration in a traditional Japanese building is inherent in the permanent architectural elements of the building. However, in some cases the architecture is designed specifically for the display of certain kinds of objects which are purely of a decorative nature. Some of these objects, like those associated with the *kamidana* (*shintō* deity shelf) or *butsudan* (Buddhist ancestral altar), are per-manently displayed and used. Others, such as the tools needed for a tea ceremony, are only displayed when the tea ceremony is being prepared or is under way. When not in use, these objects are stored out of sight in *tansu* or closets and only brought out when needed.

The one space in a traditional Japanese building that is specifically designed to display decorative objects is the *tokonoma*, the decorative alcove found in the formal reception room of a *shoin*- or *sukiya*-style building. The two items customarily displayed in a *tokonoma* are a scroll painting (*kakejiku*) and a flower arrangement (*ikebana*) or a *bonsai* plant. Both the scroll and the flower arrangement are chosen to relate to the particular time of the year and are changed often (in the case of the flowers) or at least seasonally (as for the scroll). Scroll paintings and flower arrangements also are selected or created especially for a certain guest or specific event.

While rooms in dwellings mostly are kept free of furniture and objects, some temple and shrine buildings have permanent displays of sculpture and other religious items. The altar in a Buddhist temple usually is a table placed in front of a permanent piece of sculpture, perhaps of the Buddha or a bodhisatva. Depending on the school of Buddhism, the space above the altar may be decorated with

hanging ornaments in gold or other metals, as is typical in esoteric Buddhism (*shingonshū*). Alternately, the walls of the main hall may be decorated with sculpture, such as the elegantly carved musicians floating on clouds attached to the walls in the Hōōdō of the Byōdōin Temple in Uji (figure 29), which reflect the tastes of Pure Land Buddhism (*jōdoshū*) popular in the Heian period.

Scrolls: Kakejiku

In many formal reception rooms, the scroll hung in the *tokonoma* is the only example of representational art in the room (and perhaps in the entire building). Other ornament may be abstract, but the *kakejiku* often shows a well-known person or a scene from a recognizable place. Typical scenes are landscapes or townscapes, realized with muted colors or tones of gray, or objects from nature, such as flowers, plants, birds, or animals. When these are displayed, they are selected for their expression of the current season.

Calligraphic scrolls also are quite common and feature famous verses of poetry or a single beautifully written *kanji* (Japanese ideograph based on Chinese writing). These usually are completed in black ink on a white background, often with a single dip of the calligrapher's brush into the ink. Such works can be gently flowing lines of verse with many characters covering the paper or exuberant examples of energetic brushwork. Calligraphy also is chosen to reflect the season or to make a meaningful connection to a specific person or place. In the case of calligraphy displayed in a teahouse, the significance of the character or words is important to set the tone of the tea ceremony.

The paintings and calligraphy on the *kakejiku* are completed on paper or cloth (most often silk or white satin).[40] This is attached to a colored or patterned background sheet of paper or fabric (which also might be attached to another layer) to frame the picture or poem. At the top and bottom, the scroll is wrapped around a wood dowel or a bamboo pole, and a piece of fabric ribbon is attached to the top pole for hanging. Scrolls are hung in the *tokonoma* from a beam just below the

Top An ink painting on a *washi* paper and fabric *kakejiku* scroll and a small low wood table harmonize in color and size.
Above A *kakejiku* scroll with black and white callig-raphy on a simple background hangs from a *nageshi* head beam.

ceiling. The scrolls usually are tall and narrow, similar to the proportions of the *tokonoma* itself. Because they are lightweight and can be rolled, *kakejiku* are easy to display as well as to take down and store.

Flower Arrangements: Ikebana

The most temporal element found in traditional Japanese architecture is the *ikebana* flower arrangement. Although *ikebana* (literally "living flowers," figure 35) hardly can be considered architectural, the flower arrangement is a necessary component to complete the space of the *tokonoma*, arguably the most important space within a formal reception room or a tea ceremony room. *Ikebana* also adhere to the same aesthetic principles of *shin-gyō-sō* (formal–semiformal–informal) that are used in the construction of teahouses and garden paths, among many other architectural elements. The flower arrangement is appreciated, of course, for its beauty and its relationship to the place and the current season, as the flowers used traditionally are picked from the garden outside or nearby. However, it is also appreciated for its short life span, as *mono no aware* (sensitivity to the temporality of all things) is an important concept in Japanese culture.

The bowl or vase is chosen for the arrangement to complement and enhance the flowers and to set the tone for the scale of the *ikebana*. The vase is an important element in the composition of the arrangement and may be a beautiful piece of pottery in its own right, but a vase, no matter how beautiful, is not used if it overshadows the flowers. Flowers are chosen to reflect the season and enhance the mood of a particular event, such as a tea ceremony. They are arranged very carefully, following specific rules based on the goal of harmony within asymmetry. For tea ceremony *ikebana*, flowers and greenery are chosen from the garden or the wild and are brought together in often startling combinations of color and texture. The art of *ikebana*, like all the traditional arts of Japan, is learned over many years of study and practice, and a trained eye comprehends the subtlety and skill of a beautiful arrangement.

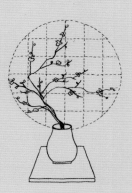

Above A simple asymmetrical flower arrangement provides a connection to the season and a bright focal point.
Left Sprays of cherry blossoms are arranged informally, suggesting the temporary nature of the seasonal flowers.
Right, figure 35 The art of *ikebana* is based on rules governing the proportional relationships of the flower arrangement.

Sculpture

On occasion, a small piece of sculpture, often (though not always) of a religious nature, is placed in the *tokonoma* instead of a flower arrangement. However, for the most part sculpture usually is found in Buddhist temples. In a typical arrangement, the *kondō* ("golden hall") is built for the purpose of displaying an image of the Buddha, and the Buddha statue is placed in the center of the space. In some instances, the *kondō* is built for one specific statue, and the form and scale of the architecture reflect the form and scale of the particular item. Two fine examples of this are the *daibutsuden* at Tōdaiji Temple in Nara and the Hōōdō Phoenix Hall of the Byōdōin Temple in Uji (figure 29).

Originally built in 751 CE (but rebuilt to its present size (two-thirds of its original length) in 1199 after fires and wars), the Tōdaiji *daibutsuden* is designed to house and display an enormous gilded bronze statue of the Buddha sitting on a lotus throne. The statue is more than 16 meters (53 feet) high and is one of the largest bronze Buddhas in the world. The building is designed with the statue placed in the center of the space, for viewing from all sides (unlike many statues in temples that can only be viewed from the front and sides but not from the back). An opening is located high in the front façade, so the face of the Buddha appears to look out from the hall.

The eleventh-century Hōōdō at the Byōdōin Temple similarly is designed so that the Buddha gazes out an opening in the front façade. At night, when the Hōōdō is lit inside, the glowing face of the Buddha is visible when the building is viewed from the garden. Carved from wood and covered with gold leaf, the Byōdōin Buddha is placed in the center of the Hōōdō, with an intricately carved leaf-shaped panel, which rises up from behind the statue to create a patterned backdrop.

Another traditional use of sculpture is within the main entrance gates of large temples. Placed in pairs, one to the left and the other to the right of the entry, these statues serve to guard and protect the temple. They typically are carved from wood and feature fierce expressions.

Far left A seated Buddha statue shows the patina of age, expressing a connection to the past.
Left A small sculpture placed in a *tokonoma* alcove creates an interesting focal point without overwhelming the space.

Above Sculptures of religious figures are common in Buddhist temples, such as this graceful Amidha Buddha sculpture at the Anrakuji Temple in Kyoto.
Left Within the grand space of the Daibutsuden Great Buddha Hall at the Tōdaiji Temple, a carved wood guardian statue commands attention.

Chapter 16
Interior ornamentation

Historically, upper-class dwellings as well as temples, shrines, and other public buildings used ornament to express wealth and power. In contrast, a country house or *minka* often has very little ornamentation, but what is used tends to be created from a functional need. For example, a *minka* may have ornament only on the ridge of the roof, with an artfully trimmed extra thick layer of thatch to reinforce the least weather-resistant part of the roof. A simple farmhouse may not have any added decoration—the beauty comes from the obvious power of the (sometimes rough) wooden structure and the straightforward use of the construction materials. The materials and structure reveal a similar power and beauty in other building

types as well, but the characteristics of the materials and structure often are enhanced by the addition of ornament. Even so, as in the *minka*, ornament is born from function. For example, a metal joint cover may be formed like a flower or a door pull may be made in the shape of a boat oar. Each serves its intended purpose very efficiently yet goes beyond pure function to become an eye-catching symbol of sophistication and wealth.

Such ornamentation can take many different forms, but there are some common themes, most notably that of geometric patterns or natural motifs. Many patterns or figures are representative of scenes or objects found in nature—of flowers and plants, birds and animals,

or mountains and rivers. Even in Edo-period buildings, which tend to have ornamentation that is more stylized and less representational, the forms and patterns are suggestive of nature.

Ceilings, walls, and even floors can be canvases for various types of ornamentation. When applied to a surface, such as a ceiling or a *fusuma*, the materials are carefully chosen to enhance the experience of the space. Ink washes (*sumi-e*) and paintings with colored pigments are used in spaces that receive enough light that the paintings can be viewed comfortably. *Washi* paper is applied to mud plaster walls to protect the walls in high traffic areas but also adds a contrasting color—perhaps, in the case of a tea ceremony room, with one color paper used at

Far left An ornamental metal plate is the base for a simple locking mechanism.
Left The *honchōna* notched surface of the heavy columns and beams catches the light of the Tenshū donjon tower at the Matsumoto Castle.
Above The painted white ends of the protruding beams protect the wood and give contrast and hierarchy to the composition of structural elements.

Left, figure 36 Undulating tree trunks are woven together in an unusual *minka* roof structure that takes advantage of the timber's natural form.
Below A small joint cover in the form of Mount Fuji with clouds is a subtle visual reference to the sacred mountain.

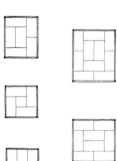

Above A triangle of bamboo makes a transitional space where two *engawa* verandas meet.
Left A chrysanthemum blossom joint cover indicates the connection to the imperial family in the Meiji Shrine.
Right, figure 37 Typical layout patterns for *tatami* mat floors take advantage of the 2:1 ratio of the mats, with some placed perpendicular to others.

the base of the walls where the guests sit and another color used where the host sits, therefore expressing the hierarchical use of the space.

Gold and silver leaf, lacquer, and mother-of-pearl are ornamental materials commonly used to reflect light in spaces that often have limited natural light. In Tanizaki's words, "The sheen of the lacquer ... reflects the wavering candlelight, announcing the drafts that find their way from time to time into the quiet room, luring one into a state of reverie. If the lacquer is taken away, much of the spell disappears...."[41]

Structural Elements

Although it is rare for columns and beams to be carved or painted, as can be found in some other Asian cultures, some examples are visible in Japan, primarily in Buddhist architecture. In these cases, brackets that support the roof and are visible in the interior or important structural beams may be carved with dragons,

clouds, or other meaningful figures. Such carved structural elements always are in visible locations and support the primary spaces of the building or complex of buildings.

Rather than applying ornament, carpenters choose wooden structural elements for their grain, color, and form, and they cut and finish the wood to best display these natural qualities. Different species of wood exhibit different grains, for example the close straight grain of *hinoki* cypress versus the figured grain of red pine, and different colors, such as the pale creamy color of paulownia or the mottled red-brown of cherry bark. Depending where and how they grew, timbers can be thick and straight or thin and curved. Carpenters work with the uneven forms of the timbers to take advantage of the natural stresses, for example in a curved beam when using it in a roof assembly or even to create a woven structure of beams in a *minka* (figure 36).

Columns are especially easy to use ornamentally. In some cases, the bark is left intact or only the outer bark is removed to expose the smooth inner surface; or a column can be planed to a silky flatness or finished to give a rough or ridged surface. It can also be shaped into a circle in section or a square, depending on the desired effect and use. Some, like the enormous columns at the Nandaimon South Gate of the Tōdaiji Temple in Nara, display gentle entasis (convex curving) along their lengths. Some wood columns, such as the *tokobashira* at the edge of the *tokonoma* decorative alcove, may be carved in low relief.

These columns are intended to have a particular aesthetic. In the case of the *tokobashira*, the column may express the form of the tree trunk as it grew naturally or perhaps utilize an exotic wood or a particular texture to give emphasis to the column as a focal point in the room. In a few cases, columns are highly

Top Fabric edging on *tatami* mats gives subtle ornamentation to the floor plane.
Center Walls and screens are painted with pastoral scenes in the Omuro Goshō Old Imperial Palace at Ninnaji Temple in Kyoto.
Above Nature is brought inside with sliding partitions ornamented with gold leaf and paintings of craggy rocks and a crane perched in a knotted pine tree.
Top right The delicate pattern of the wood transom allows light and air to pass between adjacent spaces.

ornamented. For example, columns in the seventeenth-century Tōshōgu Yōmeimon in Nikkō are completely covered with a decorative pattern in white plaster relief.

Floors

Because of their high use and the constant contact of the human body on them, floors do not tolerate applied ornament well. Often the beauty of a floor comes from the expression of the grain of the wood planks or the pattern formed by the arrangement of the *tatami* in the space (figure 37). *Tatami* mats usually are laid on the floor so that the corners of four mats do not meet at a point. For example, two mats are laid with their long sides touching, and their short sides butt against the long side of a third mat. Traditionally, mats are laid out in a spiral arrangement, starting from the middle.[42] However, many examples of other patterns can be found—apparent from the cloth edging on the mats, which also provides an opportunity for a slight amount of applied ornament to occur, even on the floor.

The most basic cloth used to edge a *tatami* mat is black linen, although other dark colors also are used. However, beautifully woven damask in richly colored patterns traditionally was used where the budget allowed or social circumstance required. The contrast of the colored fabric edging with the light green of new *tatami* or light yellow-brown of aged *tatami* creates an obvious pattern on the floor. Yet, the pattern is not overwhelming as the proportion of the cloth strip to the width of the mat (the width of the cloth band is about $1/30$ of the width of the *tatami*) and the overall size of the mats (about 182 centimeters by 91 centimeters or 6 feet by 3 feet) creates a soft background grid in the room.

Walls and Transoms

The walls are the focal point of a traditional room and their flat surfaces are easily colored and textured. Walls often are finished in mud plaster showing off the color and rough quality of the earth. Sometimes natural pigment, such as rusty orange-red *bengara* (iron oxide pigment), is added to the plaster mix, but usually the earth chosen for the plaster is used in a

way that shows off its natural color—gray, green, or brown, among others. Mud plaster walls are inherently textured, with straw and sand in the mix, but can also be finished with a brush for a ridged finish or polished with a trowel to a reflective surface.

The walls sometimes become canvases for paintings or patterns of colored handmade paper. For example, the Okushoin of the Koto-hiragū Shrine in Shikoku has walls covered with gold leaf exuberantly painted with flowers and butterflies. In the Shōkintei ("Pine Lute Pavilion") of the Katsura Imperial Villa in Kyoto, several walls are covered in a vivid checkerboard pattern of indigo blue and white *washi* paper. Walls formed with movable partitions, *shōji* and *fusuma*, also are often highly ornamented. The wood lattice of the *shōji* can be constructed in many different patterns, while the paper on the *fusuma* can be painted with ink washes or other materials. The transoms (*ranma*) above the movable partitions may be carefully carved in geometric patterns or with scenes from nature, with openings to allow the air and filter light to flow through, or they may be constructed like *shōji* or *fusuma*, embellished with ink wash or painted to match the *fusuma*.

Ceilings

A simple wood plank ceiling, accented with wood battens, radiates beauty through its fine craft and the color and grain of the wood. A more complex ceiling, such as a coffered wood ceiling in a *shoin*-style room, is beautifully patterned and needs no additional ornamentation—the proportions of the coffers, the relationship of the boards to the wood lattice, the smooth curve where the ceiling meets the walls, and the grain and patina of the wood serve as ornament. Compared to floors, ceilings are easy to ornament since they receive no human contact, nor do they have moving parts like traditional Japanese walls. As a result, there are many examples of ornamented ceilings in Japan and many methods used to apply ornament to them.

Ceilings can be painted, lacquered, or gilded in gold or silver. Often combinations of paint, lacquer, and gold or silver leaf are used to depict geometric patterns or images of nature. Some ceilings may be finished in more unusual ways, such as one ceiling in the *sukiya*-style Sumiya *ageya* (entertainment house) in Kyoto, which is covered with gold leaf and pieces of painted paper cut into the shape of fans. Such creative ornamentation is typical of Edo-period buildings designed for leisure pursuits.

Hardware

Because of the highly developed skill of Japanese carpenters and the relatively slight use of metals in Japanese architecture, traditional buildings are designed so that they could be built using few if any metal nails or other hardware. Indeed, many buildings, especially *minka*, are constructed without the use of any metal connectors. Doors slide on tracks in wood rails rather than being hinged, beams and columns are joined like puzzles rather than with bolts or metal plates, and wood shingles or battens are held in place using bamboo nails rather than metal nails. However, where the budget allowed, metal was used, perhaps to form a hinge on a *kura* door, to cover a wood pin holding together a joint, or to form a door pull (*hikite*, literally "pull hand") on a sliding *fusuma* partition.

Historically, the use of metal almost always was occasion for ornament on the metal itself, since metal primarily was used in upper-class residences as well as temples, shrines, and other buildings. Flat pieces of metal are engraved with ornamental patterns or depictions of natural objects. Joint covers are more three-dimensional and can be formed into the shapes of flowers or family crests. Door pulls are by necessity three-dimensional as they have to provide a place for the fingers to fit. They can be simply shaped, such as a well-proportioned rectangle, or take the form of a recognizable object, such as the door pulls in the Edo-period main house at the Katsura Imperial Villa in Kyoto, which depict four flower arrangements, one for each season.

In some cases, metal was used to complement the building structure or to protect the building. Thick metal straps might be wrapped around the lower ends of large wood columns to hold them together, especially if they have been repaired. To secure heavy wood doors, locks made from metal were used and often these were tastefully ornamented.

Left A textured ceiling plane and walls painted with figures and poems create two very different kinds of ornamentation in the Shisendō Temple in Kyoto.
Below left The roof structure is the ornament in the Tsutsuji-no-Chaya at the Rikugien Garden in Tokyo.
Below A dragon painting creates a lively ceiling in the Hatto Dharma Hall at Kenninji Temple in Kyoto.

Above and right Ornamental metalwork is both practical and aesthetic. Joint covers, door pulls, and reinforcing plates typically reference nature in their forms and embellishment.

Chapter 17
Exterior ornamentation

The amount of ornamentation found in a building, inside and outside, depends on the wealth and social status of the owner or the importance of the building (such as a temple or shrine) in the community. The higher the status or wealthier the owner, the more likely it is that the building has added ornamentation. The amount and kind of ornament found on temples, shrines, and similar buildings changes over time, based on the tastes and religious beliefs of a specific era. The peaceful social situation and relative wealth of people in the Heian period (794–1185) is reflected in the opulence of the buildings of that time. This persisted for dwellings up until the Edo period (1615–1868) when the Tokugawa shogunate announced sumptuary edicts that reinforced social norms, based on a family's social status, by stipulating the types of construction materials and the amount of ornamentation that could be used on dwellings.

Any architectural element can be enhanced by ornament. Almost all exterior elements in traditional Japanese buildings—the roof and roof structure, the walls, and even the foundations—may be embellished. As with interior ornament, most exterior ornament is derived from a practical function; it visually enhances a necessary element rather than being a separate added component.

As noted earlier, the roof is the dominant element in traditional Japanese architecture, whether it be a simple farmhouse or an elaborate temple. Although the main purpose of the roof is to provide shelter, it may also be the canvas for many different kinds of ornament, whether in thatch or ceramic tile. For example, in a *minka* farmhouse, the bundles of thatch used to reinforce the ridge of a thatched roof

Opposite Intricate detail and flowing forms are hallmarks of the roofs of the Kaguraden Sacred Music Hall at the Naiku Inner Shrine of the Ise Shrine.
Above As the weakest part of the roof, the ridge is reinforced with layers of ceramic tiles and mortar, topped with a line of cylindrical tiles, and finished at the gable end with a decorative *onigawara* demon tile.
Right The graceful roofs of the Nino-maru Palace at the Nijō Castle in Kyoto are ornamented with decorative metalwork, carved wood, and ceramic tiles.

may be bunched and tied in a rhythmic pattern. It is ornamental, yet it is born from necessity, using only the most readily available materials to complete the task. However, an upper-class dwelling may have a very ornate roof ridge, employing layers of ceramic tile laid in a decorative pattern and built up to an imposing height. Similarly, the roof ridge on a temple building also may have multiple layers of ceramic tile and may include highly stylized demon end tiles (*onigawara*). A temple roof may be supported by layers of wood bracketing, each bracket carefully carved and assembled to create the sense of floating clouds (*kumotokyō*).

Walls provide obvious opportunities for ornament. Wood lattices, board and batten panels, and the like, as well as coverings of mud or lime plaster or ceramic tiles can create decorative textures and patterns. Sculptural

reliefs, known as *kote-e*, formed out of lime plaster, are incorporated into walls to express a connection to nature or to help guard a building from fire, as is the case of a *kote-e* in the shape of the *kanji* (ideograph) for water on a *kura* (storage building). Although any kind of building can incorporate ornamentation, *kura*, which are covered with plaster as an aid to fireproofing, are prime candidates for wall ornament, especially *kote-e*.

Foundations, too, can be ornamented. For example, *soseki* foundation stones may be carved into recognizable shapes or covered with floral or geometric patterns. The floor surface of a podium foundation may be faced with stone or ceramic tile laid in ornamental patterns. As with the other examples, the ornamentation, though not necessary, is not extraneous but instead enhances the basic architectural elements.

Roofs and Roof Structures

Not only can the structure and surface of a roof be decorated, but the form of the roof itself may be ornamental, especially those of temples and shrines. One example is the combination of two roofs over one space, as in the Hachiman style exemplified in the main shrine of the Usa Shrine in Kyūshū, which dates from the early eighth century. In this shrine, the interior spaces could have been covered with a single roof; instead, the shrine is designed with two distinct yet attached roofs, almost identical in form. The style is thought to have been derived from earlier Buddhist temples in which a separate space for worshippers was built adjacent to an existing hall. The use of a double roof acts as a form of ornament for the building, as the interior is experienced as one continuous space rather than two separate spaces.

Roof forms may incorporate expressive curving eaves—again a type of ornament because the roof would be equally as functional and easier to construct with eaves that are straight rather than curved. The curves of a roof often are complemented by the choice and application method of the ceramic tile covering. Layers of half-cylinder tiles flow to the edge of the roof, capped with end tiles embellished with carved reliefs of flowers or family crests. The ridge of the roof provides an even greater opportunity for such elaboration, as layers of ceramic tile are built up in decorative patterns and are finished at the ends with highly ornate carved ceramic *onigawara* "demon tiles." The *onigawara* tiles function to protect the building from evil spirits.

Less elaborate roofs are also ornamented when time and finances allow. The ends of the eaves of thatched roofs can be carved to express layers or display a *kanji* character or other image, while the roof ridges can be built up in many different combinations of thatch, bamboo, wood, and tile to create an ornamental expression of shelter and permanence.

When the wood structure holding up a roof is exposed and expressed, as is the case for most temple and shrine architecture, often the structure also is ornamented. The simplest form of ornamentation is the painted ends of the exposed rafters, generally done with whitewash using pigment made from calcium carbonate (*gofun*). The paint helps to preserve the wood, as the endgrain is most likely to draw in water, and the painted rafter ends add to the architectural aesthetic. In a similar manner and for the same purpose, the ends of the rafters sometimes are covered with metal or ceramic caps carved or engraved in decorative patterns.

Opposite Carved wood beams and brackets display fierce creatures and natural scenes.
Above left The end tiles on an Okinawan house feature flower patterns embossed in the ceramic tiles.
Top right A crane flies through stylized clouds on a carved wood panel.
Above right Wood, metal, and ceramic tile each offer possibilities for ornamentation while remaining true to their practical functions.

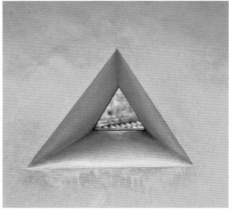

Top A high rectangular window and a low round opening in a rough mud plaster wall faced with wood reveal the thickness of the wall.

Above A tapered triangular opening in an outer castle wall covered with lime plaster is both defensive and aesthetic.

Walls

The typical wall construction with mud or lime plaster filled in between exposed wood structural columns creates an architectural aesthetic that is complete and pleasing without the addition of applied ornament. The walls can be enhanced by using special colors of mud or textured finishes, but rarely is any ornament applied to the surface of the wall. Instead, the ornament is integral to the wall itself, growing from the construction and finish of the wall. However, in certain geographic areas and for certain building types, especially the *kura* storage house and the *machiya* urban house, decorative elements may be added to walls. At the same time, these elements enhance the function of the wall, either in a practical or a spiritual way.

In many *machiya* (townhouses), the front exterior wall is finished in plaster with the lower part faced with wood paneling for added protection. The paneling may consist of simple wood planks used vertically or may be more complex, such as *shitami-ita* style (overlapped horizontal boards with battens). *Machiya* in Kyoto are famous for having skirts of split bamboo, known as *inu-yarai* ("dog fence"), which protect the walls from being splashed and can be readily replaced.

Also on the practical side is the application of an additional layer of flat ceramic tile and lime plaster over mud plaster walls. Present especially in *kura* storehouses, which are fireproofed by having the entire structure completely covered with plaster (usually finished with lime plaster), this type of wall, called *namako-kabe* ("sea slug wall"), gives an extra layer of protection from fire. Although a number of different patterns exist, the usual tile pattern for *namako-kabe* employs flat square tiles set in a diagonal grid, with thick lime plaster applied between them. *Namako-kabe* may be used only on the lower part of the wall or cover the entire height.

Kura walls are frequently decorated with *kote-e* ("trowel pictures"), which also can be found on some dwellings. These three-dimensional reliefs are carved out of plaster and applied to the wall just under the peak of the roof. *Kote-e* might take the form of a *kanji* character (most frequently the character for water to help ward off fire), a family crest, or an auspicious symbol represented by a plant or animal. *Kote-e*, crafted out of a combination of plain white lime plaster and lime plaster that is tinted with pigment, usually are colorful and playful yet perform an important spiritual role in the architecture.

Openings

Window openings in many traditional Japanese buildings are protected by a layer of vertical wood strips. Although these strips are primarily used for security, they also serve as ornamentation by adding a layer of pattern and movement to the façade of the building. Many *machiya* have such a layer of wood lattice grilles (*kōshi*) attached to the exterior of the house on the façade which faces the street. Sometimes the latticework only covers window openings, but it also may cover openings for sliding doors. Light entering these *machiya* passes through two layers of latticework—the exterior grille and the interior *shōji*, creating lovely patterns of light and shadow.

Some *machiya* also have slit openings in the mud plaster walls of the front façade of the upper story. Depending on the design, the slits may have rounded or straight corners and beveled or straight edges. The slits allow light and air to pass through the wall while providing privacy and creating another level of pattern on the building.

Kura storehouses often have wonderfully expressive window and door openings. Since these buildings are covered with plaster for fire protection, the thickness of the plaster is manipulated to serve its function as fire retardant and to act as ornament. The openings for windows and doors typically do not have simple straight edges; rather, the frames are constructed with multiple tiered layers. The windows and doors also have the same tiered layers so that they closely fit into the openings when closed and prevent any air from passing through. When open, as they often are for ventilation, the windows with their thick tiered plaster edges juxtapose sculpturally with the flat wall surfaces.

Above left Wood lattice grilles provide privacy without blocking views from inside to out.

Top right Bundles of rice straw reinforce and ornament the roof gable of a *minka* farmhouse in the mountains.

Above right A wood window frame overlaps with the wood paneling covering the lower part of the wall of a private house in Kyoto.

Right Typical shop fronts in the Hanamikōji area of Kyoto feature unusual shaped window openings, wood lattices of various sizes, and *inu-yarai* skirts of split bamboo to protect the lower walls.

PART 4
Gardens and Courtyards

山も庭もうごきいるるや
夏座敷

松尾 芭蕉

Mountains too move into the garden,
the parlor in summer.[1]

MATSUO BASHŌ (1644–94)

Chapter 18
Shaping the land

The first intentional shaping of the land by man is usually for agriculture. In Japan, the type of agriculture which most dramatically changed the surface of the land is wet rice agriculture, which was introduced from China by the third century BCE.[2] The fields or paddies for rice grown in this manner must be kept under water while the rice is planted and begins to grow. Because the rice fields are flooded and must contain the water, it is necessary to have flat areas of land. Since much of Japan is hilly or mountainous, the land had to be terraced in order to create the rice paddies, often with stone retaining walls to hold back the earth.

Once a community has achieved a certain standard of living—has moved beyond survival living and begun to prosper—it can accumulate resources, and along with that the time to enjoy the spoils of wealth. Only at that point can people begin to look at the landscape as a canvas for aesthetic and spiritual fulfillment, and a culture can begin to shape the landscape for pleasure rather than for sustenance.

The earliest known gardens and landscapes intentionally shaped for aesthetic reasons in Japan were a result of strong contact with China in the sixth and seventh centuries. Buildings and landscapes were heavily influenced by Chinese taste at that time. The gardens which were popular in China included private gardens that tried to emulate nature, with pastoral scenes of forests, hills, ponds, and streams. Rocks were used to represent mountains, and winding paths led throughout the gardens. The relationship of buildings and landscape elements was complex and carefully considered.[3] During the T'ang dynasty (618–907) there continued to be great influence from China on Japan. Chinese imperial gardens were

designed to relate to specific buildings and usually were built to one side of a particular building. The planning of the imperial residences influenced the layout of Chinese temples during the T'ang period,[4] and that in turn influenced the planning of Chinese-style Buddhist temples and later imperial and aristocratic residences built in Japan.

As can be seen in the Hōryūji Temple complex in Nara, the oldest extant temple compound in Japan (dating from 706 AD), the land was cleared to create gravel courtyards within the main area of the complex. The middle gate opens from the south into the courtyard, which is surrounded on all sides by covered corridors attached to the lecture hall on the north. The pagoda and *kondō* ("golden hall") are situated on the left and right respectively, while the lecture hall is on axis with the gate, in the center of the north side of the courtyard. The courtyard is covered with white gravel and creates a flat

Pages 148–9 Raking gravel in the dry garden at the Ryōanji Temple in Kyoto.
Opposite The rubble wall of the Nakijin Castle ruins in Okinawa follows the contours of the land, creating a defensive barrier for the buildings sited on the terraced land within the walls.
Left A landscape of moss and trees is reflected in the still water in the garden at Saihōji Temple in Kyoto.
Below A framed view reveals a raked gravel bed studded with stepping stones, trimmed azalea bushes, ornamental stones, and a lantern, with a backdrop of layered azaleas.

expanse that contrasts with the large, elaborate wood structures. In this setting, the structures are understood as objects within a defined space, not unlike pieces of sculpture that can be viewed in the round.

This same use of the gravel courtyard can be found in imperial and aristocratic residences as they also incorporated the building forms and site planning brought from China. Following geomantic principles based on climate and common sense, this type of residential compound is arranged, like the temple complexes, with a gate opening onto a courtyard on the south side of the most public building. As the functions of the buildings become more private toward the rear of the complex, the relationship of the buildings to the landscape transforms to reflect the change in formality. Gardens, which can be viewed from the buildings or walked through, are designed to include elements similar to those found in Chinese gardens of the same time period, such as streams, ponds, islands, bridges, and mountains.

As the Chinese-influenced architecture began to be altered in ways that reflected the Japanese landscape, climate, and taste, so also did the gardens transform, eventually changing so much that they no longer bore any resemblance to the gardens in China from which they originated. The first stage of this development is the paradise garden associated with Pure Land Buddhism (*jōdoshū*), which was popular toward the end of the ancient period, in the mid-eleventh century. These gardens are built together with *shinden*-style residential compounds and are designed as a representation of paradise. The gardens feature ponds constructed in front (on the south side)

of the *shinden*, the main hall of the complex, which is reflected in the surface of the water. The L-shaped corridors flanking the *shinden* reach out into the garden, strengthening the connection between the architecture and the landscape. Exotic plants and animals added to the other-worldly image, and guests could enjoy the scenery by strolling through the grounds or boating on the pond.

The next change in garden design occurred with the *shoin*-style architecture, which developed from the twelfth century. Like the earlier Buddhist temple complexes, *shoin*-style residential compounds also incorporate formal gravel forecourts as well as less formal gardens in the more private quarters behind the main reception halls. In relationship to the courtyard, the placement of the gate and entry to the main hall slightly shift off the central north–south axis, just as the buildings behind the reception halls also move off the axis. The gardens fill in the areas between the buildings and the walls that surround the compound. Similar to the earlier *shinden* gardens, these landscapes are built for pleasure and entertainment. They are meant to be viewed from inside the adjacent buildings as well as while moving through the garden.

The high point in the evolution of garden design in Japan came with the development of *sukiya*-style architecture by the fifteenth and sixteenth centuries. The layouts of residential complexes became much less formal, with entries placed off-axis, and the gravel courtyards diminishing in size or eliminated altogether. The relationship between the buildings and the gardens strengthened, with the landscape moving in under the building, and

Above left to right Religious, residential, and agricultural landscapes are opportunities for beauty through the reflection of a temple in a pond, the suggestion of a mountain path, the composition of a group of stones, the playfulness of a circular rice paddy, the surprise of a conical mound of sand, the wonder of a *torii* gate in the ocean, and the framed view of a temple path leading into a garden.

verandas and other built elements moving out into the garden. These gardens are designed with scenes and symbols that were familiar to people of the time—images from literature or places far away or symbols of longevity long known from China, for example replicas of famous landscapes or groupings of stones and plants representing tortoises or cranes.

The art of garden design flourished, as did all the arts just before and during the Edo period, and three major forms of gardens can be recognized from that time. The meditation garden, sometimes called the "scroll garden" because it is designed to be viewed like a scroll painting from a seated position within a building or on the *engawa*, is found primarily within Zen temple complexes. The stroll garden (*kaiyūshiki teien*), which is incorporated into many imperial and aristocratic residential compounds as well as some temples, is intended to be viewed not only from within a building but also by moving through the garden. The third type, the tea garden, is designed specifically to accompany a teahouse and add to the ritualistic atmosphere of the tea ceremony.

The meditation garden developed during the late fifteenth century, when Zen Buddhism was popular in Japan. It was a time of political

instability and warring, and the *samurai* ethic of discipline of the mind and discipline of the body was prevalent. The meditation garden fits with those precepts because it is designed not to be fully comprehended at first glance but rather to be understood over time, through observation and meditation.

Most meditation gardens are compact, usually built immediately adjacent to the temple abbot's residence (*hōjō*), and often contained within walls. Many of these gardens are termed *karesansui* (literally "dry mountain water" or dry landscape) because they incorporate very few plantings and use beds of gravel or groupings of stones to represent water. The *karesansui* gardens are some of the most intriguing landscapes in Japan. One of the best known is the garden at Ryōanji Temple in Kyoto (figure 38). A simple rectangle of raked gravel, the garden contains five groupings of stones and moss enclosed by walls on three sides—two magnificent rammed earth walls and one wall finished in bright white lime plaster. The garden is designed to be viewed from the *engawa* (veranda) of the abbot's quarters. The fifteen stones in the garden are placed so that from any seated position on the veranda, only fourteen stones are visible. A different viewing position reveals the hidden rock but conceals another. The quiet ambiance of the compact garden, together with the complexity of the design, provide for hours of deep meditation.

Unlike the meditation gardens, where the viewer does not enter the garden, the stroll garden allows the visitor to move through the garden and view the various scenes depicted in it as they unfold. The scenery is understood somewhat like a film, with a specific sequence that is dictated by the path. These gardens incorporate imagery from popular literature or famous scenes from faraway places—views that were familiar to people at the time the gardens were constructed. For example, the garden at the Katsura Imperial Villa in Kyoto is designed using scenes from the *Genji monogatari* ("The Tale of Genji"), one of the first great works of literature from the Heian period. The garden also incorporates a miniature version of the famous landscape of the pine tree-covered sandbar in Amanohashidate, one of the three famous sceneries of Japan (*nihon sankei*). The views can be enjoyed by following a path through the garden, while boating on the pond, or from the moon-viewing veranda (*tsukimi-dai*) of the Old Shoin section of the main house.

The garden and the main house have a very close relationship. Even though the floor level of the building is raised off the ground about 5 *shaku* (approximately 1.5 meters or almost 5 feet), the *engawa* (veranda) reaches out to the garden and the garden extends under the building. The villa opens up to framed views of the garden, designed to be seen from a seated height. Paths lead directly from the *engawa* out into the garden, past precisely placed rocks and meticulously trimmed plants, to pleasure pavilions and teahouses. Carefully constructed scenes, with views from both close and far away, are revealed as the garden unfolds.

In contrast to the sometimes sprawling stroll garden, the tea garden is often small and contained, not unlike the meditation garden. Yet, it is designed to be observed from both a stable point (the waiting bench, for example) and to be viewed by moving through it. The tea garden sets the tone for the tea ceremony, creating a sense of serenity and otherworldliness that help to put the guest into the proper frame of mind.

The tea garden typically consists of an outer garden and an inner garden adjacent to the teahouse (figure 41). The outer garden is entered through a gate, where a *samurai* must leave his sword, since the garden is a place of peace understood to be separate from the outside world. From the outer garden, the inner garden is visible through a lightly woven bamboo or similar fence, but only can be entered through a small gate once the preparations for the tea ceremony have been completed and the host signals that it is time to enter.

The outer garden usually contains carefully placed plants and stones and a waiting bench, often with a view of a carved stone lantern, and a small outhouse-style toilet pavilion out of view. A path, known as the *roji*, leads from the first gate to the waiting bench and then through the outer garden to the inner gate and through the inner garden to the entrance of the teahouse. Within the inner garden, guests see the dust pit with a few clippings from the garden (which shows that the garden has been prepared for the guests), the well from which the tea ceremony water is drawn, and a carved stone basin with a wood or bamboo dipper for cleansing the hands and mouth for purification before the tea ceremony. The process of moving along the *roji*, viewing the garden from the bench, passing through the inner gate, and rinsing the mouth creates the opportunity for the guest to leave the cares and thoughts of the day behind and enter into the proper mind-set for the tea ceremony.

These three types of gardens share some common characteristics, the most important of which is that no matter how naturalistic any of them may seem, they all are designed and formed entirely by the hand of man. The garden designer's intention is not to mimic nature but to learn from it in order to create a version of nature that, in a sense, is more perfect than nature itself. "This treatment of a landscape garden, not merely as an artistic medley of pretty contours and choice vegetation, but as a single composition, abounding in suggestions of natural spots and favorite fancies, ... seems to give to the Japanese art a rank and importance unsurpassed by any other style."[5] The garden not only offers specific scenes of known places and general scenes of nature, but it represents the cosmos, affording an understanding of man's place in the universe.

In addition to these three main categories of gardens, another significant type is the *tsuboniwa* (literally "*tsubo* garden," a *tsubo* is a unit of measurement equal to two *tatami* mats, about 180 centimeters by 180 centimeters or 6 feet by 6 feet). *Tsuboniwa* developed in urban townhouses (*machiya*) as a means of allowing light and air into the interior rooms. *Machiya* are built immediately adjacent to one another, often on long narrow lots. Tiny courtyards specially designed to complement the houses provide light and air for the adjacent rooms as well as beautiful views of designed nature. Some *tsuboniwa* are very simple in design, perhaps just a single plant and a stone

basin on a bed of gray river stones. Other *tsuboniwa* are highly complex compositions of plants, stones, bridges, and other elements. These courtyard gardens are meant to be viewed from inside the *machiya*, with rooms opening directly onto the garden or perhaps with an *engawa* creating an intermediate zone. The *tsuboniwa* typically are a surprise to the visitor, as there is no indication from the outside of the house that they exist.

There are many different design principles incorporated into traditional Japanese gardens. Overall, the most important principle—the first one listed in the *Sakuteiki* ("Memoranda on Garden Making," an eleventh-century treatise on garden design)—is to learn from nature. "According to the lay of the land, and depending upon the aspect of the water landscape, you should design each part of the garden tastefully, recalling your memories of how nature presented itself for each feature."[6] The design principles generally can be categorized into "spatial tricks," "compositional devices," and "awareness mechanisms."

Some of the most important spatial tricks in Japanese garden design are miniaturization (*shukkei*), forced perspective or foreshortening, layering of space, and *shakkei* (borrowed scenery). Miniaturization is the act of replicating a scene in nature or a known object, such as a bridge, at a scale smaller than the original. Miniaturization often is used to trick the eye into understanding the space of the garden as being larger than it actually is.

Another device used to trick the eye in a similar way is forced perspective or foreshortening, for example when a wall is constructed so that it decreases in height as it moves away from the viewer. The brain, however, understands that the wall should have a consistent height, thus the eye is tricked into understanding the space as being bigger than it really is.

Layering of space often is made by placing elements such as plantings and stone groupings of increasing heights on a slope that rises away from the viewer, giving the suggestion of greater space between the layers. *Shakkei* is created when something outside of the garden—often a tree or mountain—becomes the background for the garden in a way that makes it appear as if it is contained within the garden, thereby greatly extending the viewer's interpretation of the space of the garden.

One fine example of *shakkei* occurs in the garden of the Shūgakuin Imperial Villa in Kyoto. A path through the garden leads to a narrow stair with high uneven stone steps flanked by tall hedges composed of many different kinds of plants. The eye is drawn to the varied shapes and colors of the leaves that compose the high hedge, but the mental focus is on the feet as the visitor carefully attempts to climb the rough stairs. Directly at the top of the stairs is a beautiful teahouse, which commands attention and eclipses the recent climb up the stairs. However, upon turning around, the visitor is at the highest point of the garden with a hedge in the foreground—which blocks the view of the main part of the garden in the middle ground—and a distant range of mountains that suddenly appear to be contained within the garden.

Typical compositional devices include framing, juxtaposition, and asymmetrical harmony. Framing occurs both for views from the interior of a building looking out and within the garden itself. The structure of the building—the wood columns, floor, and roof eaves—are composed to frame specific scenes of the garden from inside the building. Sliding partitions can be opened or removed to create framed views. Within the garden, hedges, trees, and walls frame particular views as well as hide elements that are revealed from other viewpoints in the garden.

Juxtaposition is the combination of two or more contrasting elements within a particular area of a garden. For example, a typical juxtaposition is the contrast of a three-dimensional element, such as a clipped azalea, against a two-dimensional element, either a horizontal component like an expanse of raked white gravel or a vertical element like a white lime plaster wall. The colors as well as the different forms heighten the contrast, with the bright green leaves of the azalea playing off the white ground or wall surface. Juxtaposition also can comprise the contrast of a natural shape with a geometric shape, such as when a single bush clipped into a perfect cube shape is placed in an otherwise naturalistic grouping of plants.

Asymmetrical harmony is at the heart of Japanese garden design. The garden as a whole is asymmetrical yet must impart a feeling of harmony. Within the garden, each grouping of plants or stones also must convey asymmetrical harmony. "Asymmetric designs establish a sense of visual balance through a proportioning of masses and distances so that M x D = C. M is the psychological weight or mass of an object. D is the distance between it and the real or imaginary fulcrum, and C remains constant."[7] A good example is in the use of triads for groups of stones (figure 44). A tall stone is flanked by two lower stones—one of medium height but short length, the other of low height but greater length. The relative proximity of the stones to one another and their comparable sizes create a balanced yet asymmetrical composition.

Awareness mechanisms employ elements in the garden design to cause the viewer to become more aware of being within the garden. Hide-and-reveal and *mitate* ("re-seeing") are two important ways in which this is achieved. Hide-and-reveal occurs when an element, such as a tree or an unusual stone, can be viewed from a distance in a garden but the path does not lead directly there. Instead, the path leads away from the object, thus hiding it from sight. However, eventually the path leads back to it, revealing it to the viewer at a close distance and triggering the memory of the first view of the object. *Mitate* occurs when an object that is familiar from everyday use, such as a millstone or a roof tile, is utilized in a garden in a way in which it is not ordinarily used. The sight of the object, the millstone set within a run of stepping stones or the roof tile as the edge of a water channel, causes the viewer to suddenly see the object anew, and thus to see the garden with fresh eyes as well.

Everything in a traditional Japanese garden is designed. Each element and each grouping is deliberately placed and composed to evoke a certain feeling or provide a specific view. Because gardens are so carefully controlled, it is necessary that they be maintained meticulously, especially the plantings and elements like fences constructed using plant materials. Maintenance of a garden is constant. Hedges must be clipped, so they do not grow tall and block views or seem out of proportion. Trees must be pruned to avoid unpleasant shapes and unbalanced compositions. Water channels must be kept clear of debris, leaves raked, and plants protected from snow and extreme cold. Moss must be kept moist, fences in good repair, and weeds removed promptly.

The maintenance of a garden is an unending but vitally important process. It is essential to the proper viewing and understanding of the garden and to preserving the original design. It is a paradox, perhaps, that the garden is designed to represent nature, and that nature is in constant change—and while seasonal change is embraced and emphasized in a garden, the garden is painstakingly maintained to remain timeless in the face of continuous change.

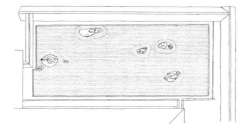

Opposite left Brightly blooming azaleas fill a view of a small courtyard garden.

Opposite right A rocky waterfall in a stroll garden creates background sound of splashing water, and stone stairs draw visitors to the water's edge.

Top An unusual composition of rocks and swirling raked gravel fills a courtyard garden at the Tōfukuji Temple in Kyoto.

Center An example of *mitate* or seeing anew, a millstone amidst set other stepping stones, is suddenly familiar and surprises the visitor into seeing both the garden and the millstone with fresh eyes.

Above, figure 38 A plan drawing of the dry garden at Ryōanji Temple in Kyoto reveals the relationship of the five groupings of stone, which are designed to hide one stone from view from any seated viewing position.

Chapter 19
Entrance gates

The purpose of a gate (*mon*) ostensibly is to create an opening in a fence or wall that can be controlled—opened and closed—as needed. This is accurate in so far as it represents the gate in its most practical function. However, gates can be more than mere entries—for example, a gate can be suggestive of something beyond, whether visible through it or not. In this way, a gate can be symbolic of another realm outside one's own. A gate is a threshold and can signal a change in attitude or stance, which is the particular purpose of the gate in a tea garden.

The way a gate is constructed affects the way it is perceived. A tall and wide gate made of solid wood planks held together with en-graved metal straps can be imposing, a show of wealth and power. The size of the gate may imply that a carriage can pass through and suggests that there is much more beyond it. On the other hand, a low gate of loosely woven strips of bamboo, which affords views through as well as over it, hardly hides what is beyond, nor does it keep out anyone or anything. Yet, it suggests an occasion for pause, creating a moment for reflection and attention when passing from one side of it to the other.

The *torii* gate of a *shintō* shrine is similarly a signal of change—a threshold from one place to another. In this case, the threshold marks the boundary of the sacred space of a *shintō* shrine in relationship to the world outside of it. A *torii* has no door and does not serve as a physical barrier. Yet, when one walks through a *torii*, whether human-scaled like many of the *torii* which march up the hillside behind the Fushimi Inari Shrine in Kyoto or grand like those at the Ise Shrine, the passage through marks a change in attitude.

Opposite A refined bamboo fence abuts the rough columns and beams of the entrance gate to the Shisendō Temple in Kyoto. **Left** Thick stone walls and a heavy roof comprise a defensive gate at Shuri Castle in Okinawa. **Below** With a framed view of the trees and sky, wide stone stairs lead up to the large entrance gate of the Hōnenin Temple in Kyoto.

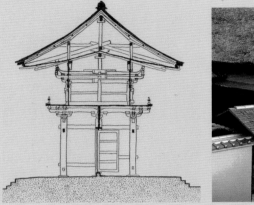

Above left, figure 39 A section drawing shows the raised podium foundation and elaborate wood structure typical of a temple gate.
Above right A single column and a simple shingle roof signify the entrance to a traditional inn.
Right A gate leading to a tea garden within a larger garden has delicate latticed bamboo doors, which create a sense of threshold without blocking the view through the gate.

Gates certainly were in use in Japan before the introduction of Buddhism in the sixth century, but their prevalence and variety of forms greatly expanded as the Chinese Buddhist architectural forms spread throughout Japan. Gates are important features of Buddhist temple complexes, as can be seen in the elaborate Great South Gate (Nandaimon) of the Tōdaiji Temple in Nara. Rebuilt in 1199 after fires and wars, the gate is set up on a high stone podium reached by a run of stairs, and has an exposed timber frame structure holding up a heavy ceramic tile roof. The most imposing element of the gate is the elaborate bracketing joined to the columns, which support the extended roof eaves. The gate is grand and imposing—a proper style for the temple that was built to be the main Buddhist temple in Japan at the time.

The Buddhist temple complex incorporates a series of gates on an axis leading from outside through enclosed courtyards to the main temple complex. The axial layout and series of gates and courtyards were brought into use in imperial and aristocratic architecture, although the axiality and symmetry virtually disappeared by the Edo period, as the architecture was transformed over time.

As noted above, gates can range from being small and open to large and closed, depending on the intended use and effect. The largest, most imposing, and elaborate gates are those of Buddhist temples, as the gates represent a change from the outside or profane world to that of the sacred Buddhist precinct. Historically, temples were not only places of worship but also acted as universities and frequently as political bodies, and the gates were built almost like rooms, with floors and roofs, but with only a central wall flanking the gate.

Likewise, castle gates were the public face of a fortress and needed to impart an appropriate sense of power and strength in addition to serving as an important defense mechanism. Castle gates are elaborate structures incorporating gatehouses and guardhouses surrounding heavily fortified doors of thick wood panels reinforced with heavy metal straps.

Imperial villas and the houses of wealthy aristocrats have scaled-down versions of temple and castle gates, some of which also incorporate gatehouses or elaborate roofs. The gates typically are found on the south side of the dwelling. The reason for this—it originates in the layout of the Chinese Buddhist temple complexes—is that a building having southern exposure gets a good amount of light. Therefore, many buildings were designed with gardens or courtyards on the south, enclosed by a fence or wall and with a gate at the southern edge, often on an axis with the ceremonial front door. These gates are large and solid, although smaller than temple and castle gates but sizeable enough to block the view and control the entrance.

Other dwellings, both in the city and in the countryside, have gates that are smaller and less imposing. However, they are large enough to block the view and often have a small roof

Above Raised up on a high stone podium foundation, the Nandaimon Great South Gate at Tōdaiji Temple in Nara has a monumental timber structure supporting long ceramic tile-covered roofs.

Above right The stepping stone path leads through an inner gate with a view of a courtyard garden at Shisendō Temple in Kyoto.

Below A gently vaulted opening appears to be carved out of the thick rubble walls of the Zakimi Castle ruins in Okinawa.

Right A low wood fence blocks entry to the gate of a subtemple set into the earthen plaster walls of the Hōryū-ji Temple complex in Nara.

Above The large timbers of a temple gate are marked with the names of businesses wishing for good fortune.
Far left Layers of refined wood structure supporting cedar shingles and a thick roof of rice straw thatch create a sophisticated tiered composition.
Left Thick columns joined to intricate systems of wood bracketing hold up the heavy roof of the Nandaimon Great South Gate at Tōdaiji Temple in Nara.

for protection from the rain. These gates, too, are symbolic of the social status and wealth of the owner. Gates also can be found within some dwelling complexes, used to separate different areas of the garden or to set off the tea garden. These gates tend to be less solid and imposing and often are constructed using materials in a rustic manner, conveying an image that is more picturesque than powerful. Many of these gates are as symbolic as they are practical, creating a threshold that suggests movement from one world to the next.

Construction

The materials used to construct gates are very similar to the materials used in the construction of houses and other traditional Japanese buildings. Stone, wood, mud and lime plasters, and ceramic tile, as well as lightweight materials such as bamboo and reeds, generally are utilized in gate construction. The methods by which the materials are used in gates also are very similar to the ways they are used in buildings, starting with the foundation and ending with the roof.

The basic elements needed to construct a gate are two columns, which often are connected at the top with a beam but may be supported from the sides. Many gates have one or two doors within the space between the columns, and these may have hinges or be on tracks for sliding. Gates, such as those at Buddhist temple complexes, may be lifted above the ground on a stone foundation or podium, sometimes with a wood beam resting on the ground at the base of the doors, or the doors may hover just above the ground, with a stone pathway flowing underneath. Gateways on stone podia or with wood beams or tracks below the doors require the act of stepping up or over, indicating a threshold that induces an awareness of place and change of attitude (figure 39).

The columns typically are made of wood but in a few rare cases may be a combination of wood and stone, such as those at the gate at Hōnenin Temple in Kyoto. Since stone is less pervious to moisture, it is advantageous to have stone below the wood part of a column. For this reason, many wood columns are set

on stone bases (*soseki*). The columns may hold up a roof with a bamboo or wood structure—an elaborate construction of brackets and beams in some cases or a simple truss in others. The roof may be surfaced with wood planks, shakes, shingles, cedar bark, thatch, or ceramic tile.

The doors of the gates customarily are constructed from wood, bamboo, reeds, or a combination of those materials, joined together with hardware (metal nails and straps) or tied with rope. A door may be a single wood panel, a series of planks attached along their lengths, or a wood frame filled with thin strips of wood in a woven pattern or a lattice of bamboo. There are innumerable combinations of materials and methods of using the materials to create gate doors. The creativity and fine craft that goes into the construction of a door (and a gate) is an important aspect of the gate, as placing a hand on the door of the gate is often a visitor's first interaction with the household.

Below Anthropomorphic stone columns contrast with the delicate wood doors of a gate to a private residence. **Bottom** Wide wood plank doors pivot open on hinges to allow entry to the Hōnenin Temple garden in Kyoto.

Chapter 20
Garden walls

The **primary purpose of a wall** is to enclose a space. Unlike a fence, which is light and often perforated, a wall is solid and frequently heavy. Some walls are designed for protection, others for privacy. Openings in walls may be for defensive purposes or they simply may allow a view. Walls can have unusual openings, as in the geometrically shaped apertures in the thick plaster walls surrounding Himeji Castle. The circular, triangular, and square openings are designed for defense—the openings diminish in size from the outside face of the wall to the inside, making it much easier to shoot from the inside out than from the outside in.

Walls in the landscape can serve as guides, leading into and through spaces and directing views. A wall may act as a backdrop, marking the edge of a garden, for example, but also providing an additional layer of color and texture. One such example is the earthen wall at the garden at the Ryōanji Temple in Kyoto. It demarcates two sides of the rectangular garden, but more than that, its construction of mud, wood, and ceramic tile is expressive of time. The discoloration, disintegration, and repair marks of the wall convey a sense of history. It is an important feature of the garden, containing the raked pea gravel ground plane and contrasting the clean whiteness of the gravel and adjacent lime plaster wall with its soft aged appearance. The wall also sets the small dry garden apart from the expansive green of the larger garden beyond.

Like gates, walls, especially retaining walls used to terrace rice paddies, certainly were in use before Buddhism was introduced in Japan, but the Buddhist temple complexes incorporated elaborate systems of walls to create covered walkways surrounding courtyards

within the complexes. One wall serves as the outermost edge of the compound, and other walls separate spaces within the complex. This layout of walled courtyards and compounds was incorporated into the design of imperial and aristocratic residences, which often included expansive tracts of land.

For houses in the countryside, a solid wall often is built around the perimeter of the property, or at least around the perimeter of the house and garden (figure 40). City houses of a certain class may have small front courtyards or gardens, and walls are used in the same way to demarcate the edge of the property. The wall and the gate together give an impression of the owner's social status, and therefore the materials and methods of construction used to build the wall play an important role.

Opposite A tall pine tree and the peak of a temple roof are visible over the earthen wall at Daitokuji Temple.
Top, figure 40 Aristocratic residential compounds had multiple buildings, gardens, and walled courtyards.
Above The refined rammed earth walls of the Ryōanji Temple in Kyoto stand on a continuous stone foundation.
Below Delicate wood grilles filter views through the majestic wall surrounding the Cloister Gallery at the Daibutsuden Great Buddha Hall of Tōdaiji Temple in Nara.

The most prevalent type of landscape wall wraps the edge or boundary of a property to separate it from adjacent land. This type of wall is often high, above eye level, and appears very solid, as is the case of most walls around temple complexes. However, sometimes the high part of the wall only occurs along the front edge of the property, and the wall is lower along the sides and back. Therefore, the wall is as much as—if not more—a symbol of privacy as it is a practical measure.

Walls that are meant to truly keep people out are those found at castles, and they are built to withstand enemy attack, with heavy timber construction and a thickly plastered finish. These walls often wind their way in the landscape, directing movement through hairpin turns and into narrow passages, making entrance into the castle difficult.

Another type of wall that relates closely to the land is the retaining wall, especially where it is used to create and support terraces for rice farming and other agriculture. Retaining walls are dug into the earth and support high ground on one side, while being exposed on the other.

Although most frequently used for practical purposes, such as terracing the ground for agricultural fields, retaining walls also sometimes are used for aesthetic purposes. For example, at the Shūgakuin Imperial Villa in Kyoto, the expansive garden is set into a hilly landscape, which was manipulated through the use of retaining walls to create terraced rice paddies and a dike to support a raised pond. The retaining walls serve a practical purpose, as the rice paddies are farmed, however the whole scene was created for its aesthetic effect.

Within temple complexes or large affluent residential compounds, walls are used to separate different areas of the complex, not only for the purpose of keeping people out but also for visual effect. Like the wall at Ryōanji described above, these walls act as sculptural elements within the garden and the landscape, directing the view and setting off other elements through contrasting color, texture, and form. The walls often are the backdrop for plantings within the gardens, as a bright white lime plaster wall sets off the green leaves and red blossoms of a camellia very beautifully.

Top A steep stone foundation supports a wood and lime plaster defensive wall at the Kumamoto Castle on Kyūshū Island.
Center Creating a composition of horizontal lines, the striated plaster garden wall of the Kaidanin Temple Ordination Hall at Tōdaiji Temple in Nara sits on a long stone foundation and is covered with a ceramic tile roof.
Above Rough blocks of stone provide a foundation for a textured earthen plaster wall in a temple complex.
Right Tall stone foundations and white lime plaster walls topped with *kawara* tile roofs create a defensive barrier between the outer guard buildings at Himeji Castle.

Construction

The materials used to construct landscape walls vary little from the materials used for interior walls, although some materials, especially mud plasters, must be protected from the rain and snow in order to last well. One material that is found in a few exterior walls but not in interior walls is rammed earth (*hanchiku*). The beauty of rammed earth lies in the striations that occur from the layers of earth tamped together to form the wall. Stones, roof tiles, and other objects can be tamped into the earth to give extra texture and coloration. Despite its beauty, rammed earth is not appropriate for most interior walls as it is structurally weak in earthquakes. But as an exterior wall material, especially for a freestanding garden wall, it offers a beautiful texture and color not found in other types of walls.

Many exterior walls are constructed with a wood post-and-beam frame filled in with a bamboo lath and finished with mud or lime plaster. Sometimes the wood columns are left exposed between the plaster panels; at other times the columns are covered over with plaster. Lime plaster walls are bright white and often are used to contrast the colors of the plants and stones in a garden. The color of mud plaster walls, however, is softer and more subtle, ranging from yellow-green to brown to reddish orange. Mud plaster walls can be used to accent the elements in a garden or to blend in with them. Most plaster walls are constructed with stone foundations so that the mud plaster does not touch the earth and does not absorb moisture from the ground. Many plaster walls also have attached ceramic tile roofs to protect them from the weather.

Stone walls, on the other hand, do not need protection from the weather. Stone walls can be made with one type of stone, all cut to the

same size and shape, different types of stone in varying sizes and shapes, or any combination thereof. Stone walls can be high or low, depending on need, although high stone walls generally require greater thickness for structural stability. Many stone walls in Japan are dry-laid—the stones are carefully fitted together without the use of any mortar. The tall curving walls at the Kumamoto Castle or at various castle ruins in Okinawa are excellent examples of this highly refined construction.

Landscape walls occasionally are constructed with large wood planks attached vertically to a wood frame or columns. These walls normally have stone foundations to raise the wood above the level of the damp ground and may have roofs made of wood or covered with ceramic tiles. The wood plank walls may be constructed with the planks attached on only one side of the columns, or the planks may alternate sides, allowing air and a glimpse of light to pass through.

Top left A playful outer wall at the Daitokuji Temple complex in Kyoto has white lime plaster walls inlaid with ceramic tiles.
Top right Yellow leaves complement the yellow plaster wall at the Kotohiragū Shrine on Shikoku Island.
Above left Wide wood planks fill in between knotted wood columns set on large base stones within a stone rubble foundation.
Above right Rows of salvaged roof tiles add texture and color to a rough earthen plaster wall.

Chapter 21
Fences

Fences perform many different roles in traditional Japanese gardens. Like walls, fences are used to divide and enclose spaces, but unlike walls, fences are light and often perforated. Some fences do create solid physical and visual barriers, as most walls do. However, many fences are built low to the ground and do not act as actual physical barriers, and many are constructed with openings between the materials that allow the view to extend through the fence and beyond. If a fence is not meant as a physical or visual barrier, what then is its role?

A fence can delineate a boundary and suggest a change in place. For example, often a tea garden—a garden designed in conjunction with a tea ceremony house (figure 41)— is divided into an inner and an outer garden. The two parts of the garden may be separated by a simple low fence, perhaps constructed of thin bamboo poles tied together in a loose diagonal grid pattern. This type of fence does little to block the view, and although it has a gate to denote the place of entry and provide a sense of entering, it is almost low enough to step over. Here, the fence merely marks the boundary between two parts of the garden. It is a device that reinforces the mind-set of the tea ceremony, as it is the threshold between two layers of space, relating to the outer world and the inner world, that must be traversed to enter into the teahouse.

In other situations, fences are employed not to enclose or mark boundaries but rather as freestanding objects in a garden. In this case, a fence may be used to set off other garden elements, to block the view beyond a particular place, or to be a focal point within the garden. One example of this is the so-called "lying cow"

fence (*gagyū-gaki*, also known as *kōetsu-gaki*) at the Kōetsuji Temple garden in Kyoto. Constructed of a long bundle of split bamboo and bamboo poles topping an open lattice of split bamboo, the fence starts high and swoops to the ground in a long gentle curve. The fence itself is a beautiful, finely crafted object and complements the surrounding greenery, yet its unusual form makes it a focal point.

Similarly, the *sodegaki* or "sleeve fence," like many of the other types of fences, is ornamental but also has a function. The *sodegaki* is a short fence that serves as an extension of a wall, either the wall of a building or a garden wall, or it may extend from a larger fence. It can serve to hide a certain feature of the house or garden or to block a view.

It is difficult to classify fences, as there are so many different variations. In the words of

Above A simple bamboo fence directs the view along a stone path at the Kotōin Subtemple of the Daitokuji Temple complex in Kyoto.
Opposite above, figure 41 An outer wall surrounds a tea garden with a less substantial fence separating the inner and outer gardens.
Right A stone path leads to a teahouse through a delicate bamboo gate and fence, which create a threshold between the outer and inner gardens.

Edward Morse, a late nineteenth-century chronicler of Japanese houses and gardens, "The variety in design and structure of fences seems almost inexhaustible. Many of them are solid and durable structures, others of the lightest possible description—the one made with solid frame and heavy stakes, the other of wisps of rush and sticks of bamboo; and between these two is an infinite variety of intermediate forms."[8] Fences can be understood by their uses, but as with walls and gates, all are both ornamental and functional. As noted previously, some create physical or visual barriers, while others suggest a delineation of space. Some fences provide focal points, where others serve as the background for objects within the garden. Some fences indicate direction, delineating the edge of a path, while others can block a path and, together with a gate, suggest—or prescribe—a place of entry.

Construction

Fences in Japanese gardens developed later than walls; they were first used extensively in the Kamakura period (1185–1332) and then in the tea garden.[9] In some cases, fences act quite similarly to walls. However, they are lighter and generally less permanent in their construction and are understood as having a much more temporal quality, as do the plantings in the garden. Because they are constructed primarily from natural materials, fences easily can blend into a garden. Their color often changes over time, and they slowly decompose as the weather wears down the materials. This act of decomposition is not seen negatively, rather, it is understood as part of the natural cycle of all living things. The idea of finding beauty in the transitory nature of life, *aware*, is an important aesthetic concept in Japanese culture.

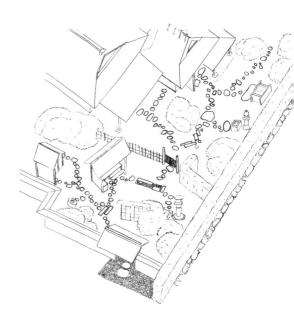

Top left The unusual *gagyū-gaki* "lying cow" fence at the Kōetsuji Temple in Kyoto has crisscrossed bamboo topped with a bundle of bamboo strips that slowly slope toward the ground.

Top center A rope carefully knotted around a wood post creates a simple fence.

Top right Tall strips of bamboo reinforced with bamboo battens provide a boundary and a backdrop in a bamboo forest.

Above A moveable wood fence blocks the stone path, which has overlapping arched strips of bamboo creating a delicate fence on one side and strips of bamboo holding bamboo poles on top of wood posts on the other.

Fences can be categorized by their physical form and construction. They can be tall, imparting a strong impression of a physical or visual barrier, or they can be low, offering a suggestion of a demarcation of space. Fences can be built to appear solid and completely block a view, or they can be very open to allow space and views to pass through. Fences can be continuous to enclose a space or create a boundary, or they can be freestanding elements that act as objects within the space of the garden.

A fence can also be constructed from many different materials—wood, bamboo, reeds, even living plants, or any combination of these. Often the main structure of a fence is wood—wood stakes driven into the ground or a framework of wood set on the ground and held up by wood bracing. Between the structure, or sometimes covering the structure, are wood planks or panels of bamboo or reeds. Wood planks might span horizontally from column to column, or a secondary horizontal structure can be used to support vertical wood planks, which may be attached on alternating sides, giving the fence two fronts rather than a front and a back.

The most elaborate fences combine panels of different materials to create lively compositions. Simpler fences are constructed with one material, often bamboo which is easy to work, light in weight, and can be cut and manipulated in innumerable ways. Bamboo can be used whole, as single poles or in bundles. It can be split into halves and tied to other materials to hold the pieces in place, or it can be split into strips which can be woven, bent, or bundled. Reeds can be lined up vertically or horizontally as a single thin layer held between bamboo poles, or they can be tied into stiff bundles and used as vertical elements, almost like columns. One ingenious style of fence uses living plants (bamboo or reeds) as a vertical panel-like element held in place with horizontal bamboo poles tied onto the front and back. This type of fence cleverly bridges between the living cultivated elements of a garden and those that are brought into the garden from outside and fixed in place.

The maintenance of fences is an important aspect of their use and the way in which they are understood in a garden. Fences are valued for having a temporal quality, and the visible aging of a fence is considered a normal and natural part of a garden. However, fences are not left to disintegrate; rather, they are maintained and when necessary are replaced. As certain parts of a fence decay, those parts are repaired or replaced. When fences outlive their usefulness, they are removed and reconstructed. Just as the aging of a fence is not considered an eyesore in a garden, the fresh quality and bright color of a new fence is not regarded to be out of place, as gardens are appreciated for their seasonal changes and the awareness of time that those changes evoke.

Top left Two bamboo rails overlap at a corner where a strip of bamboo attaches them to a wood post.
Top right A row of roof tiles protects the top of a fence constructed from tall strips of bamboo.
Below left A thin bamboo batten is tied between halved bamboo poles.
Below right Tied together with black rope, a diagonal lattice of bamboo strips creates a sense of boundary without impeding the view.

Chapter 22
Paths

The role of a path in a garden initially seems a straightforward matter. Typically, paths allow the observer to move through the garden and to be led to different areas within the garden in order to see various elements and views while keeping one's feet clean. But paths have a much more complex role in the garden than serving the practical function of permitting and aiding movement. The material and the style employed serve an aesthetic function by contributing to the degree of formality desired by the garden designer. The historic development of the garden path illustrates the crucial function of the path in the observer's understanding of a garden.

The earliest known gardens in Japan were designed in the Heian period (794–1185) and were used for leisurely amusement at aristocratic residences. The period was one of relative peace and prosperity, and the gardens featured boating ponds and pleasure pavilions. The designs were based on classical Chinese gardens, which often were large and sprawling. Oceans with craggy seaside cliffs, groves of pine trees and winding mountain streams, and other features of nature were miniaturized and expressed in exaggerated form. People interacted with the gardens, not only enjoying the views of them from inside the residences, but exploring the ponds on small boats and strolling to the pavilions for social activities such as poetry writing contests and afternoon tea. Paths allowed viewers to move through the garden from house to pavilion and to enjoy the varied views and elements of the garden.

From the late medieval period (1185–1573), gardens developed into two distinct types, those meant to be moved through, typically known as "stroll gardens," and those meant

Above right A stone path follows the perimeter of a raked gravel bed at the Kaidanin Temple Ordination Hall at Tōdaiji Temple in Nara.
Below right A narrow gravel path leads to a stone bridge in the garden of the Shūgakuin Imperial Villa in Kyoto.
Below Appearing to part the ocean, a formal stone path on an axis with a subtemple entrance leads between two narrow gardens of raked gravel, rock groupings, and manicured moss and trees at the Nanzenji Temple complex in Kyoto.

for viewing from a fixed (usually interior) position, sometimes called "scroll gardens." Both types reflected a move away from the earlier Chinese-style gardens with an incorporation of a more Japanese aesthetic, just as the architecture of the time was changing from its strictly Chinese-inspired forms toward a more Japanese "taste." The late medieval period gardens contain many of the same elements of the earlier gardens, but the two types of gardens use the elements in very different ways.

"Scroll" gardens rarely include paths. But when they do, the path—perhaps a mossy stair or a few stepping stones—is meant purely as a visual connection to a place beyond, not for physical use. In stroll gardens, on the other hand, paths are essential for experiencing and understanding the garden. Paths began to be designed with specific aesthetic qualities that also control movement and view. This concept was fully realized in the feudal period (1573–1868), when political and social stability led to a high level of development in all the traditional Japanese arts.

Every single element of the traditional Japanese garden is designed and controlled by the hand of man to provide an ever-changing experience of long and short views, simple compositions of similar elements and complex compositions of contrasting elements, visual references to famous places and scenes in literature—all in a unified composition that changes with the seasons. Paths are designed to reinforce these experiences. A wide smooth path allows for easy movement and a simultaneous wide view of the garden. A rough path of stepping stones constricts movement, especially since the visitor historically was dressed in *kimono* (which, especially for women, limits the length of a step) and *geta* (wooden sandals). An uneven path requires careful attention to where one steps, and the visual focus is on the path rather than the garden. Large flat stones within the path provide points of pause, where one can look up and observe a particular view or garden element that appears as a surprise, since the focus had been solely on the ground. Thus, the path is an essential and invaluable element in designing the experience of the garden.

Above Crossing rounded stepping stones in a *kimono* and sandals requires care and awareness, creating a heightened sensory experience of the garden.

Above, figure 42 Following typical rules of Japanese aesthetics, stone paths are compositions ranging from formal (*shin*) to semi-formal (*gyō*) to informal (*sō*).

Above left A very informal stone path meanders through the Anrakuji Temple garden in Kyoto.

Center left Millstones create a surprising path of stepping stones.

Below left Wide stones lead through a tall bamboo forest.

Left Wide stairs of random stone edged with long blocks of granite are set at an angle to the gate to the Hōnenin Temple in Kyoto.

Below Rectangular stones connect at the corner or slip past each other to create an informal path through a moss garden.

Construction

A garden path may be a simple tamped earth walkway, but more often paths are constructed of stone or perhaps incorporate pieces of old roof tile. Examples of paths using wood or bamboo can be found, but they are rare, since the dampness of the earth causes the materials to deteriorate. When wood and bamboo are utilized, however, they generally are placed as block-like elements in groups. Chunks of wood or short lengths of bamboo are driven into the ground, to the same height and close to one another, creating a rough walking surface with a beautiful pattern. In the same way, old roof tiles are set into the ground vertically, sometimes one placed right next to the other to form a continuous surface, and at other times separated with soil and moss to create softer, cloud-like configurations.

The most common material used for garden paths is stone. Stone is strong and durable and can be fashioned into various sizes and forms, making it the most appropriate material for a walking surface. Different types of stone are used for garden paths, but the most usual is granite, which has a consistent color and composition. Like other path materials, stone is laid into the ground with soil packed around it to form a stable surface. Before this can be done, however, it is necessary to compact the soil beneath the path and sometimes provide a layer of sand to create an even surface. No mortar or other adhesive is used to fix the stone in place; the compaction of the soil around it and the weight of the stone secure it.

Stone can be used in its natural state or it can be cut or chiseled to almost any desired shape. The way each stone is worked and the arrangement of stones together in a path reflect different levels of formality—*shin* (formal), *gyō* (semiformal), and *sō* (informal)—which are essential to the traditional arts of Japan (figure 42). A formal path might consist of stones cut into rectangular or square shapes and used in straight lines, or perhaps the path surface might be just a single hewn stone plank. A semiformal path combines dressed stone with rough stones or roof tiles in an asymmetrical yet bounded composition. An informal path might use large flat unfinished stones of various shapes and sizes to create a walking surface, or the oddly shaped stones might be used as stepping stones, composed to suggest the right-left-right-left movement of walking.

Paths can be opportunities to create a sense of surprise by incorporating a recognizable object, frequently a millstone or a column base stone (*soseki*), into the path. The sight of the known object, out of its typical context yet functioning as an important element within the composition of the path, causes the viewer to see the object and the path, and therefore the whole garden, in a new way. This act of "re-seeing" or "seeing anew" (*mitate*) is an important design device in Japanese gardens.

Paths are used to reinforce other design devices, such as hide-and-reveal where the viewer is given a glimpse of a garden element in the distance (a beautiful tree or composition of rocks, for example) but then is led away by the path. Later, the path leads back to the previously viewed element, revealing it at close distance after having hidden it from the viewer.

Garden paths also are an important part of connecting the garden to the architecture, as it is the path that makes the actual physical connection between building and nature. Some paths widen as they draw near a building, perhaps ending with a large stone to step up to the *engawa*. Other paths become more formal as they approach a building, reflecting the formality of the architecture as opposed to the less formal and more naturalistic character of the garden.

Top Large stepping stones lead through a stone "beach" to the water's edge.
Above Rough stones line a gently winding path in the Yoshikien Garden in Nara.

Chapter 23
Bridges

Bridges in Japanese gardens very often are admired for their graceful curves and fine craftsmanship. Their primary role ostensibly is for movement, connecting a path on one side of a body of water to another on the other side. But bridges do more than that— they also provide views as many are designed to rise vertically as well as span horizontally. The views from these bridges may vary greatly from the land-based views on either side, especially because of the increased height. Bridges also can be the objects of views as they are large enough to be visible from a distance and can be constructed as focal points within the garden. For example, the half-circle shaped "full moon" bridge (*engetsukyō*) in the Koishikawa Korakuen Garden in Tokyo is meant to be viewed from a distance, so the reflection of the bridge in the water combines with the bridge itself to form a complete circle.

Bridges were important elements in the Chinese gardens which influenced the first gardens built in Japan. Chinese-style bridges tend to be ornate geometric forms that provide a strong formal contrast to the exaggerated naturalistic forms of the plants and rocks in the gardens. Early Japanese gardens did indeed copy these bridges, but as gardens in Japan changed and developed over the centuries, the forms of bridges also changed to reflect the taste of the times.

Although Chinese-style bridges continued to be used, they often were utilized in order to make a clear reference to China in contrast to the more Japanese elements in the garden. For example, the Chitosebashi ("thousand year" bridge) in the garden at the Shūgakuin Imperial Villa in Kyoto is constructed in the Chinese style with pyramidal roofs at each end

linked by a covered path. Its use in the garden is as an exotic element that implies a connection to China. Such geographical allusions as well as literary references would have been well understood at the time by the aristocratic users of the garden. One such literary reference found in many gardens is the eight-plank bridge (*yatsuhashi*, figure 43), a bridge constructed of eight boards of wood or stone planks laid with their ends overlapping, suggestive of the landscape known as "eight bridges" described in the tenth-century classic, *Ise monogatari*.[10]

In addition to reinforcing geographic and literary references, a bridge can suggest a path to a world beyond. In some cases, a bridge connecting an island to the mainland of a garden was designed purely to be viewed from a distance and physically cannot be reached or crossed. It gives the suggestion of something beyond, close but not yet within reach. Such bridges may be used as a reference to Buddhist ideas of the Pure Land (*jōdoshū*, a popular school of Buddhist thought in the Heian period), a paradise reachable only by living according to the Buddhist tenets.

By the height of the development of Japanese gardens in the Edo period, bridges had moved well beyond their original Chinese-inspired forms and reflected the taste of the era, combining and contrasting refined shapes with rustic forms and complex structures with simple constructions. Even within a single garden, there may be a dozen or more different types of bridges, some designed as important focal points within the garden, others designed primarily to move the viewer from one place to another. Despite its shape or complexity, a bridge always suggests movement and connection, and the act of crossing a bridge is a conscious act of leaving the ground in one place and crossing over to another.

Construction

The materials that are used to lift one above the ground on a bridge typically are wood or stone. Bamboo also can be used but is not as permanent. When wood is utilized, it often is supported on a stone foundation to keep the wood above the water and the damp ground.

Above A craggy rock supports the two huge stone slabs of the Togetsukyō Bridge in the Rikugien Garden in Tokyo.
Below left A curved stone slab stretches from the bank of the pond to the flat surface of a huge block of stone in the Rinsen Garden at the Kotohiragū Shrine in Shikoku Island.
Below right An early twentieth-century stone bridge comprises a playful circular arch.
Bottom left Wood columns and beams support the gentle arch of the earth-covered log Yamakagebashi Bridge at Rikugien Garden in Tokyo.
Bottom right Stepping stones lead to low steps on a gracefully arching bridge lined with moss in the garden of the Katsura Imperial Villa in Kyoto.

Wooden bridges can be complex constructions of multiple wood members, with wood decks, railings, and even roofs. They can be either painted red or left unpainted. The Chitose-bashi at the Shūgakuin Imperial Villa noted above has a complex wooden roof supported by wood columns on a stone deck. Wooden bridges also can take simple forms, such as the gently curving wood trestle bridge that spans the pond to the teahouse island in the Ritsurin Garden in Shikoku. The bridge is composed of many small wooden members that combine to create the gently arched walkway and elegant handrail.

At the other end of the spectrum is the simple wood plank bridge—one or two planks (or as many as eight in the case of the eight-plank bridge described previously) laid horizontally to span over a body of water. If two planks are used, they usually are laid side by side with a slight shift along their lengths. One plank touches one side of the land, and the other plank touches the other side, with the two planks connected at the middle.

Many bridges that are constructed of wood also can be replicated in stone, including complex joinery carved out of stone. Large stone bridges tend to be very formal, with the stone carefully cut and finished. However, smaller stone bridges are likely to be rather informal, with the stone left in a more natural-istic form. It is not uncommon to encounter a single simple stone plank to cross a small stream or a stone version of the wooden two-plank bridge.

The shifted two-plank bridge is only one of a number of simple but ingenious bridge configurations that can be found in Japanese gardens. There are gently curving bridges covered with cedar bark, earth and moss (*dobashi*), such as the bridge connecting an island to the bank of the Ōgonchi Pond in the Saihōji Garden in Kyoto. Many of these bridges are designed for one person to cross at a time. However, there also are wider bridges, like the roofed Chitosebashi at the Shūgakuin Garden, that provide ample space for people to gather and watch the colorful carp swimming in the pond. These bridges suggest leisurely comfort, with wide planks and handrails at the proper

height for leaning and looking out over the pond and garden. They are a point of pause along a path. Other bridges are "faster" and might create a slight sensation of fear or excitement because they are narrow and have no handrail. This kind of bridge typically accommodates only one person at a time and produces a moment of self-reflection after crossing and reaching solid ground.

The experience of crossing a bridge therefore is as important as both the physical beauty of the bridge itself and the aesthetic quality of the composition of the bridge within the garden. Like a path, a bridge directs movement and visual focus and provides a connection between different elements in a garden. Both paths and bridges can reflect different levels of formality and informality and can be designed for easy movement or for focused effort. Whereas a path is understood more as a two-dimensional element, a part of the ground, a bridge is clearly a three-dimensional object. Unlike a path, a bridge elevates one above water or rough ground and therefore has the potential to heighten the senses through the act of leaving the ground.

Top left Stone supports lift the wooden Nakajima Bridge above a tidal seawater pond in the Hamarikyū Garden in Tokyo.

Top right The heavy stone foundations of the Chinese-style Chitosebashi Bridge in the Shūgakuin Imperial Villa garden support a roofed wood structure.

Opposite below With its complex structure and vermilion color, the Tsūtenkyō Bridge is a striking element in Tokyo's Koishikawa Korakuen Garden.

Above left The Ringyōbashi Bridge is a grand stone and wood structure over the Shimoyama River near Hayama.

Left The complex Keyakibashi Bridge in the Kyoto Imperial Palace garden has elaborately carved ends projecting from the wood support beams.

Above right, figure 43 A wooden *yatsuhashi* eight-plank bridge zigzags through a wet landscape.

Right Overlapping planks create a meandering *yatsuhashi* bridge.

Chapter 24
Gravel courtyards

Gravel courts first entered Japan from China with the introduction of Buddhism and its accompanying architectural forms. Court-yards covered with white gravel were used in Chinese imperial complexes to properly set off formal buildings and provide expansive space for large public activities and gatherings. Similarly, gravel courtyards were integrated into Buddhist temple complexes in China and replicated in the early Chinese-style Buddhist compounds in Japan.

In a typical configuration, the courtyards create open space in front of the main hall and are bounded by covered exterior corridors on three sides, with a formal gate in the center of the south side. The complexes are designed to face south, following geomantic principles, so the courtyard is located on the south side of the main hall, which results in sunlight reflecting off the white gravel into the hall. Pagodas and other buildings in the temple complexes also are located within the expanse of the gravel courtyard. This spatial configuration led to the buildings being understood as objects within space, rather than forms that enclose or create space.[11] It was this layout that was brought intact to Japan in the sixth century. The gravel court allows easy movement between the buildings within the temple complexes and also provides a large gathering space for special events, such as festivals and performances. The traditional Japanese *nō* drama often is performed on a stage built within a gravel courtyard, typically in a temple or shrine complex, with the audience sitting in separate structures across the courtyard.

Gravel courts in Chinese-style Buddhist temples in Japan were designed and used in the same way as they had been in China. However, the architectural forms of the Buddhist temples and the landscape integral to them were eventually appropriated into *shintō* shrine complexes, creating an ambiguity in which the building forms no longer were representative of a specific ideology. This was

understandable, since Buddhism was brought into Japan in way that allowed it to be mostly compatible with the pre-existing vernacular religion of *shintō*. To this day, many Buddhist temple complexes include small *shintō* shrines within them, so the overlap of the two religions remains present from the time Buddhism was first introduced.

The formal gravel court can be seen in early Buddhist temple complexes such as Tōdaiji and Hōryūji in Nara, as well as formal *shintō* shrines like the Heian Shrine in Kyoto, built in 1895 but replicating the Heian-era *shinden* style. Even the Ise Shrine, first constructed in the third century, reflects many of the spatial configurations found in Buddhist architecture, such as axial symmetry, layers of space, formal hierarchy, etc., and also incorporates a court-yard covered with course white gravel within which the important shrine buildings are located. Since the Ise Shrine is completely rebuilt in secret every twenty years, it is not unreasonable to conclude that some elements of the spatial configuration may have been added or altered after Buddhist forms became dominant in Japanese religious architecture.

Development

As garden styles changed and developed in Japan, the white gravel courtyard in its tradi-tional place on the south side of the main hall sometimes was replaced by a pond and garden in the *shinden*-style architecture of the Heian period. The entrance to the main hall could no longer be reached by walking through the courtyard; instead, visitors moved along the garden path and first viewed the hall from across the pond. Rather than light reflecting off the gravel court into the hall, light reflected off the surface of the pond.

The white gravel courtyard, however, did not disappear but was integrated into the garden as one of many design elements and later was transformed into a fundamental component of the traditional Japanese garden. Sometimes the expanse of white gravel is very confined; at other times, it is not so clearly bounded. In some instances, the expanse of gravel is not stepped upon, while in others it provides a place to gather, as is the case in the

garden of the Shūgakuin Imperial Villa in Kyoto. After climbing a gentle hill on a gravel road flanked by pine trees, the road ends in a rigidly bounded gravel courtyard in front of a formal gate. The expanse of white gravel adds to the sense of formality and contrasts with the narrow paths leading through lush greenery on the other side of the gate.

As the style of Japanese temple, shrine, and residential complexes developed and became more asymmetrical and generally less formal, the white gravel courtyard in its original form all but disappeared. In many gardens, it was transformed into a completely different mode, often with strong three-dimensional quali-ties—the raked gravel bed or mound—suggest-ive of flowing elements.

Opposite A long expanse of raked gravel fills the courtyard in front of the gate to an imperial mausoleum on Mount Tsukinowa at Sennyūji Temple in Kyoto.
Top The Jōmeimon Gate of the Kyoto Imperial Palace opens onto a central courtyard covered with white gravel.
Above Rounded gray stones fill a courtyard adjacent to the Honden Main Hall of the Izumo Shrine.

Chapter 25
Raked gravel beds and mounds

The decomposition of symmetry and formality in the Japanese temple, shrine, and residential complexes began with the Heian-period *shinden* style and continued through the later *sukiya* style. It resulted in the transformation of the gravel courtyard from an element that created a foreground for the buildings and plantings, setting them off as objects within space, to a stand-alone sculptural element integral to the spatial composition of the garden.

Rather than covering a great area and surrounding some of the buildings, the white gravel became much more contained and designed. It was no longer simply a surface to walk on. Instead, it was limited in size and shaped to be an element within the garden, taking on symbolic significance. It also was utilized as a clever design device.

Gravel is formed into beds, usually on the ground but sometimes mounded to a height of as much as 1 meter (about 39 inches), and is raked to create a rippled surfaced or occasionally is tamped smooth. As some components within a garden are used to represent elements from natural landscapes, the rippled expanse of white gravel came to be understood as symbolic of the ocean. In some gardens, islands float in a sea of raked white gravel. In others, the gravel ocean is bounded by craggy cliffs and wind-formed pine trees.

The symbolism is clear, yet the forms, especially that of the ocean, are abstract and immobile. This abstraction—the combination of a strong pure geometry, such as the flat plane of the raked gravel, with a naturalistic form of a tree or stone—is integral to the garden composition. In many cases, the gravel bed is the element that connects all parts of the garden, linking seemingly disparate components into a unified whole and providing the impression of a great expanse of space and a sense of continuous movement. The gravel beds are themselves static, of course, but the idea of movement is created through the undulating and curving raked patterns.

Construction

Fine white gravel (*shirakawa-suna*, "White River sand"), a smaller version of the gravel used in the expansive courtyards in temples and shrines, began to be used in the gardens by the fifteenth century. The *shirakawa-suna*, raked into rippling surfaces or formed into mounds (*sunamori*), holds its shape even in a strong rain. One of the best known examples of the use of *shirakawa-suna* is in the dry garden at the Ryōanji Temple in Kyoto (figure 38). The garden features a long rectangle of rippling gravel bounded by walls on three sides and viewed from the abbot's quarters (*hōjō*) on the north side. Within the expanse of gravel are five "islands" of stone and moss. Tall trees behind the south wall provide a variegated green background to the garden. The gravel is raked in straight lines, parallel to the front of the *hōjō* from which the garden is viewed. However, where the gravel meets the stone and moss islands, it is raked around the perimeter of the islands, suggesting, perhaps, the pattern of waves moving against the shoreline.

Left A smooth sand cone is juxtaposed with a ground surface raked in a swirling pattern in the Hōsenin Temple garden in Ōhara.
Right Two sand mounds topped with raked seasonal patterns flank a stone path in the Hōnenin Temple garden in Kyoto.

Other gardens utilize *shirakawa-suna* in a similar way to imply movement—raked into a textured background of rippled grids or swirling waves. There are many examples of different methods for raking and forming gravel beds in gardens. In the Daisenin Subtemple of the Daitokuji Temple complex in Kyoto (which has twenty-four subtemples, each with its own gardens, many of which feature raked and formed gravel beds), *shirakawa-suna* is used differently in each of the four sections of the garden surrounding the abbot's quarters. On the north side, a bounded expanse of white gravel, like a calm sea, contains small islands of stone and plants. On the northeast corner, the ripples of white gravel are in constant motion, slipping through narrow crevices between rocks, rushing around the corner of the building and under a bridge before widening out to a moment of calm on the southeast corner. A large expanse of gravel, as large as the building itself, flanks the south side of the hall with a composition of straight raked lines, parallel to the building, punctuated by two conical gravel mounds with the gravel raked in swoops around them. The final moment of the garden, a small calm expanse of gravel raked parallel to the *hōjō* but perpendicular to the lines of gravel on the south side, anchors the garden on the west.

Although gravel typically is used for horizontal planar surfaces, it can be mounded to create three-dimensional forms. For example, in the Daisenin *hōjō* garden described above, two conical mounds punctuate a long expanse of gravel. At the Ginkakuji Temple garden in Kyoto, a flat-topped smoothly finished cone of gravel (called *Kogetsu-dai*, "moon-facing platform") sits next to an amorphous raised bed of raked gravel (named *Ginsha-nada*, "Silver Sand Sea"), built up to a height of about 60 centimeters (2 feet). The geometries of the two mounds are in stark contrast to the more naturalistic forms in the rest of the garden. The lower mound reflects sunlight into the adjacent building, thus serving both a practical as well as an aesthetic role in the garden.

The raked and mounded gravel requires care and maintenance. Traditionally, it was the job of the young monks to maintain the temple gardens, which included the almost meditative task of raking the gravel each morning. In most cases, the form of the gravel is unchanging, but in a few instances the design changes seasonally. For example, the garden at the Hōnenin Temple in Kyoto features two raised flat-topped mounds of sand, one on each side of the path that leads into the complex from the main inner gate. The designs raked into the top of the mounds always reflect the season, whether cherry blossoms in a swirling sea in the spring or floating maple leaves in the fall. In this way, the mounds serve not only as permanent elements within the garden, they also reflect the season and the ephemeral quality of nature.

No matter how the gravel is used, the contrast of the almost flat white plane of gravel and the three-dimensional compositions of color and texture formed with stones and plants is an important design element in traditional Japanese gardens. Even the mounded gravel takes on a geometry that is different from the raked gravel and creates a tension that sets off the composition and intrigues the viewer, who is drawn into garden and enticed to consider the meaning and mystery inherent in the design.

Right In the early morning sunlight, a monk carefully rakes the gravel courtyard of the Ryōanji Temple garden in Kyoto.

Below Gardens work at many scales. Here, a blade of grass continues the upward extension of a conical sand mound.

Above Shadows wrap around a pair of shallow cones, which sit within an ocean of raked gravel at the Kōdaiji Temple garden in Kyoto.

Center left Contrasting textures and geometries add visual interest and complexity in traditional gardens.

Left The Eikandō Temple garden in Kyoto includes a medley of textures and patterns in the raked gravel beds.

Chapter 26

Stone borders

The sea-like expanses of raked gravel and spans of vegetation, so common in traditional Japanese gardens, are never left unbounded. Such a boundary is created with a contrasting material—a spread of closely clipped azalea hedges, a craggy rock cliff, or a simple border of low stones. This last example, the stone border, is easily overlooked as it is more modest than other elements of the garden, yet it plays an equally important role in the garden design.

The stone border, a narrow line of low stones that separates the garden into two parts or creates an edge, is both a practical element

in the garden and one that aids in the understanding of the space of the garden. Initially utilized in Chinese imperial palace and temple compounds as edging to contain the gravel in the central courtyard, the stone border also began to be used to form gutters to catch the rain falling from the eave of a roof.

Brought to Japan with the Chinese-style Buddhist temple architecture, the stone border continued its functional role as edge and container. As gardens transformed and developed, however, the role of the stone border began to change and expand, and it took on meaning

within the spatial context of the garden. The stone borders began to act as visual guides for understanding movement from one space to the next and underscored the exaggeration of visual depth within the garden. Since many of the gardens are quite small in area, they incorporate the principle of miniaturization and are designed to be understood as being much greater than their actual size.

To achieve this, plants are pruned and trained to look fully grown while in miniature form, and space is layered using different materials (plantings, stones, water) or one

Opposite below A long curb of granite separates moss and river rocks in the Daitokuji Temple complex in Kyoto.
Right A large stepping stone crosses through the granite border, which separates areas of gravel and river rocks.

material in different ways (staggered rows of clipped hedges, for example) to suggest this expansiveness. Each of these layers of space may be bounded by a line of stone, some with perfect geometries and others rough. The stone borders are understood to suggest the change in space, delineating the foreground from the mid-ground and the background.

Construction

Stone is a logical and practical choice for the purpose of creating an edge and containing other materials, as it is the most durable and unchanging of the materials used in gardens. Plants require constant maintenance and care. Water, whether real or represented by gravel, has to be contained in order to control its location and movement—and that easily can be accomplished with a layer of stone.

Stone borders typically are kept low to the ground, with just enough height to contain the area as needed and to make the suggestion of a line within the composition of the garden. Rarely is a stone border designed to be at the visual forefront of the garden; rather borders are designed to be part of the background, as quiet visual clues.

Often the stone border is of a similar material or color to the area it bounds, although sometimes the border creates a strong contrast. Stone borders are used to form gutters to catch rain falling off the edge of a roof or control the water flowing down a hill in a garden. They are used to bound paths as well as to edge expanses of gravel or plants in a garden. The stone often is granite, found commonly in Japan and durable yet able to be cut and formed. Like paths and other elements within the garden, the stone borders follow the levels

Top A narrow border of smooth stone creates a corner transition between a rocky expanse and a clipped hedge.
Center Layers of gravel and small rocks are separated by lines of rough stones.
Above Granite borders mark the edges of the stone surfaces and contain the thick moss in the Daitokuji Temple complex in Kyoto.

of formality found in Japanese aesthetics—*shin-gyō-sō*. Stone borders sometimes are very formal (*shin*), with each stone cut to the same size and shape and laid in a perfectly straight line. Other borders are semiformal (*gyō*), with roughly shaped stones in a straight line, while others are informal (*sō*), with rough stones laid along a curvy, undulating line.

One example of a garden in which all three levels of formality are apparent in the stone borders is the garden of the Ryōanji Temple in Kyoto. The garden surrounding the *hōjō* (abbot's quarters) is divided into two distinct sections, the famous dry garden with its expanse of raked gravel containing five islands of stone and moss on the south side of the hall, and a lush green garden that wraps around the other three sides of the building.

On the side with the dry garden, the rectangular expanse of gravel is contained within a formal edging of stone bounded by a gutter filled with river stones that catches the water running off the roof of the temple building and the roofs of the walls that bound the garden. The stone border that contains the river stones changes from a formal layout on the north and east, where the garden meets the building, to a semiformal edge of rough stone in a straight line on the south and west sides, where the garden is bounded by walls. As the stone borders containing the gutter move around the building, they transform from formal to semiformal and finally to informal at the point where the gutter is furthest from the building and moves into the garden to accept runoff from a small pond. In this way, the stone border is used to contain, to express spatial layers, and also to emphasize the design concept of the garden.

Chapter 27
Rocks and stones

Chinese gardens built at aristocratic residences in the T'ang dynasty incorporated large out-croppings of rock, finely figured from centuries of erosion by wind and rain or intricately carved by swirling ocean currents. These rocks were revered for their form and the figure of the lines within them. Superior examples were prized elements within a garden and were placed in prominent locations. This use of and reverence for rocks was brought from China to Japan with the art of garden design in the sixth century. Initially, rocks were used in a similar way, as the Japanese gardens mimicked those in China. However, as the gardens developed and changed over time, the forms of the rocks and stones[12] and the manner in which they were used in gardens changed as well.

Early garden manuals, secret texts like the eleventh-century *Sakuteiki* ("Memoranda on Garden Making)" and the c. fifteenth-century *Senzui narabi yagyō no zu* ("Illustrations for Designing Mountain, Water, and Hillside Field Landscapes"), explained the important princi-ples of garden design and included examples of the proper use of rock and stone in the garden. The idea of "following the request [of the stone]" (*kowan ni shitagau*)[13]—using rock in a naturalistic way—is an important principle. For example, the explanation in the *Sakuteiki* as to the method of designing a garden stream states, "The placing of stones for a garden stream should start at a place where it makes a turn and flows along. This turn is supposed to have been caused by the presence of this rock which the steam could not demolish. The stream after the turn flows with added momentum and hits hard against the object it encounters. That is the place where you will find the Flow-round Stone (*meguri-ishi*)."[14]

Opposite Stone groupings composed to represent a tortoise and a crane emerge from the clipped hedges of the Raikyūji Temple garden.
Right An old system is given a new twist—a circle filled with rocks in hues of oranges and blues is set into a concrete patio to catch rainwater dripping from a roof.

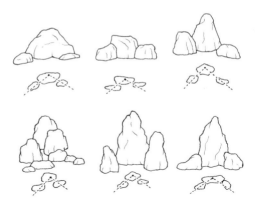

Left, figure 44 Stones often are grouped in triads with asymmetrical but balanced combinations of strong stones and supporting stones.
Right Rough rocks contrast with the smooth surface of the pond in the Sōgen Garden at the Tenryūji Temple in Kyoto.

The teachings of the art of garden design in the *Sakuteiki* also emphasize the need for rocks to be grouped together in harmonious compositions that use each rock in a way that is appropriate for its character. Rocks are understood to have "personalities" that are apparent in their size, shape, and markings. They are named according to these traits and then utilized in combinations that support each other's characters. "In the work of stone arrangement, you should first complete the placing of the principal stone having a distinct character, and then proceed to set other stones complying to the "requesting" mood of the principal stone."[15] For example, a tall rock with strong linear markings may be named a "master" rock, while a small relatively flat rock with few distinctive markings may be called an "attendant" rock. An attendant rock is too weak to stand alone but works well in combination with the stronger master rock and another attendant rock. "The Master Rock looks after its Attendants, and the Attendant Rocks look up to the Master."[16]

Composition

Rocks commonly are grouped in triads, combined to form an asymmetrical triangle in both plan and elevation (figure 44). Though asymmetrical, the triangle is a balanced, stable composition. In a typical grouping, the dominant rock creates the tall point in the middle of the triangle and is flanked by one small stone about one-third of its height, which creates the short side of the triangle, and one long low rock on the other side, creating the

triangle's long side. The combination of the different heights, lengths, and markings of the rocks, together with the distances they are placed from one another, create the stable asymmetrical composition. The asymmetrical yet balanced triangle is an important design principle in the Japanese garden and other cultural arts, such as painting and *ikebana* (flower arrangement).

Depending on the materials that surround them and where they are placed in a garden, groupings of carefully selected rocks are used to represent islands and mountains, even shorelines and waterfalls. As islands, the water, often represented by fine white gravel, is formed to swirl around the rock groupings and eddy, akin to how water acts in nature. As mountains, the groupings are placed on a high point in the garden, perhaps accompanied by a few miniature pine trees, trained and pruned to look windswept.

Rocks are used not only in freestanding groupings but also in many other ways. In some cases, they are used to represent natural features, for example the edge of a craggy seaside cliff or layers of rolling hills. In other instances, rocks are used in a completely different approach, either representational—like the rock used to denote a boat in the swirling ocean of gravel in the Daisenin garden—or symbolic, as when rocks are combined with plants to signify the form of a tortoise or a crane, both legendary symbols of longevity learned from China and frequently incorporated into Japanese garden designs.

Top right A stone with strong striations stands out against a bed of moss.
Second Emerging from the moss, a large flat stone gives the appearance of being embedded in the landscape.
Third Smooth river rocks are combined with larger rough rocks for varied color and texture.
Bottom A pile of rounded river rocks catches water dripping off a roof.

Many different kinds of rock are used in traditional Japanese gardens, and historically rocks were brought from great distances to be showcased in a garden. In his 1893 book, *Landscape Gardening in Japan*, Josiah Conder notes, "It is recorded that in the Tempo period (1830–1844), the mania for rare and costly stones became so extravagant that an edict was issued fixing a limit to the amount permitted to be paid for a single specimen."[17] Conder goes on to list almost twenty different types of stones (granites, jasper, limestones, slates, schists, etc.), which typically are used in gardens, noting that their names often denote their geologic character or the geographic region where they are found.[18]

The placing of the rocks is an integral part of the design of the garden. Size, shape, markings and coloration are all considered. A finely marked rock or one with a beautiful form or a strong character is placed in a prominent position. Since the material quality of rock is very different from that of other components of the garden, rocks easily can be used as contrasting elements against planar expanses of white gravel, mounds of low greenery such as moss or pigmy bamboo, or the smooth

verticality of a garden wall. The contrasting play of elements against each other, brought together in a unified composition, is a hallmark of Japanese gardens.

When a rock is placed, the garden designer has to consider how the rock will look from every visible angle. It must appear naturalistic unless the intention is otherwise, which is sometimes the case, as with stepping stones, and the designer learns from the way the rock sat in its original landscape. "You are not to change the position of a rock from what it was in the mountains. Placing a rock so that the part which was underneath in the mountains

Top Japanese carp swim alongside the Ōiso Isowatari Wide Stepping Stone Path in the Kiyosumi Teien Garden in Tokyo.
Above Rock groupings create a craggy edge for the Hōraijima Island in the Ninomaru Garden at Nijō Castle in Kyoto.
Far left A stone plank leads to a rocky island in the Ōhōjō Garden at the Chionin Temple in Kyoto.
Left River rocks embedded in moss give a sense of disappearing and reappearing.
Below far left A stone triad surrounded by moss is an island in the sea of raked gravel in the Ryōanji Temple garden in Kyoto.
Left Pure geometries play off each other in the surface of a stone path.
Right Swirling water of raked gravel surrounds islands of rocks in the Imperial Hotel garden in Tokyo.

is on top is called 'reversing the rock,' and is to be avoided. To do this would anger the spirit of the rock and would bring bad luck."[19]

The garden designer carefully considers the form, coloration, and markings of the rock and names it according to its aesthetic qualities, before deciding how to place it to best show it off. Rocks that are worn by water or covered with moss are used near water elements, and those that come from mountainous areas are located in a similar mountain-like setting in the garden. Some rocks are placed so that the entire form can be understood. Other rocks are sunken into the ground, so that only a small part is visible. It is not always obvious when viewing a rock in a garden just how much of that rock is being shown. This is one of the mysteries of the Japanese garden that stems from the highly developed art of garden design and construction.

A very different function for stone in the Japanese garden is the stepping stone. Stepping stones often frequently used to create or suggest a path across a body of water. Stepping stones laid in a sequence often are similar in size and shape to each other. They are chosen for or formed with a relatively flat surface and an appropriate size to accommodate their use. Stepping stones typically are placed so that they are visible just a few inches above the surface of the water or gravel. However, occasionally stepping stones are quite tall and uneven, suggesting a precarious relationship with the water below and inducing an acute awareness of the act of moving across the stones.

This role of elements within the garden to stimulate the senses and one's consciousness of being in the garden is an intriguing aspect of the Japanese garden. *Mitate* (re-seeing), as described in the section on paths, is an important example and often is designed into the stepping stones in a garden with a millstone used in place of one of the stones. The stepping stones generally are a similar size and shape to the round millstone, but the millstone is a perfect circle with the carved ridge markings used to grind grain. The sight of a millstone in the context of the garden spurs a new understanding of both the garden and the millstone and incites the viewer's self-awareness.

Chapter 28
Plants

Plants are an important element in the design of almost all gardens, as few gardens, even those termed "dry gardens" in Japan, are created without any plant material. Like most other elements of Japanese gardens, the ways plants first were used in the gardens reflected the early influence of Chinese gardens, and as gardens developed, the uses of plants and their combination with other elements similarly increased and changed.

The role of plants in Japanese gardens, as in Chinese gardens, basically is twofold. On the one hand, plants are focal points, creating moments of color and beauty within the garden. On the other hand, plants are used as background, to set off stone groupings, raked gravel beds, water features, or even other plants. Because of the dual function of plants in the garden, some are chosen for their unusual form, beautiful flowers, or distinctive leaves. Others are chosen for their diminutive size or their consistency of color or texture.

Some plant material changes its role from background to foreground depending on the season. For example, azalea bushes, with their small leaves and consistent green hue, can be grown and pruned to create thick background hedges. But when they bloom in the spring, they suddenly become foreground elements, with their bright blossoms and mass of color. Likewise, maple trees may be combined with other trees to provide a green backdrop for a garden. Yet, in the fall when the leaves change from green to deep red, maple trees become a focal point of the garden. Even moss, which can be used to create a soft carpet of green to set off groupings of stones and plants, becomes a feature in the winter, when the canopy of trees lose their leaves.

Opposite Wood supports brace the slender limbs of brightly hued maple trees extending over the pond inside Koishikawa Korakuen Garden in Tokyo.
Left Layers of clipped azaleas create a mountain adjacent to the sea of raked gravel in the Raikyūji Temple garden in Okayama Prefecture.

Below Maple leaves in autumn colors land on a closely clipped bush.

Right Rocks and trimmed azaleas combine to form a miniaturized hilly landscape surrounding a waterfall.

The four distinct seasons of Japan's temperate climate have long been a major inspiration in art, poetry, flower arrangement and landscaping. The seasonal changes of a garden are built into the design as the garden is meant to be enjoyed all year long. Flowering plants are located throughout the garden to provide points of color in different places at varying times. Deciduous trees and evergreens are used in combinations to assure that areas of the garden always are covered with a canopy of trees, though the size of the canopy might change from month to month.

These seasonal changes often bring surprise elements into a garden, such as the river of irises that blooms in the Korakuen Garden in Okayama each June or the blanket of bright pink flowers that covers the mountain of azaleas in the garden at Raikyūji near Okayama. Another way in which plants are used for seasonal surprises is as domesticated crops within the confines of the garden. In the Korakuen Garden, there is a plot of land in one corner that is divided into nine equal squares. Each square is planted with a different crop that grows during the course of the summer. Since gardens like Korakuen were designed to be a kind of idealized nature, enjoyed for its aesthetic qualities, it is highly unusual to find a working vegetable plot in such a garden. However, as a design element in the garden, the Korakuen nine-square vegetable patch is set off by a field of tea plants immediately behind it, carefully groomed to form undulating rows. Beyond the tea plants is a rising grassy slope highlighted by a sinuously curving hedge and punctuated with bushes trimmed into spheres. The whole geometrical composition is set off by a backdrop of tall bamboo.

The garden at the Shūgakuin Imperial Villa in Kyoto also incorporates agricultural fields. The extensive garden is designed in two quite distinct parts. While the inner part is a traditional garden, the outer part of the garden is designed to appear as an agricultural landscape, with terraced rice fields. The visitor is given the sense of moving through a typical Japanese landscape to get to the garden, when in fact the rice paddies are within the very confines of the garden.

The idea of incorporating crops in gardens started, of course, in China with single fruit trees or even small orchards designed into the gardens. The idea was developed in Japan to have a greater sense of the picturesque than of true functionality. Although the rice paddies, tea hedges, and vegetable plots are cultivated in the usual way, they also are designed as part of a greater composition, so their forms and sizes relate specifically to the garden overall.

The types of plants that are used in Japanese gardens range from those that commonly grow in the wild in Japan, for example certain

Above Stones and moss mingle in a playful checkerboard pattern in the Northern Hasso Garden at the Tōfukuji Temple in Kyoto.
Below Stone groupings interspersed throughout the landscape lead the eye from one feature to the next in the Kinkakuji Temple garden in Kyoto.

species of bamboo and moss to exotic plants that are brought in from other areas, such as particular types of palm trees. Plants are chosen for their specific qualities, which may include size, height, leaf color or shape, bark color or texture, and flower color, size, or quantity. All of these factors are taken into consideration by the garden designer, who places each plant alone or in combinations that show off their specific qualities and help create a unified composition.

Typical plants that are found in Japanese gardens include evergreen trees and bushes such as Japanese red pine (*akamatsu*), Japanese black pine (*kuromatsu*), and the common camellia (*yamatsubaki*); deciduous trees and bushes like Japanese maple (*momiji*), mountain cherry (*yamazakura*), and azalea (*tsutsuji*);[20] as well as grasses such as bamboo (*take*) and bamboo grass (*sasa*, also known as pygmy bamboo); and mosses (*koke*).

Left Layers of azaleas just starting to bloom build up to a plateau bedecked with trees of multiple varieties and colors and a simple viewing pavilion in the hillside garden at Mimurodōji Temple in Uji.
Below left A small cluster of greenery complements a traditional sophisticated Kyoto building.
Below center Maple leaves fall among *sasa* bamboo grass, creating a colorful autumn composition.
Below right Wooden supports prop up the fantastically curved trunk of an aged and gnarled pine tree.
Bottom Moss and stone are combined masterfully in a clever checkerboard composition in the Tōfukuji garden in Kyoto.

Maintenance

Each of these plants, like all the plants in a Japanese garden, requires specialized care and maintenance. Plants are trained to have a particular form, whether that of an old craggy wind-blown tree or a lush rolling hillside, and they require very specialized pruning and bracing systems. Gardens are maintained carefully so that no part becomes overgrown or looks unkept at any time. It is the plants that are the elements within the garden that require the greatest amount of maintenance and care. Withered flowers are picked, fallen leaves are raked, trees and bushes are pruned and trained, rain gutters are cleared, excess snow is removed, and trees are braced against strong winds and heavy snowfalls—these are just a few of the important maintenance activities.

Gardeners use a variety of traditional tools to maintain the gardens (figure 45) and can sometimes be seen working in the gardens. Often winnowers woven from bamboo strips and brooms fabricated from reeds are visible in the garden—an unintentional reminder of the constant care that is required. Most large traditional Japanese gardens require a small army of gardeners to provide the constant care they require. Some of the gardeners' jobs are demanding, such as building the support structure to brace the branches of an evergreen during the long winter. Other jobs are very detailed, such as pulling the flowers off moss plants with tweezers. Yet, just like the plants themselves, no matter the size, each task is important to the proper function and overall appearance of the garden.

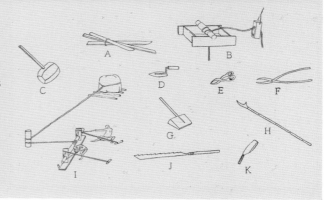

Top Rice straw wrappings protect trees from the winter cold.
Above left A gardener maintains the moss in the garden at the Mimurodō-ji Temple in Uji.
Above right Skirts of split bamboo protect the huge Japanese cedar trees leading to the Ise Shrine.
Left An artfully tied woven straw covering wraps a 300-year-old *akamatsu* red pine tree.
Right, figure 45 Traditional gardeners' tools include instruments for moving stones and earth and for trimming and maintaining plants.

Chapter 29
Water

Many traditional Japanese gardens are designed around a body of water, as were the Chinese gardens from which the Japanese gardens developed. Water is necessary for all life, and oceans and rivers have always been a major source of sustenance. Having access to a body of water for pleasure purposes is a luxury and a hallmark of wealth and prosperity.

The use of water in Chinese gardens, like other elements within the garden, was based on geomancy (*feng shui* in Chinese and *fūsui* in Japanese, both meaning "wind and water"). The direction and means by which water ran through a garden affected the *ch'i* or energy flow within the garden.[21] Proper flow of *ch'i* assured a healthy and prosperous garden. To achieve this, the garden was designed so that water, both above and below ground, would flow naturally. "The direction taken by the current of lakes and streams in gardens is considered of much moment. The inflow should if possible be from the east, the main direction of the current southerly, and the outlet towards the west; a circuitous route from north to east, then round by south and west is not uncommon, but a course from west to east is deprecated as sinister and unpropitious."[22]

Traditional garden designers observe the way water flows around rocks in a stream, how water changes speed as a river grows wider or narrower, and the effect of water entering the ocean from a river. These observations inform the way rocks are placed in a garden to control the direction of flowing water or to contain a large body of water. The gardens are meant to be naturalistic but in an exaggerated (especially in the case of Chinese gardens) or idealized way. Because gardens are designed to represent a larger expanse than their actual area, land-

scape features within the garden are placed close to one another, much closer than they would naturally occur—if they would even occur together in nature. Spatial design devices such as layering and forced perspective are used to suggest spatial distance. For example, a stream can be designed to meander down a hillside in a sinuous curve. As the distance between the stream and the viewer increases, the stream can be formed to become narrower and narrower, creating the impression that it is moving a greater distance than it actually is.

In Japanese gardens, water is incorporated in many different manners and forms. Ponds can be used for pleasure boating, but they also can be used for viewing the reflection of a building or bridge, giving a sense of ethereality. Rivers,

Above Stones dot the stream passing through the Ryūten Poetry Pavilion in the Edo-era Korakuen Garden in Okayama.
Right Sound, like the water from the Omonoigawa River rushing between rocks at the Kamigamo Shrine in Kyoto, is an important part of the experience of a garden.

streams, and waterfalls suggest movement and sound and sometimes, as noted above, spatial depth. Channels of water can be used to catch rain runoff from roofs or to express a man-made element within a natural landscape. Water is present, too, in basins for cleansing the hands and mouth before entering a tea garden. In temples and shrines, water is pro-vided near the entrance so that people can purify themselves before entering the sacred space. At the outer shrine of the Ise Shrine complex, the opportunity for such ritual cleans-ing occurs at multiple points in the journey from the first *torii* gate to the innermost shrine complex. The first occasion is at the sacred Isuzu River, which the visitor must cross on a wooden bridge at the entrance to the shrine.

The act of crossing over water, on a bridge or stepping stones, is a process of moving between two very different areas, with water serving as the divider. Water in a garden can be representative of a specific body of water in an actual geographic place, and interaction with that body of water therefore "locates" the viewer in that place. In this way, the water, perhaps combined with another element such as a bridge or pavilion, provides the idea of travel to far-off lands, those far-off locations being known to the viewers of the garden through the literature of the time. For example, the Koishikawa Korakuen Garden in Tokyo has a representation of the Ōigawa River found in a well-known aristocratic area of Kyoto. Lake Biwa near Kyoto is another famous body of water that often is re-created in gardens.[23]

Right Water follows a groove in a rough stone, falling on smooth river stones below.
Below Used to rinse the hands and mouth before entering the garden, water spouts from a hollowed-out bamboo pole onto a smooth rounded rock.
Bottom A gently curving stream meanders through grassy banks in the Korakuen Garden in Okayama.

Development

The ways in which water is used in Japanese gardens developed as the styles of gardens changed over time. Initially, garden designers closely followed the Chinese manner of incorporating water, especially lakes, which we know from the poetry of the era, although there are no extant examples of these gardens. In the *Manyōshu*, a collection of poems from the eighth century, "we can find mentioned the sparkle of a garden lake, the reflection of a rock, the green rain of young willows, and the fragrance of wisteria."[24] Later, the manner of including water was adapted to the developing Japanese taste. In *shinden*-style complexes, the buildings have a very close relationship with the landscape and specifically the pond. The main hall of the complex faces the pond and is flanked by L-shaped pavilions which extend into the garden. The whole complex is designed to be viewed from across the pond and while moving through the garden. With the pond located immediately in front of the main hall, the reflection of the building can be seen in the pond—an especially beautiful scene in moonlight.

Viewing moonlight reflected in a pond historically was a favorite pastime, and in later styles it was incorporated into the design of both the garden and the architecture. For example, the *sukiya*-style Old Shoin of the main house of the Katsura Imperial Villa in Kyoto features a large bamboo-covered deck that extends from the building to the pond, constructed specifically for moon-viewing.

Shoin-style residential compounds do not face gardens in the same manner as *shinden*-style complexes; rather, the most public buildings generally face a formal gravel forecourt. However, the architecture becomes less formal as it moves away from the ceremonial entry area, and the buildings have a stronger relationship to the landscape. Garden elements, often including water, are used to enhance this connection. For example, in the Kyoto Imperial Palace, a fine example of *shoin*-style design, this condition is clearly expressed. The formal entry to the compound is a gate that opens into a white gravel courtyard facing the most public building, the Shishinden ceremonial hall. The buildings directly connected to the Shishinden also are very formal and have a similarly abstract relationship to the ground. But as the buildings in the complex and their relationships to one another become more informal as they move further from the entry court area, the relationship of the buildings to the landscape becomes more informal as well. The landscape evolves into a lush garden, which moves up to and in some places under the buildings, and a pond is used to denote the transition between the formal and less formal areas. Placed at the corner of a building where the garden also turns the corner, the pond can be viewed from both areas, setting the tone for the rest of the garden.

Far left The gentle banks of the Yokuryuchi Pond in Shūgakuin Imperial Villa garden in Kyoto impart a sense of serenity and tranquility to the landscape.
Left The stream running through the Ryūten Poetry Pavilion is a playful element in the Korakuen Garden in Okayama. Cups of *sake* were floated from one end to the other, and participants had to complete poems before the cup passed them by.
Above The moat surrounding the Nijō Castle in Kyoto was a defensive element that now adds to the monumentality of the landscape.

As the formality of the architecture breaks down at the point furthest from the formal entry, the garden and the architecture are joined in a very strong relationship. The buildings appear to reach out to the garden, while the landscape almost seems to seep into the buildings. This is best exemplified at the corner of the Chōsetsu Teahouse, where the building hovers low over the garden, and a stream runs beneath it. At that point, the stream is the focal point of the garden, drawing the viewer in and offering itself up to be touched or simply watched at close range. In this way, water is used to connect buildings, landscapes, and people.

At the Korakuen Garden in Okayama, the Ryūten Pavilion is built with a stream running through it. Designed as a resting place, the open ground level of the pavilion is shaded by overhanging eaves and the enclosed upper story, which was used by the feudal lord owner to look over the garden. On the lower level, wood platforms for sitting are raised above the ground and provide views of the surrounding garden as well as the stream running through the pavilion. Although the stone foundations for the wood platforms form straight-edged walls for the stream, the water is punctuated by rough rocks which create a rippled meandering flow through the pavilion. The form of the pavilion suggests that it was used for the social game known as *kyokusui-no-en* ("meandering stream party"), a poetry-writing game that originated in China in which the participants must each write a poem by the time a cup of *sake* floats past them.

Water, as a liquid, is of course different from the other physical elements used in garden design. It has no specific shape and always must be contained. Thus the "container" is an integral part of the body of water, despite the fact that the container frequently is designed to disappear in order to highlight the water. Ponds often are lined with rocks or river stones, depending on the desired effect. Rough rocks can be set into the ground at the periphery of a pond or lake, to retain the earth and create a jagged edge depicting a craggy cliff, whereas river stones can be placed on a gentle bank to represent the seashore. A pond requires a source of constantly flowing water and typically also has at least one outlet for the water to flow into the garden.

The garden designer must also work with gravity to assure a proper flow of water, creating hills and valleys as needed. Rivers and streams also must be contained besides being made to look realistic with the placement of rocks and stones to control the direction and speed of the flow. Waterfalls are an important element in many Japanese gardens. "Contained" by rocks placed to control the direction and speed of flow, a waterfall may appear to meander gently down a hillside or rush in torrents through craggy boulders before spilling out into a calm sea.

Chapter 30
Garden objects

Although the primary focal points in traditional Japanese gardens are naturalistic features created by plantings, compositions of large rocks, and flat expanses of white gravel, there are other smaller elements that are used intentionally to show the hand of man. Also constructed using natural materials like stone, wood, and bamboo, these elements serve to heighten the sensory experience and create small moments of pause or surprise within the garden. Some of the objects have practical functions while others are included purely for aesthetic reasons.

These garden objects include benches, basins (*chōzubachi,* "hand water bowl," *or tsukubai,* "stooping basin," when used in a tea garden), lanterns (*tōrō*), and animal-scaring devices known as *shishi-odoshi* ("deer startler," figure 46). For example, basins provide a place to rinse the hands and mouth before entering a garden, especially in the case of a tea garden fronting a tea ceremony house. Lanterns, carved from stone, are used to light the garden at night. *Shishi-odoshi* make sharp sounds that scare away deer, wild boar, and other animals from the garden.

Gardens that are meant to be moved through may have pavilions for resting and viewing scattered around the garden. Gardens that are designed together with a small building for tea ceremonies include benches where guests can sit and enjoy the garden while waiting to enter the teahouse. A typical waiting bench is like a small pavilion, with two or three walls and a roof to protect the bench and give direction to the views of the garden. A waiting bench often has a stone foundation, a wood structure, and walls of wood, bamboo, or plaster. The roof is covered with wood

shingles or shakes or perhaps layers of cedar bark, and the bench itself is made of wood or bamboo. Such a bench is designed to enhance the experience of the garden and the architecture of the teahouse but not to overshadow any other part of the garden.

Basins developed from the reservoirs of water provided at shrines for worshippers to cleanse themselves before entering the sacred precinct in order to be pure of mind and body. This idea of purification was brought into the tea ceremony gardens as they developed over time. A small basin, usually carved out of stone, is placed along the *roji* garden path, just inside the second gate (figure 41). As a guest passes through the gate, the basin is visible, a reminder of the process of purification and another step toward attaining the appropriate mind-set for tea. The *tsukubai* creates a moment of pause, where the guest immerses a bamboo or wood dipper into the basin and uses the water to rinse the hands and mouth before proceeding to the teahouse entrance.

Basins are found in many shapes and heights, though most are low, at a stooping height, and are used to accentuate the design of the garden. Some basins are very geometric, with each surface formed and finely polished, but many basins combine mostly natural forms with a dash of geometry. For example, the top of a rough vertical oblong stone may be carved into a smooth perfect circle for the basin. The combination of the natural texture of the stone and the perfect geometry of the circle, with its polished surface, exemplifies the typical contrast of nature and artifice found in the garden.

Basins usually are placed at a height that requires the user to bend over slightly to dip the water (hence the name "stooping basin"). The act of stooping forces the body to remain at a slight distance away from the basin, which helps avoid splashing water. Most basins are set at a comfortable height, but some very intentionally are placed at unusual heights. In one famous story, the tea master Sen no Rikyū constructed a teahouse and garden on a piece of property with a beautiful view of the ocean. His friends waited anxiously for the garden to be completed so they could view the sea.

Opposite An artistic stack of old roof tiles creates a focal point in the foreground of this framed view of Anrakuji Temple in Kyoto.
Top A stone lantern is partially concealed by the branches of the surrounding maple trees.

Above A stone carved in the shape of a coin serves as a basin in the Ryōanji Temple garden in Kyoto.

Left Stone steps and orange lanterns lead up to the mountainside Kibune Shrine outside of Kyoto.
Below In the garden at the Hōnenin Temple in Kyoto, camellia blossoms adorn a cylindrical stone basin.
Bottom A carved stone lantern sits on a naturalistic stone at the edge of the pond at the Tōji Temple garden in Kyoto.

However, they were stunned to find, upon entering the garden, that Sen no Rikyū had planted two tall hedges that blocked the view of the sea. Rikyū's friends could not understand why he blocked the beautiful view—until they bent down low to use the basin. They then discovered that Rikyū had created an opening in the hedges that provided a perfectly framed view of the ocean, visible only when stooping down to the basin.[25]

It is clear from this example that the basin, like all the elements in traditional Japanese gardens, has more than a single purpose. In Rikyū's garden, the basin served the customary functions of holding water and acting as a beautiful object, thereby adding to the aesthetic quality of the garden, but it also served as a device that induced a more complete understanding of the garden and an awareness of one's place within it as well as the place of the garden within the world.

Lanterns (tōrō), brought to Japan with the Chinese-style Buddhist architecture, were donated to temples as offerings and used in temple complexes to give light at night, where they often stood quite tall so that the light was at eye level. By the sixteenth century, lanterns began to be used in gardens, especially tea ceremony gardens,[26] and their forms and heights became more varied. At temples, lanterns often were lined up on both sides of a path leading to the main hall, reinforcing the hierarchy of buildings within the complex and giving a clear sense of direction. When

Top left A heavy stone basin provides a place to cleanse the hands and mouth before entering a garden.

Top right Garden objects can be temporary or permanent or a combination of both, as with the camellia flower adorning a flower-shaped stone basin.

Above left Salvaged roof tiles are fashioned into ornamental and eye-catching objects.

Above right A simple stone tied with a rope temporarily blocks access to a path.

lanterns were introduced into gardens, they were not arrayed in lines as they had been in temples. Instead, they were placed singly, at strategic moments in the garden so that they could provide light at night but also be a focal point during the day.

Lanterns are carved out of stone in order to be fireproof, and light traditionally is provided by a small pot of oil or a candle placed in an opening near the top of the lantern. The opening typically is enclosed with a small *shōji*-like screen composed of a wood frame covered with *washi* paper. The flickering flame filtered by the *washi* gives off a gentle glow, illuminating the area near it with a cloud-like light rather than a strong or direct light.

Left Peaking out from the azalea bushes, a stone lantern creates a contrasting focal point in the garden of the Anrakuji Temple in Kyoto.
Above The sound of the *shishi-odoshi* striking a rock enhances visitors' awareness of the garden.
Above center A candle in a portable metal lamp provides a gentle glow to a garden in the evening hours.

Similar to carved stone basins, lanterns often are a combination of geometric and naturalistic forms and finishes. They usually are either columnar in form or are supported on three or more legs. Most lantern bases are stone pedestals carved into geometric forms, although more rustic ones are softly curved oval-shaped stones used as they were found in nature and reworked just enough so that they can be stacked, with a lamp housing in the middle. The lantern typically has a frame of carved stone—like an open cube—with panels of wood and *washi* which fit into each of the four open sides to enclose the flame. The cap often matches the pedestal—perhaps a carved hexagon or a square with a gently curving convex top, or perhaps a flat rounded stone

with a small spherical stone placed on it serving as a more naturalistic cap. The stone can be polished or left in its natural state, or it can combine parts that are polished with others that are left natural.

A *shishi-odoshi* is a device that uses a bamboo lever arm hitting against a rock or block of wood to make a loud crack that scares away animals. The device is constructed of a length of bamboo (about 1 meter or 3 feet long), cut so that the solid joint (*fushi*) of the bamboo is slightly offset from the middle of the piece and the two ends are open. Typically, the pole is attached to a bamboo or wood frame and set in a stream near another bamboo pole that has been hollowed out and arranged to form a spout. The water from the stream runs

through the hollow bamboo pole into the pole with the joint, filling up the shorter end of the pole. As it fills, the weight of the water causes that end to lower and the other end to rise, like a see-saw. As the pole lowers, the water spills out, and the opposite side, which is heavier, drops and hits a block of wood or stone set below it. The sound of the bamboo hitting against the block is meant to scare away deer or other animals, but it also has another purpose. As a visitor walks through the garden, the sudden loud crack of the *shishi-odoshi* causes that person to focus on the sound and the experience of the garden with a momentary intensity. In this way, the *shishi-odoshi* plays an important role of the sensory experience of a garden.

Above A carved stone lantern on a cylindrical base is an obviously human-made element within a naturalistic garden landscape.
Left, figure 46 A *shishi-odoshi* scares deer away from a garden with the clacking sound it makes when it strikes a stone after water flowing into the bamboo lever increases its weight, causing it to drop, pour out the water, and then strike the stone when returning to its original position.

Chapter 31
Temporary and seasonal elements

Seasonal ornaments and objects are an important way to emphasize and strengthen ties to nature and the continuous cycle of the seasons and time. These elements enhance the landscape, giving a new perspective of something that may have become familiar. Temporary objects also are used to create a festive atmosphere for a special occasion, many of which relate to seasonal celebrations such as the New Year or Children's Day. A few of these temporary objects are unrelated to a specific season but still are used to emphasize the connection to and the temporal quality of nature.

One example of this is a leaf that is placed in a carved stone *chōzubachi* basin along a garden path at the Hōnenin Temple in Kyoto. The leaf is held in place with a small stone and positioned so that it channels a slight amount of water from the upper bowl to the lower basin, creating a slow drip. The dripping water and the simple yet ingenious leaf spout create a moment where the viewer's focus is brought into a very small scale within the context of the garden as a whole. The leaf is kept fresh and therefore must be replaced almost daily, a reiteration of the idea that nature is a continuous cycle of life. A visitor to the garden

sees a leaf in the *chōzubachi* on every visit, regardless of the season. Although the leaf always may be from the same kind of tree, used in the same spot in the basin and fulfilling the same function, it will be a different leaf each time. The care required to maintain this level of detail in a small part of a garden serves as a reminder of the care necessary to maintain the entire garden.

This type of temporal element is unusual, as most temporary elements are used only for a specific season or event. Many of the objects that might be found in a traditional Japanese landscape or garden during different seasons

Far left Changed daily, a fresh green leaf spouts water from a stone fountain in the Hōnenin Temple in Kyoto.
Left Rain dripping from cherry blossoms is a short-lived spring sight and a reminder of the transience of life.
Above A cup of green tea and a sweet in the shape of a maple leaf accompany an autumn garden view from a veranda covered with red felt and adorned with falling maple leaves.

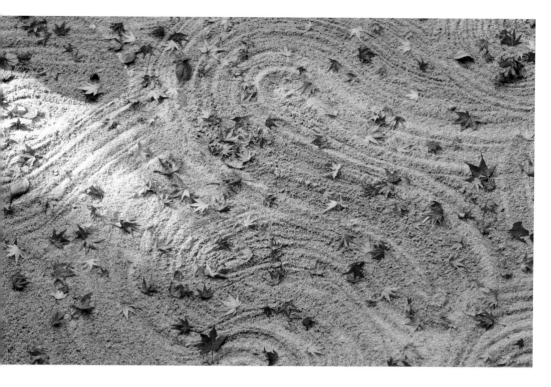

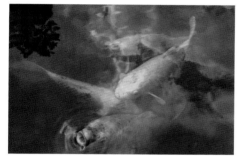

Left A late autumn scene at the Hōsenin Temple garden in Ōhara is highlighted by maple leaves scattered on an ocean of swirling raked gravel.
Below Multihued carp add lively movement and vibrant color to a garden pond.

have particular symbolism. For example, special displays of symbolic plants are used to welcome in the New Year. The large ornamental arrangement (*kadomatsu*) includes plants having specific meaning, such as bamboo (longevity), pine boughs (prosperity), and plum branches (steadfastness). Generally, three lengths of bamboo, representing heaven, humanity, and earth, are used in the display. By placing these arrangements in front of a house or building, the household welcomes the *shintō* deities.

At the end of March, when Japan's cherry blossoms are at their peak, many people enjoy the sight of the petals floating to the ground, and parties are held to celebrate the beauty of the falling blossoms. Large pieces of fabric are placed on the ground to indicate sitting areas, and sometimes the areas are demarcated by panels of fabric strung horizontally between bamboo poles driven into the ground, which give direction to the view and a sense of protection and the intimate scale within the larger landscape.

The same kinds of horizontal banners are used to define spaces for outdoor tea ceremonies. Large traditional paper umbrellas also might be incorporated to provide shade if the tea ceremony takes place during the day, while paper lanterns may be hung from trees or bamboo poles if the ceremony occurs at night. These same elements are used to create temporary spaces within open areas of gardens or landscapes for social gatherings during warm weather.

Annually, on May 5, long colorful banners in the shape of carp (*koinobori*) are hung from tall bamboo poles to celebrate Boys' Day (now called Children's Day). One carp banner is hung for each son (or child), and in houses where there are multiple children, the carp banners are of graduated lengths and hung at different heights on the pole, with the longest carp closest to the top. Each bamboo pole is topped with a colorfully striped windsock. The carp symbolizes perseverance and aspiration. Hanging the banners annually reflects the desire for each child to have a strong and healthy future.

A very different type of temporary element within the landscape is the *himorogi*, a sacred plot of land used to demarcate the space of a temporary shrine for the traditional *shintō* groundbreaking ritual (*jichinsai*, figure 2). Like many other temporary objects, the elements used to demarcate the space of the *himorogi* are natural materials having specific symbolic meaning. First, four bamboo poles are driven into the ground, forming a square with its sides facing the cardinal directions. The poles are connected at the top with a *shimenawa*, a twisted rope made of rice straw that marks the separation between the profane space of the everyday world and the sacred *shintō* space. Folded ornamental paper streamers (*shide*) are attached to the *shimenawa*. A temporary altar with offerings of food, salt, and *sake* is set up facing south within the space defined by the *himorogi*. Although now usually performed by a *shintō* priest, the *jichinsai* traditionally was led by the master carpenter. This simple setting for the ritual offering to the deities of the place combines the reverence for the natural world, awareness of the temporality of all things, respect for craft, and attention to detail that are inherent in traditional Japanese culture.

Endnotes

Introduction

1 Translation based on William J. Higginson's translation in Faubion Bowers (ed), *The Classic Tradition of Haiku: An Anthology*, Mineola, NY: Dover, 1996, p. 31.

Part 1 Context

1 Donald Richie, *A Tractate on Japanese Aesthetics*, Berkeley, CA: Stone Bridge Press, 2007, p. 37.

2 The total land area of Japan is 374,744 square kilometers (144,689 square miles) and the population was estimated at 127,288,419 in July 2008, according to the Central Intelligence Agency's *The 2008 World Factbook*, available online at https://www.cia.gov/library/publications/the-world-factbook/print/ja.html.

3 Marc P. Keane, *Japanese Garden Design*, Rutland, VT, and Tokyo: Charles E. Tuttle, 1996, p. 6.

4 The height of Mount Fuji is 3,776 meters.

5 The other two are Amanohashidate, a sandbar covered with more than 6,000 pine trees at the Tango Peninsula in the Sea of Japan, and the sacred island of Miyajima in the Seto Inland Sea.

6 The winner was Matsuo Bashō with his *haiku*, "Matsushima ya, ā Matsushima ya, Matsushima ya" (Matsushima! Ah, Matsushima. Matsushima!).

7 Ritchie, *A Tractate*, p. 71.

8 Ibid, p. 72.

9 Kurokawa Kisho, *Rediscovering Japanese Space*, New York and Tokyo: Weatherhill, 1988, p. 58.

10 Tanizaki Jun'ichirō, *In Praise of Shadows*, New Haven, CT: Leete's Island Books, 1977, p. 13.

11 Ibid, p. 18.

12 R. H. P. Mason and J. G. Caiger, *A History of Japan*, Rutland, VT, and Tokyo: Charles E. Tuttle, 1997, p. 21.

13 For example, see the discussion of Yayoi and Jōmon styles in Isozaki Arata, *Japan-ness in Architecture*, Cambridge, MA: MIT Press, 2006, pp. 39–46.

14 Nishi Kazuo and Hozumi Kazuo, *What is Japanese Architecture?*, Tokyo and New York: Kodansha, 1983, p. 54.

15 Norman F. Carver Jr, *Japanese Folkhouses*, Kalamazoo, MI: Documen Press, 1984, p. 10.

16 Ibid, p. 43.

17 Ono Sokyo, *Shintō: The Kami Way*, Rutland, VT, and Tokyo: Charles E. Tuttle, 1962, p. 20.

18 *Encyclopedia of Shintō*, Tokyo: Kogakuin University, 2002–6; online English translation of *Shintō Jiten*, Tokyo: Kobundo, 1994, at http://eos.kokugakuin.ac.jp/modules/xwords/.

19 Ono, *The Kami Way*, p. 20.

20 Laurence G. Liu, *Chinese Architecture*, London: Academy Editions, 1989, p. 148.

21 Kawazoe Noboru, "The Ise Shrine and its Cultural Context," in Tange Kenzō, Kawazoe Noboru, and Watanabe Yoshio, *Ise: Prototype of Japanese Architecture*, Cambridge, MA: MIT Press, 1965, p. 169, notes, "The colored *hoju* [metal ornaments] on the railings of the main sanctuaries are definitely not Japanese in origin but are considered an influence from China...." Isozaki Arata, *Japan-ness in Architecture*, Cambridge, MA, and London: MIT Press, 2006, p. 140, writes, "It is likely that during the half century after establishment of the periodic alteration of sites, the eastern and western treasure houses of the inner shrine came to be placed behind the main structure (Shōden) with its balustrade, while in the outer shrine they remained in front. If so, the latter arrangement with its emphasis on symmetry is certain to have been based on Chinese cosmology."

22 Unno Taitetsu, *River of Fire, River of Water*, New York: Doubleday, 1998, p. 11.

23 Ibid, p. 13.

24 Murasaki Shikibu (trans. Arthur Waley), *Genji Monogatari*, in Donald Keene (ed.), *Anthology of Japanese Literature*, New York: Grove Press, 1980, p. 112.

25 Mason and Caiger, *A History of Japan*, p. 121.

26 Nishi and Hozumi, *What is Japanese Architecture?*, pp. 74–5.

27 Sen Sōshitsu XV (trans. V. Dixon Morris), *The Japanese Way of Tea: From Its Origins in China to Sen Rikyū*, Honolulu: University of Hawai'i Press, 1998, pp. 3–4.

28 Suzuki Daisetz T., *Zen and Japanese Culture*, Princeton, NJ: Princeton University Press, 1973, p. 385.

29 Yamasaki Masafumi, "Kyoto: Its Cityscape Traditions and Heritage," in *Process: Architecture*, No. 116, April 1994, pp. 46–7.

30 Gehō Taku, "Mejia: Kontentsu no Nashōnarichi" (Media: The Nationality of Contents), IIPS Policy Paper 322J, Tokyo: Institute for International Policy Studies, 2007, p. 16.

31 *Webster's New Collegiate Dictionary*, 8th edn, Springfield, MA: G & C Merriam, 1981.

32 William Coaldrake, *The Way of the Carpenter*, New York and Tokyo: Weatherhill, 1990, p. 8.

33 Gehō, "Mejia," pp. 15–16.

34 Robert J. Smith, *Japanese Society*, Cambridge, UK: Cambridge University Press, 1983, p. 9.

35 Jonathan M. Reynolds, *Maekawa Kunio and the Emergence of Japanese Modernist Architecture*, Berkeley, CA: University of California Press, 2001, p. 20. Also in Don Choi, "Educating the Architect

in Meiji Japan," in *Architecture and Modern Japan*, symposium proceedings, New York: Columbia University, 2000, p. 4.

36 David B. Stewart, *The Making of a Modern Japanese Architecture: 1868 to the Present*, New York and Tokyo: Kodansha, 1987, p. 19.

37 Mason and Caiger, *A History of Japan*, p. 265.

38 Stewart, *The Making of a Modern Japanese Architecture*, p. 22.

39 Jonathan M. Reynolds, "The Bunriha and the Problem of 'Tradition' for Modernist Architecture in Japan, 1920–1928," in Sharon A. Minichiello (ed.), *Japan's Competing Modernities: Issues in Culture and Democracy 1900–1930*: Honolulu, University of Hawai'i Press, 1998, p. 228.

40 Ibid, pp. 231–2.

41 Jonathan M. Reynolds, "Ise Shrine and a Modernist Construction of a Japanese Tradition," *The Art Bulletin* 83, No. 2, 2001, pp. 321–3.

42 Smith, *Japanese Society*, p. 35.

43 Yanagita's influential publications include his 1934 *Minkan denshōron* (On Folklore Studies) and his 1937 *Dentō ni tsuite* (On Tradition).

44 Kishida Hideto, *Japanese Architecture*, Tokyo: Japan Travel Bureau, 1936, p. 13.

45 Ibid, p. 29.

46 Ibid, p. 40.

47 Ibid, p. 42.

48 Reynolds, "Ise Shrine," p. 321.

49 Ralph Adams Cram, *Impressions of Japanese Architecture and the Allied Arts*, New York: The Baker and Taylor Co., 1905, pp. 86–7.

50 Isozaki, *Japan-ness in Architecture*, p. 13, emphasis original.

51 Ibid, p. 17.

52 Tange Kenzō, *Katsura: Tradition and Creation in Japanese Architecture*, New Haven: Yale University Press, 1960, p. v.

53 Arthur Drexler, *The Architecture of Japan*, New York: The Museum of Modern Art, 1955, p. 262.

54 Ibid, pp. 41, 43, 53, 262.

55 Kawazoe, "The Ise Shrine and Its Cultural Context," pp. 200–6.

56 Tange Kenzō, Kawazoe Noboru, and Watanabe Yoshio, *Ise: Prototype of Japanese Architecture*, Cambridge, MA: MIT Press, 1965, p. 16.

57 Ibid.

58 Reynolds, "Ise Shrine," p. 316.

59 Itō Teiji, with Noguchi Isamu and Futagawa Yukio, *The Roots of Japanese Architecture*, New York, Evanston, and London: Harper & Row, 1963, p. 9.

60 Nishi and Hozumi, *What is Japanese Architecture?*, p. 9.

61 Ibid.

62 Ibid, pp. 9–11.

63 Isozaki Arata, *Island Nation Aesthetic*, London: Academy Editions, 1996, pp. 46–52.

64 Ibid, p. 41.

65 Ibid, p. 47.

66 Isozaki Arata, "The Teahouse as a Manifestation of Manmade Anti-nature," in Isozaki Arata, Ando Tadao, and Fujimori Terunobu, *The Contemporary Tea House: Japan's Top Architects Redefine a Tradition*, Tokyo: Kodansha, 2007, p. 28.

67 Fujimori Terunobu, "The Development of the Tea Room and Its Meaning in Architecture," in Isozaki, Ando, and Fujimori, *The Contemporary Tea House*, p. 22.

68 Ando Tadao, "The Conflict between Abstraction and Representation," in Isozaki, Ando, and Fujimori, *The Contemporary Tea House*, p. 60.

69 Isozaki, "The Teahouse," p. 29.

70 Kuma Kengo, "Tea Room Building as a Critical Act," in Isozaki, Ando, and Fujimori, *The Contemporary Tea House*, p. 108.

71 Ibid.

72 Fujimori Terunobu, "The Tea Room: Architecture Writ Small," in Isozaki, Ando, and Fujimori, *The Contemporary Tea House*, p. 80.

73 Ibid, p. 78.

Part 2 Forms and Materials

1 Lady Sarashina (trans. Ivan Morris), *As I Crossed a Bridge of Dreams*, London and New York: Penguin, 1975, p. 54.

2 Suzuki Daisetz T., *Zen and Japanese Culture*, Princeton, NJ: Princeton University Press, 1973, p. 361.

3 Mitchell Bring and Josse Wayembergh, *Japanese Gardens: Design and Meaning*, New York: McGraw-Hill, 1981, p. 3.

4 Simon J. Gale, "Orientation," in *Process: Architecture No. 25, Japan: Climate, Space, and Concept*, Tokyo: Process Architecture Publishing, August 1981, p. 45.

5 Bring and Wayembergh, *Japanese Gardens*, p. 154.

6 Inoue Mitsuo (trans. Watanabe Hiroshi), *Space in Japanese Architecture*, New York and Tokyo: Weatherhill, 1985, p. 5.

7 Ibid.

8 Ibid.

9 Paola Mortari and Vergara Caffarelli, "China," in Mario Bussagli (ed.), *Oriental Architecture/2*, New York: Rizzoli, 1989, p. 94.

10 Koizumi Kazuko, *Traditional Japanese Furniture*, Tokyo, New York, and San Francisco: Kodansha, 1986, p. 149.

11 Arthur L. Sadler, *A Short History of Japanese Architecture*, Sydney and London: Angus and Robertson, 1941, p. 11.

12 Koizumi, *Traditional Japanese Furniture*, p. 150.

13 Witold Rybczynski, *Home: A Short History of an Idea*, New York: Penguin, 1986, p. 96.

14 Paul Oliver, "Symbolism and Decoration," in Paul Oliver (ed.), *Encyclopedia of Vernacular Architecture of the World*, Cambridge, UK, New York, and Melbourne: Cambridge University Press, 1997, Vol. 1, p. 497.

15 Nakagawa Takeshi (trans. Geraldine Harcourt), *The Japanese House: In Space, Memory, and Language*, Tokyo: International House of Japan, 2005, p. 136.

16 Edward S. Morse, *Japanese Homes and Their Surroundings*, New York: Dover, 1961, pp. 337–8.

17 Watanabe Hitoshi, "The Ainu Ecosystem," in William W. Fitzhugh and Chisato O. Dubreuil (eds), *Ainu: Spirit of a Northern People*, Washington, DC: National Museum of Natural History, Smithsonian Institution, 1999, p. 199.

18 Morse, *Japanese Homes*, p. 77

19 Itoh Teiji, *Traditional Domestic Architecture of Japan*, New York and Tokyo: Weatherhill/Heibonsha, 1982, pp. 150–1.

20 Ibid, p. 150.

21 William H. Coaldrake, *The Way of the Carpenter: Tools and Japanese Architecture*, New York and Tokyo: Weatherhill, 1990, p. 19.

22 Guntis Plēsums, "Structure System [of *Minka*]," in Paul Oliver (ed.), *Encyclopedia of Vernacular Architecture of the World*, Cambridge, UK, New York, and Melbourne: Cambridge University Press, 1997, Vol. 2, p. 991.

23 An excellent resource (although only available in Japanese) is the *Nihon no komyunichi (Communities of Japan)* issue of *SD* No. 7, Tokyo: Kashima Shuppan Kai, 1975.

24 S. Azby Brown, *The Genius of Japanese Carpentry: An Account of a Temple's Reconstruction*, New York and Tokyo: Kodansha, 1989, p. 69.

25 Coaldrake, *The Way of the Carpenter*, pp. 90, 103.

26 Ibid, p. 94.

27 Ibid, p. 90.

28 Ibid, pp. 90–1, 193–4.

29 Ibid, p. 124.

30 Ibid, p. 146.

31 Ibid, p. 157.

32 Ibid, p. 128.

33 Ibid, p. 30.

34 Ibid, p. 9.

35 Ibid, pp. 32–47.

36 Heino Engel, *Measure and Construction of the Japanese House*, Rutland, VT, and Tokyo: Charles E. Tuttle, 1985, p. 30.

37 Coaldrake, *The Way of the Carpenter*, p. 44.

38 Ibid, p. 132.

39 *Mushi-cho shi* (History of Mushi Village), Mushi-cho, 2005; available online at http://www.city.takamatsu.kagawa.jp/6133.html.

40 Compiled from Seki Mihoko, *Kokenchiku no waza nehori hahori* (Minute Details of Traditional Architectural Techniques), Tokyo: Rikōgakusha, 2000; and Ueda Atsushi, *Nihonjin to sumai* (Japanese People and Dwellings), Tokyo: Iwanami Shoten, 1974.

41 Brown, *The Genius of Japanese Carpentry*, pp. 56–7.

42 The list of woods was prepared by master carpenter Edo Tamotsu.

43 Watanabe Masatoshi, "Bamboo in Japan," available online at http://www.kyoto.zaq.ne.jp/dkakd107/E02-e.html.

44 From the website of the Yamaguchi Marble Onix Union: http://dairiseki.sugoihp.com/kumiai/history.htm.

45 Josiah Conder, *Landscape Gardening in Japan*, New York: Dover, 1964, pp. 44–5; and Fukuda Kazuhiko, *Japanese Stone Gardens: How to Make and Enjoy Them*, Rutland, VT, and Tokyo: Charles E. Tuttle, 1970, pp. 197–8.

46 Marc P. Keene, *Japanese Garden Design*, Rutland, VT, and Tokyo: Charles E. Tuttle, 1996, p. 148.

47 Nakagawa, *The Japanese House*, p. 7.

48 Nishi Kazuo and Hozumi Kazuo, *What is Japanese Architecture?*, Tokyo and New York: Kodansha, 1983, p. 17.

Part 3 Architecture

1 Translation based on Janine Beichman's translation in Faubion Bowers (ed.), *The Classic Tradition of Haiku: An Anthology*, Mineola, NY: Dover, 1996, p. 75.

2 *JAANUS Online Dictionary of Japanese Architectural and Art Historical Terminology* (comp. Mary Neighbour Parent), Japanese Architecture and Art Net Users System, 2001; http://www.aisf.or.jp/~jaanus/deta/k/karahafu.htm.

3 Itoh Teiji, *Traditional Domestic Architecture of Japan*, New York and Tokyo: Weatherhill/Heibonsha, 1982, pp. 44, 47.

4 Mary Neighbour Parent, *The Roof in Japanese Buddhist Architecture*, New York and Tokyo: Weatherhill/Kajima, 1985, p. 68.

5 Florence Du Cane and Ella Du Cane, *The Flowers and Gardens of Japan*, London: Adam & Charles Black, 1908, p. 23.

6 Edward S. Morse, *Japanese Homes and Their Surroundings*, New York: Dover, 1961.

7 David Young and Michiko Young, *Introduction to Japanese Architecture*, North Clarendon, VT, and Singapore: Tuttle, 2004, p. 81.

8 Nishi Kazuo and Hozumi Kazuo, *What is Japanese Architecture?*, Tokyo and New York: Kodansha, 1983, p. 54.

9   Nihon Kenchiku Gakkai, *Nihon kenchikushi zushu* (Collected Illustrations of Japanese Architectural History), Tokyo: Shokokusha, 1980, p. 157.

10 Ibid, p. 157.

11 Ibid.

12 Nishi and Hozumi, *What is Japanese Architecture?*, p. 94.

13 Nihon Kenchiku Gakkai, *Nihon kenchikushi zushu*, pp. 157–8.

14 *JAANUS*; http://www.aisf.or.jp/~jaanus/deta/s/soseki.htm.

15 Nihon Kenchiku Gakkai, *Nihon kenchikushi zushu*, p. 158.

16 William H. Coaldrake, *The Way of the Carpenter: Tools and Japanese Architecture*, New York and Tokyo: Weatherhill, 1990, p. 102.

17 *JAANUS*; http://www.aisf.or.jp/~jaanus/deta/b/bengara.htm.

18 Nakagawa Takeshi (trans. Geraldine Harcourt), *The Japanese House: In Space, Memory, and Language*, Tokyo: International House of Japan, 2005, p. 77.

19 Heino Engel, *Measure and Construction of the Japanese House*, Rutland, VT, and Tokyo: Charles E. Tuttle, 1985, p. 112.

20 Nakagawa, *The Japanese House*, p. 81.

21 *JAANUS*; http://www.aisf.or.jp/~jaanus/deta/g/genkan.htm.

22 Nakagawa, *The Japanese House*, p. 176.

23 Ibid, p. 174.

24 *JAANUS*; http://www.aisf.or.jp/~jaanus/deta/t/tatami.htm.

25 Engel, *Measure and Construction*, pp. 34–42.

26 Nishi and Hozumi, *What is Japanese Architecture?*, p. 74.

27 Arthur Drexler, *The Architecture of Japan*, New York: The Museum of Modern Art, 1955, p. 71.

28 Morse, *Japanese Homes*, pp. 156–7.

29 *JAANUS*; http://www.aisf.or.jp/~jaanus/deta/c/chigaidana.htm.

30 Morse, *Japanese Homes*, p. 137.

31 *JAANUS*; http://www.aisf.or.jp/~jaanus/deta/o/oshiita.htm.

32 Morse, *Japanese Homes*, p. 154.

33 Ibid, p. 192.

34 Tanizaki Jun'ichirō, *In Praise of Shadows*, New Haven, CT: Leete's Island Books, 1977, pp. 3–4.

35 Ibid, p. 35.

36 Morse, *Japanese Homes*, p. 183.

37 Ibid, p. 212.

38 Susan B. Hanley, *Everyday Things in Premodern Japan: The Hidden Legacy of Material Culture*, Berkeley, Los Angeles, and London: University of California Press, 1997, p. 158.

39 Ty Heineken and Kiyoko Heineken, *Tansu: Traditional Japanese Carpentry*, New York and Tokyo: Weatherhill, 1981, pp. 23–4.

40 *JAANUS*; http://www.aisf.or.jp/~jaanus/deta/k/kakemono.htm.

41 Tanizaki, *In Praise of Shadows*, p. 14.

42 Morse, *Japanese Homes*, p. 123.

Part 4 Gardens and Courtyards

1   Yamagata Saburō, *Kenchiku Tsurezuresa* (Architectural Idleness), Kyoto: Gakugei Shuppansha, 1982, p. 148. Translation adapted from David Landis Barnhill, *Bashō's Haiku: Selected Poems of Bashō*, Albany, NY: SUNY Press, 2004, p. 89.

2   Boye Lafayette De Mente, *Kata: The Key to Understanding and Dealing with the Japanese*, Tokyo and Rutland, VT: Tuttle, 2003, p. 18.

3   Lou Qingxi (trans. Zhang Lei and Yu Hong), *Chinese Gardens*, Zurich: China Intercontinental Press, 2003, p. 13.

4   Mario Bussagli, *Oriental Architecture/2*, New York: Electa/Rizzoli, 1981, p. 95.

5   Josiah Conder, *Landscape Gardening in Japan*, New York: Dover, 1964, p. 12.

6   Tachibana-no-Toshitsuna (attrib., trans. Shimoyama Shigemaru), *Sakuteiki: The Book of Garden*, Tokyo: Town & City Planners, 1976, p. 1.

7   Mitchell Bring and Josse Wayembergh, *Japanese Gardens: Design and Meaning*, New York: McGraw-Hill, 1981, p. 188. The formula is based on Shimode Kunio (ed.), *Nihon no Toshikukan* (Japanese Urban Space), Tokyo: Shokokusha, 1969, p. 36.

8   Edward S. Morse, *Japanese Homes and Their Surroundings*, New York: Dover, 1961, p. 266.

9   Josiah Conder, *Landscape Gardening in Japan*, New York: Dover, 1964, p. 75.

10 Irmtraud Schaarschmidt-Richter and Mori Osamu, *Japanese Gardens*, New York: William Morrow and Company, 1979, p. 61.

11 Inoue Mitsuo (trans. Watanabe Hiroshi), *Space in Japanese Architecture*, New York and Tokyo: Weatherhill, 1985, pp. 18–19.

12 I utilize the definitions of "rock" and "stone" laid out by David A. Slawson in *Secret Teachings in the Art of Japanese Gardens: Design Principles and Aesthetic Values*, Tokyo: Kodansha, 1987, p. 200. He states, "Japanese *ishi* (*seki*) I translate as "rock(s)" when they are used in the garden to suggest rock formations in nature, and "stone (s)" when they are used (for their naturally or artificially flattened upper surfaces) as stepping stones or paving stones, or when they have been sculpted (stone lanterns, water basins, pagodas) or split or sawed (stone slabs used for bridges, paving, curbing)."

13 Shimoyama Shigemaru, "Translator's Preface," in Tachibana-no-Toshitsuna (attrib., trans. Shimoyama Shigemaru), *Sakuteiki: The Book of Garden*, Tokyo: Town & City Planners, 1976, p. ix.

14 Tachibana-no-Toshitsuna, *Sakuteiki: The Book of Garden*, Tokyo: Town & City Planners, 1976, p. 20.

15 Ibid, p. 23.

16 Zōen, *Senzui narabi ni yagyō no zu* (Illustrations for Designing Mountain, Water, and Hillside Field Landscapes), 15th century; reproduced in *Secret Teachings in the Art of Japanese Gardens: Design Principles and Aesthetic Values* (trans. David A. Slawson), Tokyo: Kodansha, 1987, 153.

17 Conder, *Landscape Gardening*, p. 45.

18 Ibid, pp. 44–5.

19 Zōen, *Senzui narabi ni yagyō no zu*, p. 156.

20 Bring and Wayembergh, *Japanese Gardens*, pp. 208–11.

21 Ibid, pp. 154–5.

22 Conder, *Landscape Gardening*, p. 96.

23 Schaarschmidt-Richter and Mori, *Japanese Gardens*, p. 57.

24 Loraine Kuck, *The World of the Japanese Garden: From Chinese Origins to Modern Landscape Art*, New York and Tokyo: Weatherhill, 1989, p. 71.

25 Ibid, pp. 196–7.

26 *JAANUS Online Dictionary of Japanese Architectural and Art Historical Terminology* (comp. Mary Neighbour Parent), Japanese Architecture and Art Net Users System, 2001; http://www.aisf.or.jp/~jaanus/deta/t/tourou.htm.

Below Detail of a painting at the Kyoto Imperial Palace.

Glossary

aburashōji 油障子 "oil *shōji*," wood lattice screen covered with oiled paper to protect from rain, usually found in teahouses (also known as *amashōji*)

ageya 揚屋 elegant entertainment house, typically a *machiya* in an urban pleasure quarter

akamatsu 赤松 red pine (*Pinus densiflora*)

amado 雨戸 "rain door," removable wood shutters used to protect openings in exterior walls

amashōji 雨障子 "rain *shōji*," wood lattice screen covered with oiled paper to protect from rain, usually found in teahouses (also known as *aburashōji*)

anzangan 安山岩 andesite

arakabe 荒壁 "rough wall," first coat of mud plaster

ara-nuri 荒塗り "rough coat," roughly textured mud plaster

asobi 遊び "play" for pleasure or amusement

asunarō 翌檜 hatchet-leafed arborvitae (an evergreen of the pine family)

atebishi 当てビシ heavy steel-headed hammer used by blacksmiths to flatten metal

aware あわれ, 哀れ awareness of beauty in the ephemeral nature of all things

bai バイ wood or bamboo stick (used in papermaking to pound fibers into pulp)

bengara 弁柄 red pigment made from iron oxide

bishan ビシャン bush hammer used by stone workers

bonsai 盆栽 miniaturized tree or plant

bu 分 traditional unit of measurement equal to 10 *rin* or 1/10 of 1 *sun* (3.03 millimeters, approximately 0.12 inch)

butsudan 仏壇 ancestral Buddhist altar, usually in the form of a table and cabinet

byōbu 屏風 portable screen of two or more hinged panels; see also *tsuitate*

cha-dansu 茶箪笥 chest for tea ceremony utensils

chashitsu 茶室 "tea room" for traditional tea ceremony

ch'i (Chinese) 気 energy flow (Japanese, *ki*)

chigaidana 違い棚 "different shelf," decorative staggered shelves typically found in an alcove in a formal reception room; see also *usu-kasumi-dana*

chōba-dansu 帳場箪笥 chest for merchant wares

chōdaigamae 帳台構え doorway in *shoin* room, normally with four ornamental *fusuma*

chōna 釿 adze

chōzubachi 手水鉢 "hand water bowl," a stone or ceramic bowl used in gardens for rinsing hands or as an ornamental element; see also *tsukubai*

dabo 太枘 dowel or pin (short for *daboso*, "fat tenon")

daibutsuden 大仏殿 "great Buddha hall," a hall housing a huge statue of Buddha, typically within a Buddhist temple complex

dai-ganna 台鉋 "block plane"

daikokubashira 大黒柱 "god of wealth column," central structural column in a *minka*

daiku 大工 carpenter

daimyō 大名 feudal lord

dairi-seki 大理石 "Dàli stone," marble (named after the Chinese city of Dàli)

danjōzumi kidan 壇正積基壇 stone podium

dentō 伝統 "transmit control," tradition

dobashi 土橋 bridge covered with earth and moss

dodai 土台 wood sill or footplate

doma 土間 "earth space," earthen-floored area within a building

doro-nuri 泥塗り coating of metal shavings from the sharpening process mixed with water, used by a metalsmith to cool hot metal

dōtsuki-noko 胴付き鋸 tenon or back saw

ebizuka 海老束 thin vertical post used between two staggered shelves (*chigaidana*)

engawa 縁側 indoor–outdoor veranda-like extension of the floor plane that is protected by overhanging eaves

engetsukyō 偃月橋 "half-moon bridge," half-circle shaped bridge that forms a complete circle with its reflection

enza 円座 circular seat cushion woven from straw or similar material

e-shi 絵師 master painter

ezo-matsu 蝦夷松 Yezo-spruce (*Picea jezoensis*)

ezu-ita 絵図板 carpenter's floor plan drawn on a thin wood board (also known as *ita-zu*)

feng shui (Chinese) 風水 ancient Chinese geomantic system responding to astronomic and geographic indicators to organize space embodying positive *ch'i* (in Japanese, *fūsui*)

fudegaeshi 筆返し "brush return," curved wood edge piece added to a shelf or counter to stop brushes and other objects from rolling off, often used decoratively on *chigaidana*

fuigo 鞴 bellows

furo 風呂 bath

fushi 節 solid joint within bamboo culm

fūsui 風水 "wind–water," geomantic system based on Chinese *feng shui* utilizing astronomic and geographic indicators to organize space embodying positive *ki*

fusuma 襖 sliding screen of wood lattice covered with opaque paper

futon 布団 sleeping mat

gagyū-gaki 臥牛垣 "lying cow fence" of woven and bundled bamboo at the Kōetsuji Temple garden in Kyoto and elsewhere (also known as *kōetsu-gaki*)

gampi 雁皮 gampi shrub (*Wikstroemia sikokiana*, also known as *kaminoki*)

gasshō 合掌 "hand clasp," hands pressed together as in prayer

gasshō-zukuri 合掌造り "hand clasp style" steep roof

found in many *minka* in the Hida region

genbugan 玄武岩 basalt

genkan 玄関 enclosed entrance area with the floor surface at ground level

gennō 玄能, 源翁 hammer with two faces (one flat and the other convex), sledge hammer; see also *kanazuchi*

geta 下駄 wooden sandals

giyōfū 擬洋風 "pseudo-Western style" used for buildings built in the early Edo period by master carpenters using traditional methods

goemonburo 五右衛門風呂 large iron cauldron used for bathing, filled with water, and heated over a wood fire

gofun 胡粉 white calcium carbonate pigment used in whitewash

gotoku 五徳 metal stand set into a hearth to support a kettle

goza 茣蓙 lightweight woven grass mat, used to cover *tatami*

gundera グンデラ double-headed mallet used by stoneworkers

gyō 行 semiformal

gyōkaigan 凝灰岩 tuff or tufa

hachiku 淡竹 Henon bamboo (*Phyllostachys nigra f. henonis*)

haiku 俳句 poem written in three phrases of 5, 7, and 5 syllables

haitsuchi migaki 灰土磨き smoothly troweled earthen plaster finish using pulverized straw and seaweed or casein glue to bind finely ground dried earth

hanamaru-noko 鼻丸鋸 "round-nose saw," round-nose roughing saw

hanchiku 版築 rammed earth

haniwa 埴輪 ceramic funerary image

hari 梁 beam

hashira 柱 column

hatagane 端金 clamp

hazama-ishi 狭間石 continuous footing foundation constructed with many medium-sized stones between *soseki* base stones

heichi jūkyo 平地住居 literally "flat-land dwelling"

hiba 檜葉 type of Japanese cypress (*Thujopsis dolabrata*)

hibachi 火鉢 "fire box," charcoal brazier

hidana 火棚 "fire shelf," wood rack or panel suspended over a hearth in a *minka*, used to dry food and keep heat down

hikite 引手 "pull hand," door pull

himorogi 神籬 sacred plot of land demarcating the space of a temporary shrine for the traditional *shintō* groundbreaking ritual

hinoki 檜 Japanese cypress (*Chamaecyparis obtusa*)

hira-ganna 平鉋 smoothing plane

hiraya tatemono 平家立物 one-story building

hiwada-bōchō 檜皮包丁 knife used to trim the edges of bark shingles on a *hiwadabuki* roof *hiwadabuki* 桧皮葺 Japanese cypress (*hinoki*) bark shingled roof

hiwadabuki-ya 桧皮葺屋 Japanese cypress (*hinoki*) bark roof craftsman

hōchō 包丁 knife

hōjō 方丈 temple abbot's residence

hokubo 火窪 forge

honchōna 本釿 type of adze, can be used to create a grooved surface

hondō 本堂 "main hall" of a Buddhist temple complex

honmikage 本御影 granite (also known as *ikoma-ishi*, *kaji-ishi*, *kakōgan*, *mikage-ishi*, *okushū-mikage*, *ōshima-ishi*)

horigotatsu 掘炬燵 "dug out" *kotatsu*, a sunken space around the *irori* to allow people to sit on the floor and have their legs warmed by the hearth

hozo 柄 tenon

hozoana 柄穴, 柄孔 mortise

hyōgu-ya 表具屋 paper mounter (attaches paper to *shōji* and *fusuma*)

ibushi-kawara 燻瓦 "smoked tile," typical gray Japanese roof tile with oxidized finish

ichi-no-ma 一の間 "first room," most important room in a suite of *shoin*-style rooms, typically contains the *tokonoma*, *chigaidana*, and *tsukeshoin*

ichō 銀杏 ginkgo tree (*Gingko biloba*)

igusa 藺草 type of rush (*Juncus alatus*) woven into a thin covering for *tatami*

ikebana 生花 flower arrangement

ikō 衣桁 wood rack for hanging *kimono*

ikoma-ishi 生駒石 granite (also known as *honmikage*, *kaji-ishi*, *kakōgan*, *mikage-ishi*, *okushū-mikage*, *ōshima-ishi*)

ima 居間 "living space," room used for daily activities

imono-ya 鋳物屋 cast metal craftsman

inakadatami 田舎畳 "countryside *tatami*," sized to fit between columns

inaka-ma 田舎間 distance between the centers of adjacent structural columns (varies depending on the locale); see also *kyōma*

inu-yarai 犬矢来 "dog fence," skirt of split bamboo protecting the lower part of building walls

irimoya 入母屋 hip-and-gable roof

irori 囲炉裏 sunken hearth

ishi 石 rock or stone

ishi 倚子 throne-like chair

ishihama 石浜 stone beach

ishi-ya 石屋 stonemason

ishō-dansu 衣装箪笥 clothing chest

ita-ishi 板石 "board stone," slate stone (also known as *surēto*)

itako イタコ spirit medium

ita-shōji 板障子 "board *shōji*," wood panel screen

ita-zu 板図 carpenter's floor plan drawn on a thin wood board (also known as *ezu-ita*)

ito 糸 string

jari 砂利 gravel or small stones

jibukuro 地袋 "earth pouch," cabinet placed on the floor below the *chigaidana*

jichinsai 地鎮祭 *shintō* groundbreaking ceremony

jifuku 地覆 horizontal wood member placed on top of the foundation stones or directly on the ground

jikuzuri 軸吊り pivot hinge

jimune 地棟 inner ridge pole, longitudinal beam located below the ridge pole

jizai 自在 pot hook, used to hold a kettle over a hearth (also known as *jizaikagi*)

jizaikagi 自在鈎 pot hook, used to hold a kettle over a hearth (also known as *jizai*)

jō 丈 10 *shaku* (3.03 meters or about 10 feet)

jōdoshū 浄土宗 Pure Land Buddhism

jōgi 定規 measuring gauge

jōshō 縄床 chair used by Buddhist priests

kabuki 歌舞伎 traditional form of theater

kabuto 兜 helmet

kabuto-yane 兜屋根 helmet-style roof

kadomatsu 門松 ornamental arrangement of plants displayed at New Year

kaidan-dansu 階段箪笥 "stair chest," storage unit built within a staircase

kaikashiki 開化式 "Restoration mode," style of build-ing having an eclectic combination of Western and Japanese elements, often designed and built by master craftsmen

kaimentetsu 海綿鉄 iron bloom, sponge-like mass of iron and slag containing some carbon

kaiyūshiki teien 回遊式庭園 stroll-style garden

kajihibashi 鍛冶火箸 long pincers used in metal-smithing

kaji-ishi 庵冶石 granite (also known as *honmikage*, *ikoma-ishi*, *kakōgan*, *mikage-ishi*, *okushū-mikage*, *ōshima-ishi*)

kaji-ya 鍛冶屋 metalsmith

kakejiku 掛け軸 hanging scroll

kaki-shibu 柿渋 persimmon tannin

kakōgan 花崗岩 granite (also known as *honmikage*, *ikoma-ishi*, *kaji-ishi*, *mikage-ishi*, *okushū-mikage*, *ōshima-ishi*)

kakume 角目 increments of *sun* multiplied by the square root of 2 on a *sashigane*

kamado 竈 earthen cook stove

kamakiri-nomi かま切り鑿 type of chisel used by *tategu-ya* (also known as *kama-nomi*)

kama-nomi 鎌鑿 type of chisel used by *tategu-ya* (also known as *kamakiri-nomi*)

kami 神 *shintō* deity

kamidana 神棚 "deity shelf"

kaminoki カミノキ "paper tree," gampi shrub (*Wikstroemia sikokiana*, also known as *gampi*)

kamoi 鴨居 upper track for sliding partition

kamuy 神威 Ainu spirits

kanashiki 鉄敷 anvil

kanazuchi 金槌 hammer with two faces, one flat and the other pointed; see also *genno*

kanejaku 曲尺, 矩尺 carpenter's square (also known as *sashigane*)

kanji 漢字 pictographic characters based on the Chinese writing system

kanna 鉋 plane

kanna-mi 鉋身 cutting blade of a plane

karesansui 枯山水 "dry mountain–water," garden type incorporating very few plantings but using beds of gravel or groupings of stones to represent land- and seascapes

kaseigan 火成岩 igneous rock

kashi 樫 oak (*Quercus serrata*)

katana-dansu 刀箪笥 chest for sword blades

kawara 瓦 ceramic roof tiles

kawarabuki-ya 瓦葺屋 ceramic tile roofer

kaya 茅 miscanthus or Japanese torreya (*Torreya nucifera*)

kayabuki 茅葺 thatched roof, literally with miscanthus but can be any number of reeds or grasses

kazari kanagu-ya 飾金具屋 ornamental metal craftsman

kazari kanamono 飾金物 decorative metal fittings

kebiki 罫引 marking gauge

keisodo 珪藻土 diatomaceous earth

ken 間 the distance of one structural bay, 6 *shaku* (equal to about 180 centimeters or 6 feet)

kenchiku 建築 architecture, also means building or construction

kenzao 間竿 measuring rod (also known as *shaku-zue*)

kesshōhengan 結晶片岩 crystalline schist

keta 桁 purlin

keyaki 欅 zelkova (*Zelkova acuminata*)

ki 気 energy flow (Chinese, *ch'i*)

kibori-shi 木彫師 woodcarver

kikkō-chiku 亀甲竹 tortoiseshell bamboo

kikori 樵 woodcutter, lumberjack

kimono 着物 clothing (often used to refer to tradi-tional Japanese clothing in particular)

kiri 桐 paulownia tree (*Paulownia imperialis*)

kiri 錐 gimlet

kiridome-hōchō 切留包丁 type of knife used by *tategu-ya*

kirikane-shi 截金師 metal leaf craftsman

kiri-yoki 切斧 chopping ax used by lumberjack

kiryokugan 輝緑岩 dolerite (also known as diabase)

kiwari 木割り "wood divide," traditional proportional system

kizuchi 木槌 wood mallet

kobiki 木挽き sawyer

kōetsu-gaki 光悦垣 "lying cow fence" of woven and bundled bamboo at the Kōetsuji Temple garden in Kyoto and elsewhere (also known as *gagyū-gaki*)

kogatana 小刀 small marking knife used by *tategu-ya*

koguchi kanagu 小口金具 decorative metal (typically bronze) plate (also known as *koguchi kanamono*)

koguchi kanamono 木口金物 decorative metal (typi-cally bronze) plate (also known as *koguchi kanagu*)

koinobori 鯉幟 carp banner

koke 苔 moss

kokerabuki 柿葺き thin wood shingle roofing, typically cedar

kokutan 黒檀 ebony or blackwood

komai 小舞, 木舞 lath, typically made from bamboo strips

komisen 込栓 wood draw pins

komo 菰 mat of roughly woven straw used on the floor, hung from eaves, or attached to an exterior wall for protection from winter weather

konohagata-noko 木葉形鋸 leaf-shaped crosscut push saw

kondō 金堂 "golden hall," centrally located main hall in a Buddhist temple complex

kōshi 格子 lattice, typically made of wood

koshiki 甑 large wooden tub used to steam branches for papermaking, also refers to a rice steamer

kotatsu 炬燵 small brazier placed under a wood frame or table with a quilt over the top to keep the heat in (also known as *okigotatsu*)

kote 鏝 trowel

kote-e 鏝絵 "trowel picture," sculptural relief formed from lime plaster

kote-ita 鏝板 wood palette or hawk

kowan ni shitagau 乞わんに従う "following the request," an expression used in garden design that refers to learning from nature

kōyōju 広葉樹 broad-leafed or deciduous trees, hardwoods

kōzo 楮 fibrous inner bark of the paper mulberry tree (*Broussonetia kajinoki*), also used to refer to the tree

kugikakushi 釘隠し "nail hider," ornamental nail cover

kuma-zasa 熊笹 kuma bamboo grass (*Sasa veitchii*); see also *sasa*

kumotokyō 雲斗拱 floating cloud pattern bracketing

kura 倉 storehouse

kuri 栗 chestnut (*Castanea crenata*)

kurobe 黒檜 Japanese arbor vitae (*Thuja standishii*)

kuro-chiku 黒竹 black bamboo (*Phyllostachys nigra*)

kurokaki 黒柿 black persimmon (*Diospyros nitida* Merr.)

kuromatsu 黒松 black pine (*Pinus thumbergii*)

kurumi 胡桃 walnut (*Juglans ailantifolia*)

kusabi 楔 wedge

kusu 樟, 楠 camphor (*Cinnamomum camphora*)

kuwa 桑 mulberry (*Broussonetia papyrifera*)

kyokuroku 曲彔 throne-like chair

kyokusui-no-en 曲水の宴 "meandering stream party," poetry-writing game in which participants must each write a poem by the time a cup of *sake* floats past them

kyōma 京間 distance from the center of one column to the center of the next column, used in the Kansai region; see also *inaka-ma*

kyōmadatami 京間畳 Kyoto-style *tatami*, sized to fit from the center of one column to the center of the next column

ma 間 interval or space (between two columns, for example)

machiya 町屋 "townhouse," urban artisan or merchant house

madake 真竹 madake bamboo (*Phyllostachys bambusoides*)

maebiki-noko 前挽鋸 rip saw

maebiki-oga 前挽大鋸 wide-bladed ripsaw

magusa 楣 lintel

maki-gane 巻矩 tool similar to a *sashigane* used by *tategu-ya*

makura 枕 pillow

marume 丸目 dimensions equal to *sun* multiplied by the multiplicative inverse of *pi* (or $1/3.1416$), used on *sashigane*

masago 真砂 course granite sand used in gardens; see also *shirakawa-suna*

masu-gumi 枡組 "square framing," bracketing to support eaves

matsu 松 pine (*Pinus densiflora*)

medake 女竹 simon bamboo (*Pleioblastus simonii*)

meguri-ishi 廻石 "flow-round stone" used in garden design to direct the flow of water (or stone repre-senting water)

mikage-ishi 御影石 granite (also known as *honmikage*, *ikoma-ishi*, *kaji-ishi*, *kakōgan*, *okushū-mikage*, *ōshima-ishi*)

minka 民家 "people's house" or "folk house"

mino 蓑 straw raincoat

misu 御簾 blinds made from thin strips of bamboo used at shrines, temples, palaces, and aristocratic residences; see also *su* and *sudare*

mitate 見立 "re-seeing," used objects incorporated into a design in a new way, especially in gardens

mitsuba tsutsuji 三葉躑躅 azalea (*Rhododendron dilatatum*)

mitsumata 三椏 paperbush or giant leaf paper plant (*Edgeworthia papyrifera*)

mizuya kasane-dansu 水屋重ね箪笥 chest to hold everyday items

momi 樅 white fir or Japanese fir (*Abies firma*)

momiji 紅葉 Japanese maple (*Acer palmatum*)

mon 門 gate

mono no aware 物の哀れ sensitivity to the temporality of all things

mōsō-chiku 孟宗竹 Moso bamboo (*Phyllostachys heterocycla f. pubensis*)

motokawa-shi 原皮師 craftsman who removes bark from cypress trees for *hiwada-buki*

mujō 無常 concept from Buddhism related to impermanence, mutability, and transience

munagi 棟木 ridge pole

nageshi 長押 head beam (tie beam that runs the perimeter of a room)

nageshi-suki 流し漉き Japanese papermaking process

nakabashira 中柱 "center column" found only in tea ceremony rooms

nakanuri 中塗り "middle coating" of earthen plaster

namako-kabe 海鼠壁 "sea slug wall," wall surface of ceramic tiles, typically set in a grid pattern with lime plaster

nara 楢 Japanese oak (*Quercus crispula*)

nekoguruma 猫車 wheelbarrow

neri ねり glutinous vegetable material used to slow the drainage of water from the pulp mixture in papermaking

nezuko 鼠子 white cedar (*Thuja standishii*)

nezumi-gaeshi 鼠返し "rat turn-around," flat board at the top of a stair to deter rodents

nihon sankei 日本三景 three famous sceneries of Japan

nijiri-guchi 躙口 "crawl-in entrance" of a tea ceremony room

nō 能 traditional drama combining poetry, music, dance, and theater (also written *noh*)

noboribari 登り梁 rising beam or raking beam

nokikarahafu 軒唐破風 cusped gable roof at the end of an eave

noko-giri 鋸 saw

nomi 鑿 chisel

noren 暖簾 curtain-like hanging panels of fabric sewn together at the top and left separate for about the lower three-quarters

nori 海苔 red algae (*Porphyra yezoensis* and *Porphyra tenera*)

nuno-ishi 布石 long rectangular stone used in continuous stone footing; see also *renzoku-kiso*

nusumi-geiko 盗み稽古 "stolen lessons" in which an apprentice observes the master and learns tech-niques to refine through practice

ōbiki 大引 sleeper or beam which supports a floor system

oga 大鋸 two-man frame ripsaw

okigotatsu 置き炬燵 small brazier placed under a wood frame or table with a quilt over the top to keep the heat in (also known as *kotatsu*)

okoshi-ezu 起絵図 drawing combining floor plan and elevations that can be folded to create a three-dimensional model of a room, primarily used in the design of tea ceremony rooms

okushū-mikage 奥州御影 granite (also known as *honmikage*, *ikoma-ishi*, *kaji-ishi*, *kakōgan*, *mikage-ishi*, *ōshima-ishi*)

omoteme 表目 front side of *sashigane*; see also *urame*

onigawara 鬼瓦 "demon tile," ornamental tile located at the ends of the roof ridge

oni-shi 鬼師 *onigawara* ornamental tile craftsman

osae-ba 押え刃 chip breaker or capping iron in a plane

oshiire 押入 wardrobe or closet-like space, often outfitted with shelves

oshi-ita 押板 desk-like board in a *tokonoma* serving as the top surface of the *jibukuro* (also known as *toko-oshi-ita*), originally the name of a shallow alcove with a raised floor (the precursor to the *tokonoma*)

ōshima-ishi 大島石 granite (also known as *honmikage*, *ikoma-ishi*, *kaji-ishi*, *kakōgan*, *mikage-ishi*, *okushū-mikage*)

oya-ishi 大谷石 Oya stone or Oya tuff

ranma 欄間 transom

renzoku-kiso 連続基礎 continuous stone footing; see also *nuno-ishi*

rin 厘 traditional unit of measurement equal to ¹/₁₀ of 1 *bu* (0.303 millimeter, approximately 0.012 inch)

ro 炉 hearth used in tea ceremony rooms

rodan 炉壇 box, typically made from cypress with a thick clay liner, filled with ash and burning charcoal for use in tea ceremony rooms

roji 露地 "dewy ground," path leading from the gate through the tea garden to the tea ceremony house

rokujō 六畳 "six mats," six *tatami* mat-sized room

rokuro 轆轤 pulley or lathe

sado-akadama-ishi 佐渡赤玉石 Sado red stone of architecture; see also *zōkagaku*

sagan 砂岩 sandstone

sagefuri 下げ振り plumb line

sakaki 榊 Japanese evergreen tree (*Cleyera japonica*)

sakan-ya 左官屋 plaster craftsman

sake 酒 rice wine

sakuketa 簀桁 wood frame used in papermaking

sakoku 鎖国 "closed country," national isolation policy in place from 1639 to 1858

sakura 桜 cherry (*Prunus japonica*)

samurai 侍 member of aristocratic warrior class

sankarado 桟唐戸 heavy wood-paneled doors incorporating decorated bronze straps

sansui 山水 "mountain–water" garden type incorporating streams, ponds with islands, and rough rock outcroppings

sarusuberi 百日紅 crape myrtle (*Lagerstroemia indica*)

sasa 笹 bamboo grass (*Sasa veitchii*); see also *kuma-zasa*

sashigane 指矩 carpenter's square (also known as *kanejaku*)

sawara 椹 Sawara cypress (*Chamaecyparis pisifera*)

sekkaigan 石灰岩 limestone

sen 鐇 draw knife

sentokodai 鏟床台 special platform used by metal-smiths when smoothing blades

shachi 車知 wood key or draw pin used to fix wood joinery together

shachi-gawara 鯱瓦 roof ridge end tile in the shape

Above, figure 47 *Nokikarahafu* cusped gable roof.

of a legendary fish-shaped creature with tiger head

shakkei 借景 borrowed scenery, technique used in garden design to extend the perceived limits of the garden

shaku 尺 traditional unit of measurement equal to 10 *sun* (30.3 centimeters, approximately 1 foot)

shaku-zue 尺杖 measuring rod (also known as *kenzao*)

shiage 仕上 "finish," used to refer to the final surface coat of plaster as well as other finish surfaces

shiage-nomi 仕上鑿 chisel used for finishing surfaces

shiagenuri 仕上塗り "finish coat" of plaster (also known as *uwanuri*)

shibamune 芝棟 roof ridge reinforced with planks

shichirin 七輪 small brazier for cooking, typically made from baked clay tile, mud plaster, or *keisodo*

shide 四手, 垂 strips of folded paper (or sometimes cloth) attached to *shimenawa*

shihōbuta 四方蓋 "covers on four sides," roof type with hipped upper roof and lower eaves which skirt the perimeter

shikii 敷居 lower track for sliding partition, also refers to a threshold or sill

shikkui 漆喰 lime plaster

shimenawa 注連縄 twisted rice straw rope used to mark the separation between the space of the everyday world and sacred *shinto* space

shin 真 formal

shinden 寝殿 formal architectural style primarily used for aristocratic residences during the Heian period, also refers to the main hall of an aristocratic residential compound in the *shinden* style

shingonshū 真言宗 esoteric Buddhism

shin-gyō-sō 真行草 formal–semiformal–informal

shinyōju 針葉樹 needle-leafed tree

shintō 神道 "the way of the gods," the *shintō* faith indigenous to Japan

shioji 塩地 ash (*Fraxinus spaethiana* Lingelsh)

shiragaki 白書 metal-marking tool used by *tategu-ya* similar to a *sumisashi*

shirakawa-suna 白川砂 "White River sand," fine white gravel used in gardens; see also *masago*

shīsā シーサー legendary Okinawan guardian lion-dog

shishi-odoshi 鹿威し "deer startler," device used in gardens which makes a sharp sound to scare away

deer and other animals

shitajimado 下地窓 rough ornamental lattice window opening found in tea ceremony houses

shitami-ita 下見板 "see-below board," exterior wood clapboards with overlapping horizontal planks and thin vertical rails

shitan 紫檀 red sandalwood or rosewood (*Dalbergia latifolia* Roxb.)

shitomido 蔀戸 wood lattice shutters which hinge upward

sho-dansu 書簞笥 chest used to store books

shoin 書院 formal architectural style primarily used for aristocratic residences from the Momoyama period, also refers to a building in the shoin style or a formal reception room with a writing desk and is the abbreviated term for *tsukeshoin*

shōji 障子 wood lattice screen covered with translucent paper

shukkei 縮景 "shrunken scenery," miniaturization technique used in garden design to alter the perceived scale of elements in the garden

shura 修羅 log used by stonemasons to roll large pieces of stone

sō 草 informal

sōda ソーダ, 曹達 alkali

sodegaki 袖垣 "sleeve fence," short fence that serves as an extension of a wall and/or is used to limit a view

sodekabe 袖壁 thin partial wall which limits a view, used in tea ceremony rooms to block the guests' view of the host's entrance

sokosarai-nomi 底浚鑿 long-handled chisel used by *tategu-ya* to clean out mortises

soseki 礎石 "foundation stone," base stone used to support a column

su 簾 blinds made from thin strips of bamboo; see also *misu* and *sudare*

sudare 簾 loosely woven blinds made from thin strips of bamboo, reeds, or other material, used to block views or sunlight; see also *misu* and *su*

sudare-shōji 簾障子 *shōji* that use *sudare* in place of *washi* paper

sugi 杉 Japanese cedar or cryptomeria (*Cryptomeria japonica*)

sukiya 数奇屋 "abode of empty" or "abode of refinement," architectural style combining elements of the *shoin* style with less formal features, also refers to a tea ceremony house

sukiya-shoin 数奇屋書院 a *shoin* room built in the *sukiya* style

sumi-e 墨絵 ink wash painting

sumisashi 墨刺 bamboo marking pen

sumitsubo 墨壺 ink pot with snap line

sun 寸 traditional unit of measurement equal to 10 *bu* or ¹/₁₀ of 1 *shaku* (3.03 centimeters, approximately 1.2 inches)

suna 砂 sand

sunamori 砂盛り sand or gravel mounded to create a three-dimensional form

surēto スレート slate (also known as *ita-ishi*)

tagane 鏨 graver used in metalsmithing and stone work

tagayasan 鉄刀木 Indian ironwood (*Mesua ferrea* L.)

takakura 高倉 "high storehouse," raised-floor store-house

takayuka 高床 "high floor," building with a floor elevated above the ground

take 竹 bamboo

takekugi 竹釘 bamboo nail

tama-ishi 玉石 "ball stone," rock with a rounded form

tansu 箪笥 storage chest

taruki 垂木 rafter

tataki 叩き, 三和土 tamped earthen floor

tataki-nomi 叩鑿 striking chisel

tatami 畳 woven rush-covered straw mat used as flooring material

tatami-ya 畳屋 *tatami* maker

tateana jūkyo 竪穴住居 "vertical hole dwelling," pit dwelling

tategu-ya 建具屋 door and screen carpenter

teikan yōshiki 帝冠様式 "imperial crown style," early twentieth-century architectural style promoted by the Japanese government which featured a "Japanese" roof on a Western-style building

teko 梃子 lever used to move stone

temoto-dansu 手元箪笥 chest for personal objects

tenbukuro 天袋 "heaven pouch," cabinet located just above the *chigaidana*

tenjōbito 殿上人 "person on the palace floor," a high-ranking person allowed on the raised floor in an aristocratic residence

tenjō-nageshi 天井長押 ceiling rail (tie beam running the perimeter of a room, just below the ceiling)

teppei-seki 鉄平石 "flat iron stone," pyroxene andesite

tobukuro 戸袋 "door container," box attached to the building exterior used to store *amado*

tochi 栃, 橡 horse chestnut (*Aesculus turbinata*)

to-ishi 砥石 whetstone

tokobashira 床柱 "alcove column" which separates the *tokonoma* from the alcove containing the staggered shelves

tokonoma 床の間 decorative alcove

toko-oshi-ita 床押板 desk-like board in a *tokonoma* serving as the top surface of the *jibukuro* (also known as *oshi-ita*)

torii 鳥居 "bird perch," post-and-beam gate marking the entrance to a *shintō* precinct

tōrō 灯篭 lantern

tororo 黄蜀 pounded root of the *Hibiscus manihot* used in papermaking

tōryō 棟梁 "ridge pole," chief master carpenter

tsubaki 椿 camellia (*Camellia japonica*)

tsuba-nomi 鐔鑿 "sword-guard chisel" used to cut

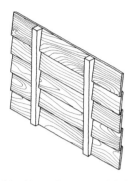

Above, figure 48 *Shitami-ita* overlapping wood clapboards.

square holes for nails

tsubo 坪 a unit of measure equal to two *tatami* mats or approximately 90 centimeters by 90 centimeters or 6 feet by 6 feet

tsuboniwa 坪庭 "*tsubo* garden," very small interior courtyard garden

tsuchi 槌 mallet or hammer

tsuchikabe 土壁 "mud wall," solid wall coated with mud plaster

tsuga 栂 hemlock-spruce (*Tsuga siekoldii*)

tsuitate 衝立 portable standing single-panel screen; see also *byōbu*

tsuitate-shōji 衝立障子 fabric-covered movable partition (typically freestanding but may be attached to a column)

tsuka 束 struts

tsukeshoin 付書院 built-in writing desk in a *shoin* room

tsukimi-dai 月見台 moon-viewing veranda

tsuki-nomi 突鑿 paring chisel used for finishing surfaces or mortise holes

tsukubai 蹲踞 "stooping basin," a stone or ceramic bowl used in a tea garden for rinsing hands or as an ornamental element; see also *chōzubachi*

tsuri-kanamono 釣金物, 吊り金物 hardware (metal rods and hooks) used to support *shitomido*

tsunami 津波 tidal wave

tsunomata 角叉 red algae (*Gingartinaceae Chondrus*) used to make glue

tsutsuji 躑躅 azalea (*Rhododendron indicum*)

ukiyo-e 浮世絵 woodblock print

ume 梅 plum (*Prunus mume*)

urame 裏目 back side of *sashigane* with square root scale; see also *omoteme*

urushi 漆 lacquer, also short for Japanese lacquer tree; see *urushi-no-ki*

urushi-no-ki 漆の木 Japanese lacquer tree (*Toxicodendron vernicifluum*)

urushi shokunin 漆職人 lacquer craftsman

usu-kasumi-dana 薄霞棚 "thin mist shelf" or *chigaidana*

uwanuri 上塗り "top coat" of plaster (also known as *shiagenuri*)

wabi 侘 aesthetic concept incorporating the under-standing of beauty in humbleness, imperfection, and loneliness

wabi-cha 侘茶 "*wabi* tea," tea ceremony style based on the concept of *wabi*

wagoya 和小屋 Japanese roof structure system

wara 藁 rice straw

warabuki 藁葺 rice straw thatch

waraji 草鞋 woven straw sandals

wara no hai 藁の灰 straw ash

waraza 藁座 metal socket used with pivot hinge

washi 和紙 paper typically made from the inner bark of the paper mulberry tree

washi shokunin 和紙職人 paper maker

washitsu 和室 "Japanese-style room" with a floor covered with *tatami* mats

ya 矢 wedge used to split stone or wood

yaki-ire 焼入れ tempering hot metal by quenching it in water

yakisugi 焼杉 *sugi* charred to a dark black finish

yamatsubaki 山椿 common camellia (*Camellia japonica*)

yamazakura 山桜 mountain cherry (*Prunus denarium* var. *spontanea*)

yane-ya 屋根屋 roofer

yari-ganna 槍鉋 spear-head plane

yasuri 鑢 file, typically used to sharpen metal saw blades

yatsuhashi 八橋 "eight bridges," eight-plank bridge

yojōhan 四畳半 "four and a half mats," four and a half *tatami* mat-sized room

yokobiki-noko 横引き鋸 crosscut saw

yōma 洋間 "Western-style room"

yoshi 葭 ditch reed (*Phragmites australis*)

yū 木綿 30-centimeter length of tree bark fiber attached to a *shimenawa*

yukimi shōji 雪見障子 "snow-viewing *shōji*"

yūyaku 釉薬 glaze, used on ceramic tile

zabuton 座布団 "sitting *futon*," cushion

zashiki 座敷 *tatami*-floored formal reception room

zōkagaku 造家学 "building studies," early Meiji-era translation of academic discipline of architecture; see also *zōkajutsu*

zōkajutsu 造家術 "building arts," early Meiji-era translation of academic discipline of architecture;

Below Young boy in a *kimono* at the Yasukuni Shrine, Tokyo.

Bibliography

Barnhill, David Landis, *Bashō's Haiku: Selected Poems of Bashō*, Albany, NY: SUNY Press, 2004.

Blaser, Werner, *Classical Dwelling Houses of Japan*, Teufen AR, Switzerland: Arthur Niggli, 1958.

Blofeld, John Eaton Calthorpe, *The Chinese Art of Tea*, London: Allen & Unwin, 1985.

Bowers, Faubion (ed.), *The Classic Tradition of Haiku: An Anthology*, Mineola, NY: Dover, 1996.

Bring, Mitchell, and Josse Wayembergh, *Japanese Gardens: Design and Meaning*, New York: McGraw-Hill, 1981.

Brown, S. Azby, *The Genius of Japanese Carpentry: An Account of a Temple's Reconstruction*, New York and Tokyo: Kodansha, 1989.

Bussagli, Mario (ed.), *Oriental Architecture/2*, New York: Rizzoli, 1989.

Carver, Norman F., Jr., *Japanese Folkhouses*, Kalamazoo, MI: Documen Press, 1984.

Central Intelligence Agency, *The 2008 World Factbook*; available online at https://www.cia. gov/library/publications/the-world-factbook/ print/ja.html.

Chamberlain, Basel Hall, *Japanese Things: Being Notes on Various Subjects Connected with Japan*, Rutland, VT, and Tokyo: Charles E. Tuttle, 1971.

Choi, Don, "Educating the Architect in Meiji Japan," in *Architecture and Modern Japan*, symposium proceedings, New York: Columbia University, 2000.

Coaldrake, William H., *Architecture and Authority in Japan*, London and New York: Routledge, 1996.

_____, *The Way of the Carpenter: Tools and Japanese Architecture*, New York and Tokyo: Weatherhill, 1990.

Conder, Josiah, *Landscape Gardening in Japan*, New York: Dover, 1964; first published 1893.

Cram, Ralph Adams, *Impressions of Japanese Architecture and the Allied Arts*, New York: The Baker and Taylor Company, 1905.

De Mente, Boye Lafayette, *Kata: The Key to Understanding and Dealing with the Japanese*, Tokyo and Rutland, VT: Tuttle Publishing, 2003.

Drexler, Arthur, *The Architecture of Japan*, New York: The Museum of Modern Art, 1955.

Du Cane, Florence, and Ella Du Cane, *The Flowers and Gardens of Japan*, London: Adam & Charles Black, 1908.

Encyclopedia of Shintō, Tokyo: Kogakuin University, 2002–6; online English translation of *Shintō Jiten*, Tokyo: Kobundo, 1994, at http://eos.kokugakuin. ac.jp/modules/xwords/.

Engel, Heino, *Measure and Construction of the Japanese House*, Rutland, VT, and Tokyo: Charles E. Tuttle, 1985.

Fitzhugh, William W., and Chisato O. Dubreuil (eds), *Ainu: Spirit of a Northern People*, Washington, DC: National Museum of Natural History, Smithsonian Institution, 1999.

Frampton, Kenneth, and Kunio Kudo, *Japanese Building Practice: From Ancient Times to the Meiji Period*, New York: Van Nostrand Reinhold, 1997.

Fujioka Michio, *Genshoku Nihon no Bijutustu: 12— Shiro to Shoin*, Tokyo: Shōgakan, 1968.

Fukuda Kazuhiko, *Japanese Stone Gardens: How to Make and Enjoy Them*, Rutland, VT, and Tokyo: Charles E. Tuttle, 1970.

Fukuyama Toshio, *Heian Temples: Byodo-in and Chuson-ji*, New York and Tokyo: Weatherhill/ Heibonsha, 1976.

Gehō Taku, "Mejia: Kontentsu no Nashōnarichi" (Media: The Nationality of Contents), IIPS Policy Paper 322J, Tokyo: Institute for International Policy Studies, 2007.

Guth, Christine, *Art of Edo, Japan: The Artist and the City, 1615–1868*, New York: Harry N. Abrams, 1996.

Hanley, Susan B., *Everyday Things in Premodern Japan: The Hidden Legacy of Material Culture*, Berkeley: University of California Press, 1997.

Heineken, Ty, and Kiyoko Heineken, *Tansu: Traditional Japanese Carpentry*, New York and Tokyo: Weatherhill, 1981.

Hirai Kiyoshi, *Feudal Architecture of Japan*, New York and Tokyo: Weatherhill/Heibonsha, 1973.

Hirota, Dennis, *Wind in the Pines: Classic Writings of the Way of Tea as a Buddhist Path*, Fremont: Asian Humanities Press, 1995.

Hume, Nancy (ed.), *Japanese Aesthetics and Culture: A Reader*, Albany: State University of New York Press, 1995.

Inoue Mitsuo (trans. Watanabe Hiroshi), *Space in Japanese Architecture*, New York and Tokyo: Weatherhill, 1985.

Isozaki Arata, *Island Nation Aesthetic*, London: Academy Editions, 1996.

_____, *Japan-ness in Architecture*, Cambridge, MA: MIT Press, 2006.

Isozaki Arata, Ando Tadao, and Fujimori Terunobu, *The Contemporary Tea House: Japan's Top Architects Redefine a Tradition*, Tokyo: Kodansha, 2007.

Itō Teiji, with Noguchi Isamu and Futagawa Yukio, *The Roots of Japanese Architecture*, New York and London: Harper & Row/Evanston, 1963.

Itoh Teiji, *The Elegant Japanese House: Traditional Sukiya Architecture*, New York and Tokyo: Walker/Weatherhill, 1967.

_____, *Traditional Domestic Architecture of Japan*, New York and Tokyo: Weatherhill/Heibonsha, 1982.

JAANUS Online Dictionary of Japanese Architectural and Art Historical Terminology (comp. Mary Neighbour Parent), Japanese Architecture and Art Net Users System, 2001; www.aisf.or. jp/~jaanus/deta/k/karahafu.htm.

Kawashima Chuji, *Minka: Traditional Houses of Rural Japan*, Tokyo: Kodansha, 1986.

Keene, Marc P., *Japanese Garden Design*, Rutland, VT, and Tokyo: Charles E. Tuttle, 1996.

Kishida Hideto, *Japanese Architecture*, Tokyo: Japan Travel Bureau, 1936.

Koizumi Kazuko, *Traditional Japanese Furniture*, Tokyo, New York, and San Francisco: Kodansha, 1986.

Kuck, Loraine, *The World of the Japanese Garden: From Chinese Origins to Modern Landscape Art*, New York and Tokyo: Weatherhill, 1989; first published 1968.

Kurokawa Kisho, *Rediscovering Japanese Space*, New York and Tokyo: Weatherhill, 1988.

Lady Sarashina (trans. Ivan Morris), *As I Crossed a Bridge of Dreams*, London and New York: Penguin, 1975.

Liu, Laurence G., *Chinese Architecture*, London: Academy Editions, 1989.

Lu Yu (trans. Francis Ross Carpenter), *The Classic of Tea*, Boston: Little Brown, 1974.

Mason, R. H. P., and J. G. Caiger, *A History of Japan*, Rutland, VT, and Tokyo: Charles E. Tuttle, 1997.

Morse, Edward S., *Japanese Homes and Their Surroundings*, New York: Dover, 1961; first published 1886.

Murasaki Shikibu (trans. Arthur Waley), *Genji Monogatari*, in Donald Keene (ed.), *Anthology of Japanese Literature*, New York: Grove Press, 1980.

Mushi-cho shi (History of Mushi Village), Mushi-cho, 2005; available online at http://www.city.takamatsu.kagawa.jp/6133.html.

Nakagawa Takeshi (trans. Geraldine Harcourt), *The Japanese House: In Space, Memory, and Language*, Tokyo: International House of Japan, 2005.

Nihon Kenchiku Gakkai, *Nihon kenchikushi zushu* (Collected Illustrations of Japanese Architectural History), Tokyo: Shokokusha, 1980.

Nihon Minka-en: Japan Open Air Folk House Museum Catalog, Kawasaki, Japan: Nihon Minka-en, n.d.

Nihon no komyunichi (Communities of Japan), issue of *SD*, No. 7, Tokyo: Kashima Shuppan Kai, 1975.

Nishi Kazuo, and Hozomi Kazuo, *What is Japanese Architecture?*, Tokyo and New York: Kodansha, 1983.

Nitschke, Günter, *Japanese Gardens: Right Angle and Natural Form*, Cologne: Benedikt Taschen Verlag GmbH, 1993.

Okakura Kakuzo, *The Book of Tea*, New York: Dover, 1964.

Oliver, Paul (ed.), *Encyclopedia of Vernacular Architecture of the World*, Cambridge, UK: Cambridge University Press, 1997.

Ono Sokyo, *Shintō: The Kami Way*, Rutland, VT, and Tokyo: Charles E. Tuttle, 1962.

Paine, Robert Treat, and Alexander Soper, *The Art and Architecture of Japan*, Harmondsworth: Penguin, 1958.

Parent, Mary Neighbour, *The Roof in Japanese Buddhist Architecture*, New York and Tokyo: Weatherhill/Kajima, 1985.

Process: Architecture No. 25, Japan: Climate, Space, and Concept, Tokyo: Process Architecture Publishing, August 1981.

Qingxi Lou (trans. Zhang Lei and Yu Hong), *Chinese Gardens*, Zurich: China Intercontinental Press, 2003.

Reynolds, Jonathan M., "Ise Shrine and a Modernist Construction of a Japanese Tradition," *The Art Bulletin*, 83(2), 2001, pp. 316–41.

_____, *Maekawa Kunio and the Emergence of Japanese Modernist Architecture*, Berkeley, CA: University of California Press, 2001.

_____, "The Bunriha and the Problem of 'Tradition'

for Modernist Architecture in Japan, 1920–1928," in Sharon A. Minichiello (ed.), *Japan's Competing Modernities: Issues in Culture and Democracy 1900–1930*, Honolulu: University of Hawai'i Press, 1998.

Richie, Donald, *A Tractate on Japanese Aesthetics*, Berkeley, CA: Stone Bridge Press, 2007.

Rudolfsky, Bernard, *Architecture without Architects*, Albuquerque: University of New Mexico Press, 1987.

Rybczynski, Witold, *Home: A Short History of an Idea*, New York: Penguin, 1986.

Sadler, Arthur L., *The Art of Flower Arrangement in Japan*, London: Country Life, 1933.

_____, *A Short History of Japanese Architecture*, Sydney and London: Angus and Robertson, 1941.

Schaarschmidt-Richter, Irmtraud, and Mori Osamu, *Japanese Gardens*, New York: William Morrow, 1979.

Seiki Kiyoshi, *The Art of Japanese Joinery*, New York, Tokyo, and Kyoto: Weatherhill/Tankosha, 1977.

Seki Mihoko, *Kokenchiku no waza nehori hahori* (Minute Details of Traditional Architectural Techniques), Tokyo: Rikōgakusha, 2000.

Sen Sōshitsu XV (trans. V. Dixon Morris), *The Japanese Way of Tea: From Its Origins in China to Sen Rikyū*, Honolulu: University of Hawai'i Press, 1998.

Shimode Kunio (ed.), *Nihon no Toshikukan* (Japanese Urban Space), Tokyo: Shokokusha, 1969.

Slawson, David A., *Secret Teachings in the Art of Japanese Gardens: Design Principles and Aesthetic Values*, Tokyo: Kodansha, 1987.

Smith, Robert J., *Japanese Society*, Cambridge, UK: Cambridge University Press, 1983.

Stewart, David B., *The Making of a Modern Japanese Architecture: 1868 to the Present*, New York and Tokyo: Kodansha, 1987.

Stierlin, Henri (ed.), and Masuda Tomoya, *Architecture of the World: Japan*, Lausanne, Benedikt Taschend Verlag GmbH, n.d..

Sumiyoshi Torashichi and Matsui Gengo, *Wood Joints in Classical Japanese Architecture*, Tokyo: Kajima Institute Publishing, 1989.

Suzuki Daisetz T., *Zen and Japanese Culture*, Princeton, NJ: Princeton University Press, 1973.

Tachibana-no-Toshitsuna (attrib., trans. Shigemaru Shimoyama), *Sakuteiki: The Book of Garden*,

Tokyo: Town & City Planners, 1976.

Tanaka Sen'o and Tanaka Sendo, *The Tea Ceremony*, Tokyo: Kodansha, 1988.

Tange Kenzō, *Katsura: Tradition and Creation in Japanese Architecture*, New Haven: Yale University Press, 1960.

Tange Kenzō, Kawazoe Noboru, and Watanabe Yoshio, *Ise: Prototype of Japanese Architecture*, Cambridge, MA: MIT Press, 1965.

Tanizaki Jun'ichirō, *In Praise of Shadows*, New Haven, CT: Leete's Island Books, 1977; first published as *In'ei raisan* 1933.

Ueda Atsushi, *Nihonjin to sumai* (Japanese People and Dwellings), Tokyo: Iwanami Shoten, 1974.

_____, *The Inner Harmony of the Japanese House*, Tokyo, New York, and London: Kodansha, 1990; first published 1974.

Unno Taitetsu, *River of Fire, River of Water*, New York: Doubleday, 1998.

Varley, Paul, and Kumakura Isao (eds), *Tea in Japan: Essays on the History of Chanoyu*, Honolulu: University of Hawai'i Press, 1989.

Watanabe Masatoshi, "Bamboo in Japan," available online at http://www.kyoto.zaq.ne.jp/dkakd107/E02-e.html.

Webster's New Collegiate Dictionary, 8th edn, Springfield, MA: G & C Merriam Co., 1981.

Yamagata Saburō, *Kenchiku Tsurezuresa* (Architectural Idleness), Kyoto: Gakugei Shuppansha, 1982; first published 1954.

Yamaguchi Marble Onix Union website: http://dairiseki.sugoihp.com/kumiai/history.htm.

Yamasaki Masafumi (ed.), "Kyoto: Its Cityscape Traditions and Heritage," *Process: Architecture*, No. 116, April 1994.

Yanagita Kunio, *Minkan denshōron* (On Folklore Studies), Tokyo: Kyōritsusha, 1934.

Yoshida Kenko (trans. Donald Keene), *Essays in Idleness*, New York: Columbia University Press, 1967.

Young, David, and Michiko Young, *Introduction to Japanese Architecture*, Singapore: Periplus Editions, 2004.

Zōen, *Senzui narabi ni yagyō no zu* (Illustrations for Designing Mountain, Water, and Hillside Field Landscapes), 15th century, reproduced in *Secret Teachings in the Art of Japanese Gardens: Design Principles and Aesthetic Values* (trans. David A. Slawson), Tokyo: Kodansha, 1987.

Index

The Tuttle Story

Many people are surprised to learn that the world's largest publisher of books on Asia had its humble beginnings in the tiny American state of Vermont. The company's founder, Charles E. Tuttle, belonged to a New England family steeped in publishing.

Tuttle's father was a noted antiquarian dealer in Rutland, Vermont. Young Charles honed his knowledge of the trade working in the family bookstore, and later in the rare books section of Columbia University Library. His passion for beautiful books—old and new—never wavered throughout his long career as a bookseller and publisher.

After graduating from Harvard, Tuttle enlisted in the military and in 1945 was sent to Tokyo to work on General Douglas MacArthur's staff. He was tasked with helping to revive the Japanese publishing industry, which had been utterly devastated by the war. When his tour of duty was completed, he left the military, married a talented and beautiful singer, Reiko Chiba, and in 1948 began several successful business ventures.

To his astonishment, Tuttle discovered that postwar Tokyo was actually a book-lover's paradise. He befriended dealers in the Kanda district and began supplying rare Japanese editions to American libraries. He also imported American books to sell to the thousands of GIs stationed in Japan. By 1949, Tuttle's business was thriving, and he opened Tokyo's very first English-language bookstore in the Takashimaya Department Store in Ginza, to great success. Two years later, he began publishing books to fulfill the growing interest of foreigners in all things Asian.

Though a westerner, Tuttle was hugely instrumental in bringing a knowledge of Japan and Asia to a world hungry for information about the East. By the time of his death in 1993, he had published over 6,000 books on Asian culture, history and art—a legacy honored by Emperor Hirohito in 1983 with the "Order of the Sacred Treasure," the highest honor Japan can bestow upon a non-Japanese.

The Tuttle company today maintains an active backlist of some 1,500 titles, many of which have been continuously in print since the 1950s and 1960s—a great testament to Charles Tuttle's skill as a publisher. More than 60 years after its founding, Tuttle Publishing is more active today than at any time in its history, still inspired by Charles Tuttle's core mission—to publish fine books to span the East and West and provide a greater understanding of each.

Acknowledgments

From the Author
This book could be built only from the teaching, inspiration, support, assistance, and encouragement of many people over many years. They are too numerous to thank individually, but I am deeply grateful to all. The foundation for the book was laid by Tony Atkin, who showed me that first slide of a stone lantern in a lush mossy garden twenty years ago, and Maruyama Kinya, who has been educating and inspiring me ever since. Many wonderful teachers have given me the structure—the columns and beams—for my research, including Dana Buntrock, Edo Tamotsu, Fujimori Terunobu, Kohyama Hisao, Kuma Kengo, Kusumi Naoki, and Sugimoto Takashi. The walls and the openings in them were built with the support and encouragement I have received, especially from Susan Cohen, Paula Deitz, Joann Gonchar, Ikeda Erika, Amy Katoh, Kimura Sachiko, Zeuler Lima, Sato Noriko, Leslie Van Duzer, illustrator Yamamoto Atsushi, and my colleagues and students at the places I have worked and taught. My parents, Nancy C. Locher and the late Jack S. Locher, taught me to recognize the sound of the *hototogisu*. They gave me the ability and opportunity to slide open that first door, and they watched quietly as I walked through. The construction of this book would not be complete without the roof, as shelter and symbol, layers bound together by Eric Oey, June Chong and Chan Sow Yun from Tuttle Publishing, editor Noor Azlina Yunus, and photographer Ben Simmons. But most of all, the book could not have been built without my *daikokubashira*, Murakami Takayuki.

From the Photographer
I would like to sincerely thank Chan Sow Yun, Naoto Ogo, Atsuro Komaki, Atsunori Komaki, Yoko Yamada, Toshio Okada, Kumeto Yamato, Yasaburo Hiraki, Mariya and Mineo Hata, Teiji Shinkei and Son, Ryorijaya Uoshiro Restaurant, Friends of Mikuni, Shoi, Colleen and Oshin Sakurai, Katharine Markulin Hama, Tim Porter, Toshio and Kumiko Wakamei, Takuji Yanagisawa, Yuri Yanagisawa, Yamada Sakan, Dennis "Bones" Carpenter, Kathryn Gremley, Greg, Maki and Marina Starr, and Rie, Rika, and Tsuneko Nishimura for all their kind support and assistance, and Mira Locher for her inspiring insights and unique perspective on Japan.

Illustrations
The publisher and author are grateful to the following individuals, institutions and publishers for help and permission in drawing and/or reproducing the line drawings in this book: **Fujimori Terunobo:** p. 41 (top and bottom); **Kuma Kengo:** p. 36; **Murakami Takayuki:** pp. 22 (top), 127, 136 (with Yamamoto Atsushi); **Yamamoto Atsushi:** pp. 17, 18, 22 (bottom), 29 (after Young and Young, *Introduction to Japanese Architecture*, p. 103), 31, 48, 58 (after Chikatada Kurata, *Minzoku Tambo Jiten*, Tokyo: Yamakawa Shuppansha, 1983), 60 (after Rudolfsky, *Architecture without Architects*, p. 132, with permission of Bungeishunjū), 65 (after Engel, *Measure and Construction of the Japanese House*, p. 31), 67, 74, 79 (after an image of *minka* structure, exhibition room guide, homepage of Hiratsuka City Museum (http://www.hirahaku.jp/tenji-shitsu/p24-25.html), 82, 85, 89, 93 (after Chūji Kawashima, *Minka: Traditional Houses of Rural Japan*, Tokyo: Kodansha, 1986, p. 20), 95, 96, 100, 102, 103, 105, 107, 110, 115, 118, 119 (top and bottom), 121, 132, 139 (top, after *Nihon Minka-en*, n.d.), 139 (center), 155, 158 (after Parent, *The Roof in Japanese Buddhist Architecture*, p. 122, with permission of Kyoto Prefectural Board of Education and Kūhonji Temple), 163 (after *Uesugi-bon rakuchū rakugaizu byōbu*, screen by Kano Etoku, c. 1560), 167 (after Keene, *Japanese Garden Design*, p. 79), 171 (after Keene, *Japanese Garden Design*, p. 77), 177, 188 (after Slawson, *Secret Teachings in the Art of Japanese Gardens*, p. 136), 197 (after Slawson, *Secret Teachings in the Art of Japanese Gardens*, p. 45), 207, 216, 217.

門しめに
出 聞て居る
蛙かな

mon shime ni
dete kitte oru
kawazu kana

Coming out
to close the gate,
I end up listening to frogs.[1]

MASAOKA SHIKI (1867–1902)
正岡 子規